PASSAGES
TO THE
PRESIDENCY

PASSAGES
TO THE
PRESIDENCY
FROM CAMPAIGNING TO GOVERNING

CHARLES O. JONES

BROOKINGS INSTITUTION PRESS
Washington, D.C.

Copyright © 1998
The Brookings Institution
1775 Massachusetts Avenue, N.W., Washington, D.C. 20036

Library of Congress Cataloging-in-Publication Data

Jones, Charles O.
    Passages to the presidency : from campaigning to governing /
Charles O. Jones.
        p. cm.
    Includes bibliographical references and index.
    ISBN 0-8157-4714-4 (cloth : alk. paper)
    ISBN 0-8157-4713-6 (pbk. : alk. paper)
    1. Presidents—United States—Transition periods. 2. Presidential
candidates—United States. 3. United States—Politics and
government—1945–1989. 4. United States—Politics and
government—1989–1993. I. Title.
    JK516 .J64 1998
    324.6´3´0973—ddc21

                                                                    98-9041
                                                                       CIP

9 8 7 6 5 4 3 2 1

The paper used in this publication meets the minimum requirements of the American National
Standard for Information Sciences—Permanence of Paper for Printed Library Materials, ANSI
Z39.48-1984.

Set in Times Roman

Composition by Oakland Street Publishing
Arlington, Virginia

Printed by R. R. Donnelley & Sons Co.
Harrisonburg, Virginia

FOREWORD

EXCELLENT STUDIES and reports have been produced concerning the vital process of one president moving out and another moving in: the transition from one president to another. This book, by Charles O. Jones, focuses on a parallel passage, from campaigning to governing.

The book includes detailed examination of four recent transitions: Lyndon B. Johnson to Richard M. Nixon in 1968, Gerald R. Ford to Jimmy Carter in 1976, Carter to Ronald Reagan in 1980, and George Bush to Bill Clinton in 1992. Jones conducted extensive interviews with presidential aides, public officials, scholars, journalists, and other political observers.

Jones finds that campaigning and governing are experiencing important changes that will affect future transitions. His sources uniformly criticized the Clinton transition as the least effective, yet they were applying standards drawn from the conventional wisdom while important changes were occurring in campaigning and governing. He sees Clinton's public-oriented style of governing as one that future transitions will have to accommodate.

Another finding was that the press plays a significant role in upholding and disseminating expectations for the transition. Reporters had clear opinions about subtle and important differences between campaigning and governing, as well as how the new team should behave in setting up a government.

In addition, Jones concludes that presidential transition can be understood in advance by knowing the candidate's background, status, and purposes in seeking the office. Knowing what presidential candidates have done, who their friends are, and why they want to serve in the White House reveals much about how they proceed to create a new administration.

Brookings and the author gratefully acknowledge financial support from the Alcoa Foundation, the Douglas Dillon Chair in Governmental Studies at Brookings, and the Glenn B. and Cleone Orr Hawkins Chair in Political Science at the University of Wisconsin-Madison.

The views in this study are those of the author alone and should not be attributed to those acknowledged above or to the trustees, officers, or other staff members of the Brookings Institution.

Michael H. Armacost
President

May 1998
Washington, D.C.

AUTHOR'S PREFACE

IN THE SPRING of 1993 noted presidential scholar Richard E. Neustadt proposed that the Brookings Institution undertake a study of presidential transitions: "Brookings should review in depth, interviewing extensively, what went right and wrong during the eleven weeks between election and inaugural." He proposed examining the three most recent transitions in which there was a change of party—Carter in 1976, Reagan in 1980, and Clinton in 1992—suggesting, as well, that Nixon's transition in 1968 could be used as a baseline for comparison. "Lessons should be derived in terms of what helps/hurts the president-elect himself, and also his key incoming associates, to function effectively (and learn fast) after January 20."

Later that same year, I was appointed the Douglas Dillon Visiting Fellow in Governmental Studies at Brookings for 1994–95. Having just completed a study of the presidency in the postwar period (*The Presidency in a Separated System*), I was pleased to undertake a study of presidential transitions as Neustadt had recommended. *Passages to the Presidency* is the result.

Much of what I have learned in this study is a result of interviews and conversations with transition aides, public officials, scholars, journalists, and other political observers. I have quoted liberally from these interviews, all of which were transcribed. The words are theirs; the interpretation and ordering of these words are mine. I judged that it was not essential to identify who spoke the words for an understanding of the dynamics of the transition.

Further, because I wanted respondents to be cooperative and candid, I assured them that I would not divulge their identity. An attributed quote was necessary in just one instance, and I appreciate that Michael K. Deaver approved that citation.

I do want to acknowledge with gratitude the generosity of the many persons who willingly gave of their time to relate their experiences and impart their judgment. First and foremost among these is Richard E. Neustadt. It was not only his idea to conduct this study, but he contributed in many ways. His own writing on this subject is classic, always the place to start. He permitted me to read memorandums he prepared for several presidents-elect that seemingly, in some cases, offered more wisdom than they or their staffs could absorb. We corresponded frequently about the project, and he did me the enormous favor of providing a constructively critical reading of the manuscript. Though I never had the chance to study with Dick Neustadt, I am, nonetheless, his devoted and grateful student.

Interviews with transition aides and others with knowledge or experience included James A. Baker III, Andrew H. Card Jr., Dick Cheney, Michael K. Deaver, Frank J. Donatelli, Kenneth M. Duberstein, Eugene Eidenberg, Frank Fahrenkopf, Marlin Fitzwater, Bill Frenzel, Al From, Robert Healy, Stephen Hess, Constance Horner, Michael Jackson, Robert A. Katzmann, Harry MacPherson, Edwin Meese III, William Murphy, Eli Segal, Donna E. Shalala, George Stephanopoulos, Margaret Tutweiler, Jack H. Watson Jr., Harrison Wellford, and Anne Wexler.

Conversations about the topic (rather than a formal interview) were held with Douglas Dillon, Lawrence S. Eagleburger, William A. Galston, Edwin Harper, Harold M. Ickes, Paul C. Light, Richard E. Neustadt, and James P. Pfiffner.

Interviews and conversations with reporters included Jeffrey H. Birnbaum, David S. Broder, Adam Clymer, Ann Devroy, Albert R. Hunt, Carl P. Leubsdorf, Mara Liasson, Susan Page, Robert Rankin, Steven Roberts, David E. Rosenbaum, and Paul West. Previous interviews with Dom Bonafede, Richard E. Cohen, Janet Hook, Dick Kirschten, Cokie Roberts, and Gerald F. Seib were also useful for this project.

James P. Pfiffner has written importantly on the subject of transitions, often studying the subject firsthand. He generously allowed me to read and transcribe several of his excellent interviews. Included were Richard Beal, Chuck Bingman, Hugh Carter, Dick Cheney, Clark M. Clifford, Bowman Cutter, John Ehrlichman, Stuart Eizenstat, H. R. Haldeman, Charles Kirbo,

Bruce Kirschenbaum, Bert Lance, Edwin Meese, Theodore Sorenson, Jack Watson, and Harrison Wellford.

Mark J. Rozell also made available to me transcribed interviews, associated with his several works on the press and the presidency. Among those provided were Marlin Fitzwater, Gerald R. Ford, Robert Hartmann, John W. Hushen, Ronald H. Nessen, Larry Speakes, Jerald F. terHorst, Louis Thompson, and Gerald Warren.

Also useful was the transcript of a conference on the presidential transition held at the Brookings Institution on October 25, 1996. Participants included former transition aides Frank Donatelli, Harrison Wellford, and Anne Wexler and journalists Adam Clymer, Susan Page, and David M. Shribman.

Finally, I found many of the oral history interviews conducted by the Lyndon Baines Johnson Library at the University of Texas to be valuable, principally as background material for framing the study and confirming some of the findings.

Conducting research at the Brookings Institution is a satisfying and rewarding experience. The surroundings are accommodating, colleagues are supportive, research assistance is impressive, and the Brookings reputation eases access. I am especially indebted to Thomas E. Mann, director of the Governmental Studies program, who invited me to spend time at Brookings and to undertake this study. It is hard to imagine a more enthusiastic, responsive, and understanding director of research anywhere. The intellectual neighborhood on the sixth floor contributes to each and every study. In my case, and for this book, Bill Frenzel, Stephen Hess, Constance Horner, Robert Katzmann, and Pietro S. Nivola were particularly helpful.

I profited immensely from the talents of several research assistants at the University of Wisconsin-Madison and Brookings. Among these, Corey Cook at Wisconsin and Laurel Imig at Brookings worked the longest and provided the most assistance. They not only fulfilled assignments, they sensibly modified requests when they knew more than I did what would be helpful. But there were others whose help differed only in quantity, not quality: David Howat, Andrew Shaw, and Kevin den Dulk at Wisconsin and Stephanianna Lozito at Brookings.

I also want to acknowledge the assistance of Brookings staff: Ingeborg Lockwood, who arranged most of the interviews and helped in many other ways; Susan Stewart, who made the arrangements for my time at Brookings; and Judith Light, who cheerfully handled every request. The marvelous Brookings library staff was helpful and cooperative, as always.

Paul C. Light, Richard E. Neustadt, and James P. Pfiffner read the manuscript and made excellent suggestions for improvement. Alice Honeywell was the copy editor for the manuscript, providing needed improvements in order and wording. As the verifier, Tara Adams Ragone caught errors in transcription and references. Carlotta Ribar proofread the pages, and Sherry L. Smith prepared the index. And Nancy Davidson managed the editing and publishing phases with a deftness admired by all.

As always, my wife, Vera, helped me in many ways. The book is dedicated to our granddaughters, each of whom was born during the life of this project, thus confirming our own passages.

CONTENTS

TABLES

FIGURES

To
Annabel Sage Jones
and
Phoebe Rose Hanauer Jones

1

TRANSITIONS AND DEMOCRACY

PERSONS become presidents. Presidents are variously prepared to do the job by reason of what they know, whom they know, and whether this knowledge is an asset or a liability in Washington, D.C. Persons as presidents differ from one another in most critical characteristics—experience, style, temperament, intelligence, and savvy. Yet they enter an office (literally and figuratively) that symbolizes stability and continuity. Our expectations of new presidents are often pure and hopeful, as with any new beginning. Accordingly, we tend to exaggerate presidential power at the start of a new administration, even as we support the conditions that limit its exercise (notably the constitutional separation of institutions, bolstered by a sharing of powers).[1] Discerning these inflated expectations is what is involved in a person becoming a president. Managing their effects is what is involved in successfully serving. These challenges distinguish the passages from campaigning to governing.

My purpose in this book is to explore the challenges faced by those elite persons who survive the arduous workings of presidential selection. I concentrate on the last four party shifts in the twentieth century: Lyndon B. Johnson to Richard M. Nixon (1968), Gerald R. Ford to Jimmy Carter (1976), Carter to Ronald Reagan (1980), and George Bush to Bill Clinton (1992). A candidate who wins is said to undergo a transition from the very special experience of campaigning to the very demanding service as president. I explore how that happens—from the decision to run until the inau-

1

guration. I identify the changes that affect this process of persons as candidates assuming the role of president. Throughout the book I draw heavily on formal interviews and informal discussions with those who experienced and observed the four most recent transitions involving party change. My goal is to consolidate and synthesize their analysis so as to provide lessons from the past and anticipations of the future. The principal focus is on the passages from declared candidate to nominee to president-elect to president.[2]

I confess to imagining in advance that contemporary campaigning deprives candidates of the experiences that prepared past presidents to govern. For example, candidates now surround themselves with merchandising specialists, not politicians upon whom they can depend later to bargain with other politicians. Consequently, today's presidents have a task for which their predecessors were better prepared—that is, connecting with other major decisionmakers. Further, they are likely to employ a coterie of advisers oriented more to the outside than the inside, more to the public and media than to legislators, governors, and bureaucrats. Samuel Kernell writes about the increasing tendency of presidents to "go public," as though doing so was a choice rather than an inevitability in today's politics or, as he puts it, their "preferred course."[3] Yet modern campaigning may leave them unprepared for classic bargaining and may require them to govern differently than in the past. On the other hand, after looking at recent cases I conclude that future transitions may feature a less sharp distinction between campaigning and governing, thus calling into question what it is we think we know about preparing for office.

Here then are some of my contentions:

—A president-elect's personal, political, policy, and organizational experience sends strong signals as to the type of transition to expect. Likewise, stature in the Washington community aids in identifying the advantages and disadvantages of assuming the presidency.

—Outsiders as presidents-elect face special problems in acquainting themselves with the politics of the inside. Often lacking stature, they need help from those in the know, and yet they may deny themselves this aid.

—The canons of an effective transition are based on a distinction between campaigning and governing, with election day as the marker: campaigning before, preparing to govern after.

—The press serves as the public's "window" for the transition, with reporters relying primarily on the conventional tests for judging effectiveness.

—Campaigning has lessons for governing for those prepared to learn them.

—Preelection planning is a vital, yet sensitive, enterprise best integrated into the campaign organization and leadership.

—The Nixon, Carter, Reagan, and Clinton transition teams all acknowledged the standard criteria; Nixon and Reagan had more success in meeting these criteria, Carter and Clinton had less.

—Campaigning and governing are undergoing important changes: campaigning is increasingly professionalized, requiring direction by skilled technicians more than experienced politicians; governing is more public, requiring skilled opinion specialists.

—These changes are blurring the distinction between campaigning and governing, suggesting an ancillary passage from campaigning for election to campaigning for policy.

—The conventional canons for an effective transition must now be supplemented by revised standards of governing that incorporate campaigning on issues.

—The Clinton transition is the watershed case. Dubbed the "worst" for having failed to meet many of the tests for a conventional transition, the Clinton White House developed a campaigning style of governing over the first term.

—The "biggest mistakes" for transitions—not establishing leadership, mismanaging time and opportunity, misjudging or mishandling appointments, failing to connect with Congress—are related to a failure to project competence and clear direction.

Changing Transitions

Transitions are themselves in transition. The new is often tested by the familiar for the good reason that it is all we know and it is hard to prepare for that which is unrecognizable. In the case of transitions, judgments continue to be based on conventional standards, and yet a campaign-oriented style of governing has developed. The passage continues to be one from campaigning to governing, but within that generic transition is a shift from campaigning for election to campaigning for policy. Among other demands of this revised transition is the integration of political consultants and pollsters into White House staff operations without disrupting regular operations, a not inconsiderable challenge.

This alteration in transitions relates to a style or manner of governing, not simply to a continuation of election campaigning. The shift is not only a result of electing a postwar-generation leader, though Clinton's arrival surely symbolized change. Quantum increases in access to information, as well as in the speed and sources of communication, have contributed to a substantially more public and participatory policy process. The very terms of governance are changing.

Current transition rules do not reflect these important developments, and yet new rules have not been formed and codified. Further, the changes, while acknowledged by sophisticated observers, are resisted as distortions to be refocused and clarified rather than realities to be confronted. I concede my own misgivings about a future for which I know we must prepare. Yet I acknowledge that it is quite possible that an effective transition in the standard mode may leave the new president unprepared in the next millennium to participate effectively in a more public governing process. Change must, and will, be absorbed in a democracy. This book, then, specifies a challenge for future presidents-elect: how best to achieve an ancillary passage following the election, while satisfying the standards of the conventional transition.

Thinking about Transitions

Representative democracy is about transitions. Citizens are chosen in free elections to become agents. As such, they no longer speak just for themselves. Agents have the responsibility to speak and act for others. And so every election is a time of transition, with first-time winners experiencing the challenge of assuming another's stead and incumbents reading the results as a measure of their performance.

Democratic government is also about transitions. Most of the time the newcomers try to fit in. They accept current institutional practices in their effort to learn what is expected of them. Occasionally, however, institutional norms are themselves at issue in an election, and fresh representatives or new presidents seek change. For example, the elections in 1932, 1964, and 1980 for president and Congress, or 1974 and 1994 for Congress, produced transition-like impacts within institutions. The effect of the old on the new and the new on the old is at the heart of political or institutional transitions. A misreading of political conditions by newcomers, therefore, can lead either to loss of effectiveness if the support is not there for change or to a failure to capitalize on the opportunity if it is.

Attention here focuses on presidents as newcomers to government. They are currently among the least-tenured public servants. The Twenty-Second Amendment imposes a two-term limit. Between 1951, when it was ratified, and 1992, however, the average length of presidential service was five, not eight, years.[4] Meanwhile, the Senate carries over two-thirds of its membership by constitutional design, and the House of Representatives has had impressively high incumbent return rates in the post–World War II period.[5] The bureaucracy is based on a merit system, not election, and service in the federal courts is for a life term.

Expectations of presidents are high since they have come to symbolize the national government for the public, the political parties, the media, and other nations. But when they take office, presidents are imagined to lead a government mostly already in place, a government selected *independently* of its newly elected chief. Followership must be earned by the person who will be designated by others as the most powerful leader in the western world. Meanwhile other transitions may be occurring in Congress and state governments—changes that are responsive to developments separate from those that brought the new president to Washington.

Here then is the task undertaken in this book: to explore why people run for president, how they campaign, who their friends are, what they believe the job is like, what they want to accomplish, whether and how they think organizationally, how they manage the transition from being a candidate to serving as president, and what the role of the press is in this vital function of creating a presidency. A basic premise of this study is that the transition begins when a person decides to seek the presidency.[6] Candidates vary in the extent to which they contemplate, at the start, what is involved in serving as president and why it is that they are willing to undertake the arduous task of seeking the office and then creating an administration. Those actively weighing these matters wonder how it is that a person-as-president can be fitted atop the executive and alongside the other branches. To delay such considerations until after the election is to be tempted to rely heavily on the recent campaign experience in creating a presidency (a dependency unlikely to prepare a president-elect to manage even a revised transition effectively—that is, to govern by campaigning).

Put otherwise, those candidates who decide early why they want to be president and whether they have the personal, political, and organizational resources to meet the demands of the job will likely have an advantage in the transition. A first requirement for realizing this edge is a working knowledge

of what is expected of presidents, then tested by the personal qualifications
of any one chief executive. Nicholas Johnson, former member of the Federal
Communications Commission, had exactly these issues in mind when he
wrote about the "questions they [the candidates] never get asked":

> Have they read Richard Neustadt's "Presidential Power" and com-
> parable studies of process? What did they learn? How do they pro-
> pose to build the coalitions and political support necessary to
> accomplish those things in "the public interest" that are of low pri-
> ority for the mass media and public but of high priority to the spe-
> cial interests that oppose them? How will they break the grip of the
> sub-governments. . . ?
>
> Is the candidate interested in the management of the federal
> government at all? What management experience, theories, prefer-
> ences—or "style"—will he or she bring? How will the candidate
> collect, evaluate and select nominees for presidential appoint-
> ments—or proposals for legislation? How will he or she apportion
> functions and staff between Cabinet departments and the White
> House?[7]

Johnson pointed out that "few if any such questions are ever put to the
candidates," and yet they should be since "the qualities it takes to govern are
different from the qualities it takes to be elected."

Granting that it is important to ask such questions, I believe it is also possible to extrapolate from a president's previous political and administrative
experience to predict how he or she might perform as president. Presidential
candidates are not blank slates. The overwhelming majority have made
appointments, created staffs, made political and policy decisions, and managed an organization. As Richard E. Neustadt advised, presidents arrive at
the White House with their "own operating style." "Harry Truman," he said,
"was instinctively a judge. . . . Franklin Roosevelt, by comparison, was an
intelligence operative."[8] Thus it is possible to answer certain of the questions raised by Johnson even if they are not asked directly of the candidates.
An attempt is made here to relate presidents' earlier experiences to the transition from candidate to president-elect to president. The crucial point for
now simply is that inquiry regarding transitions should not be shelved until
a candidate wins. Those interested in effective governance, presumably
including the candidates themselves, are well advised to confront the issues

of leadership long in advance of the celebration of victory and the ceremony of inauguration.

A Leisurely Pace

Most political systems install new leadership in a matter of days following an election. The rationale for a quick transition is persuasive. The people have made their decision; why not install a new government? Thus, for example, Jacques Chirac was elected president of France on May 7, 1995, and the sitting president, François Mitterrand, announced that he would step down even before the end of his term on May 20, 1995. On May 1, 1997, British voters chose a Labour party majority, and on May 2 the moving vans were removing the defeated prime minister's household goods from No. 10 Downing Street.

By comparison, the United States maintains a leisurely pace in changing the head of state, waiting two and one half months to install the new president, during which time the transition—that uniquely American political exercise—takes place. Yet however slow-paced the process is today, it was tortoise-like before the ratification of the Twentieth Amendment. An act of Congress in 1788 dictated that the president be inaugurated on March 4, about four months after the election. The previous Congress typically met in a lame-duck session between the election and the inauguration.[9] Here then was the spectacle of the president-elect watching from the sidelines as the old Congress, populated with many retired and defeated members, acted on the issues of the day. Another oddity, provided for in Article I, Section 4 of the Constitution, was that a new Congress would meet on the first Monday in December, some thirteen months after being elected.[10]

Led by George W. Norris, Republican of Nebraska, in the 1920s, the Progressives sought, to no avail, to change the dates for both the inauguration and the meeting of Congress. According to constitutional scholar Carl Brent Swisher, "it was lethargy which stood in the way of the amendment rather than overt opposition."[11] Differing versions of the proposed amendment passed the House and Senate in 1929 and 1930 but died in conference for lack of agreement on a House provision that sessions should end on May 4 during even-numbered years. In 1932, with the Democrats a majority in the House, the Norris proposal received the requisite two-thirds vote in both chambers. It was quickly ratified by

Table 1-1. Lame-Duck Presidents and Congresses, 1940–94[a]

President and party	Election year	Party change	Reason for leaving
	Presidents		
Truman (D)	1952	Yes	Retired
Eisenhower (R)	1960	Yes	Term limit
Johnson (D)	1968	Yes	Retired
Ford (R)	1976	Yes	Defeated
Carter (D)	1980	Yes	Defeated
Reagan (R)	1988	No	Term limit
Bush (R)	1992	Yes	Defeated

Congress and majority party	Election year	Party change	Adjournment date
	Congresses		
76th (D)	1940	No	Jan. 3, 1941
77th (D)	1942	No	Dec. 16, 1942
78th (D)	1944	No	Dec. 19, 1944
81st (D)	1950	No	Jan. 2, 1951
83d (D)	1954	Yes	Dec. 2, 1954[b]
91st (D)	1970	No	Jan. 2, 1971
93d (D)	1974	No	Dec. 20, 1974
96th (D)	1980	Senate	Dec. 16, 1980
97th (split)	1982	No	Dec. 23, 1982
103d (D)	1994	Yes	Dec. 1, 1994

SOURCE: Compiled by the author.
a. Following ratification of the Twentieth Amendment in 1933.
b. Senate only.

three-fourths of the states, to be in effect for the next session of Congress and the inauguration of the president in 1937.[12]

The ratification of the Twentieth Amendment, however, did not eliminate lame-duck or transitional government. Rather it shortened its life and reduced substantially the possibility of having the old Congress meet after the election. The amendment provides that "the terms of the President and Vice President shall end at noon on the 20th day of January, and the terms of Senators and Representatives at noon on the 3d day of January . . . and the terms of their successors shall then begin." The date for the annual assembly of Congress was also changed from the first Monday in December to the "3d day of January." So we were left with two lame-duck forms: a defeated or retiring president serving with the old Congress (until January 3) and this same president serving for over two weeks with the new Congress.[13]

As table 1-1 shows, presidents were lame ducks seven times after the ratification of the Twentieth Amendment. Four of those had retired (two voluntarily, two having reached the two-term limit), and three were defeated. Six of the seven cases involved party changes and therefore represented instances where the losing party in the presidential race managed the two-and-one-half-month transitional government. After 1933, lame-duck Congresses—those in which the previous membership met after the election—occurred during the war years of 1942, 1944, and 1950 (Korea), and in seven other years. Just three of these sessions (1940, 1944, 1980) followed presidential elections.

To what extent did lame-duck sessions have political or policy significance? Five in particular are worthy of comment. In 1942 the Republicans rebounded from their nadir in the 1930s, realizing a net gain of forty-seven House seats and ten Senate seats. But the war effort reduced the probability of partisanship. In 1950 Republicans also had notable gains of twenty-eight House seats and five Senate seats. Once again the United States was engaged in a significant military engagement, this time in Korea. The lame-duck session was devoted to what President Truman dubbed his "must list"—"supplemental defense appropriations, an excess profits tax, aid to Yugoslavia, . . . extension of federal rent controls and statehood for Hawaii and Alaska." All except the statehood proposals were acted on in this lengthy session.

In 1954 and again in 1980 party power shifted as a result of the elections: to Democratic majorities in both houses in 1954 and to a Republican president and Senate in 1980. The 1954 case was special in that the Senate met to act on a recommendation to censure Senator Joseph R. McCarthy, Republican of Wisconsin. The 1980 session was quite active, to include the final budget resolution, Alaska land preservation, the toxic waste "superfund," and an extension of general revenue sharing to the states. The Republicans suffered significant net losses in the House and Senate in the post-Watergate election of 1974. As in 1950 and 1980, the 1974 session was active: a mass transit bill, appropriations measures, and a foreign aid package passed; several vetoes were overridden; and the nomination of Nelson A. Rockefeller as vice president was approved.[14]

A lame-duck congressional session along with a lame-duck president has occurred just once since the ratification of the Twentieth Amendment (Carter in 1980). Such a session is more common following the midterm elections. This record, however, is a reminder to presidents and presidents-elect that the period between the general election and the constitutional ending of a Congress has characteristics that require adaptive strategies.

Budgeting for Transitional Government

In a letter of transmittal to Congress with the report of his bipartisan Commission on Campaign Costs, President John F. Kennedy stated: "There are important reasons, aside from costs, to institutionalize the change in party power from one administration to another."[15] Budgeting is surely the ultimate stage in the institutionalization of a practice. Presidents-elect and their appointees had previously arranged for their own financing during this period. The national party committees and private individuals had contributed funds for this purpose. In testimony before a House subcommittee, Elmer B. Staats, then deputy director for the Bureau of the Budget, stated: "It has been estimated that a special Republican committee expended in excess of $200,000 in 1952–53 and that the Democratic National Committee spent over $360,000 in 1960–61." Staats also observed that appointees to major positions had to endure "considerable personal sacrifice" in working "without pay for 2 to 3 months while incurring the increased personal expenditures caused by absence from the family residence."[16]

A bill providing for transition costs of up to $1.3 million for the incoming and outgoing president and vice president passed the House on a voice vote on July 25, 1963. The bill permitted 20 percent of the expenditures to be certified as "confidential." The Senate did not act until October 17, providing just $500,000 for expenditures, with no funds designated as confidential. The compromise in conference was $900,000 for expenditures, with 10 percent allowable as confidential. No expenditures were permitted if an incumbent was reelected. The measure became law with the president's signature on March 7, 1964, and its first application followed the 1964 election for the new vice president only (Lyndon Johnson was an incumbent serving out Kennedy's term and therefore was not eligible for monies under the act).[17] The first full application of the 1963 act occurred in 1968 with the election of a new president and vice president. The $900,000 was split evenly between the incoming and outgoing administrations. The Nixon administration reportedly also used an estimated $1 million in private funds.[18]

With the passage of the Presidential Transition Act, the postelection, preinaugural period was officially sanctioned as a government- and taxpayer-sponsored event. It is therefore reasonable to expect accountability during this time. Judgments about effectiveness are justified, and presidents-elect have a responsibility to perform competently. They should be answerable if their transition is not efficacious.

The 1963 act was amended in 1976 and again in 1988. The principal changes were to increase the amount available and to specify more clearly how the funds might be used. In 1976 the authorization for expenditures was increased to $3 million: $2 million for the incoming administration, $1 million for the outgoing administration. It was also provided that any detailees from departments or agencies would be paid for from transition funds. In part the urgency of an increase was due to a Federal Election Commission ruling that prohibited the use of privately raised funds for transition purposes if the president- and vice president–elect accepted public financing for the campaign.[19]

In 1988 Congress reviewed a number of issues associated with the cost and management of the transition. First, the authorization of expenditures was again increased: to $3.5 million for the incoming administration, $1.5 million for the outgoing, with inflation-adjusted amounts in the future.[20] Second, the issue of using private funds was more fully engaged than in the past. The president- and vice president–elect were permitted to solicit and spend private funds but were required to make full disclosure of the contributions as well as the sources of funding for each transition team member. A limitation of $5,000 was set for contributions. Additionally, the incoming administration was required to report an estimate of in-kind contributions to the administrator of General Service.[21]

Third, attention was devoted in the Senate to providing appropriations for preelection planning, with each of the national committees receiving reimbursements after the election (to prevent use of public funds for campaign-related purposes). This proposal was innovative in acknowledging that what happened the day after the election was related to what happened before. The Senate report noted:

> In addressing the funding issue, the Committee [on Governmental Affairs] also recognized the near-unanimous agreement among past transition officials that a President-elect must undertake at least some advance planning during the general election campaign. A President-elect cannot wait until the morning after the election to start planning for the transition. In order for the President-elect to "hit-the-ground-running," the candidate must lay the administrative groundwork before the campaign is over.[22]

Both of the sitting national committee chairs favored the provision, which was subsequently passed by the Senate, with an allocation of $200,000 for any political party receiving 25 percent of the popular vote or more.[23] This provision did not survive, in part because of a concern that reimbursements would be made for planning by losing candidates, in part because of the problem of judging legitimate preelection transition costs and the belief by some that preparations before election were the responsibility of the candidate.[24]

Several other relevant issues in the Senate report deserve attention since they will be visited throughout this book.[25] Perhaps the most important of these concerned the preparation of the budget. There are few more awkward arrangements in government than the transition in budgeting, particularly given the long lead time required for a budget and the lack of experience common for a new White House team. Cooperation between the old and new administrations was recommended by the Senate Committee on Governmental Affairs, a goal more easily stated than realized given the partisan nature of most budget planning. Another large issue identified by the Senate report was the problem of recruiting the best talent at a time of increasing attention to ethical standards for government service. As Marshall Berger, chairman of the Administrative Conference, explained it: "What remains to be studied is the application of current conflict-of-interest restrictions to transition personnel. Obviously, we should seek requirements that are appropriate to such activities—not so harsh as to chill participation in these necessary efforts or so loose as to allow untoward conduct."[26] One proposal by the committee was that the White House Personnel Office forward a list of position descriptions for major appointments to the national party committees, in part to encourage preelection planning for the transition.

Just as important as people are the records and documents necessary for building a new presidency. The committee report addressed this issue, even to the point of undertaking a study. The problem itself was described in testimony by Stuart Eizenstat, former domestic policy adviser to President Carter:

One major disability during transitions is the absence of access by the incoming Administration to records, documents, and key papers in the Executive Branch bureaucracy. Even more troubling is the absence of documents at the White House from the outgoing Administration, to which reference could be made on important decisions. For example, it is nearly impossible to envision a new corporate CEO confronting the same situation each new President faces—assuming the top position in his company with no available records of his predecessor's decisions and no background on those decisions; the offices he and his new team enter are empty of past memos and files on major events—records which had been there the day before. . . . A structure such as this makes it virtually impossible from the onset to instill institutional memory and to make transitions effective.[27]

Again, the committee did not deem it necessary to legislate in regard to this problem, but they did contact the National Archives and Records Administration, which agreed to provide briefings, training, and advice to current and incoming White House staff regarding records management and responsibilities.

Clearly, there has been a gradual recognition of the organizational and management issues associated with transferring power from an incumbent administration to an emergent one. This began with the 1963 act, when Congress recognized the period as officially associated with governing by providing funds to assist in managing the process. The expenditure of public funds is logically followed by an auditing of expenditures and that function leads to inquiry about effectiveness. Therefore by 1988 there was increased attention to the practical matters associated with moving a new president into the White House. As it happens, this quarter century of time was characterized by a significant increase in the reach and complexity of the federal government, further justifying the need to try to do it right.[28]

Another dimension of transition is not well accommodated by attention to the more strictly administrative issues. That is, not all presidents-elect have the experience or the aptitude to manage an effective transition. Furthermore, their most recent political exercise—the campaign—furnishes training of limited value for forming a presidency, yet it is extraordinarily demanding of time, energy, and resources. Presidents-elect enter the critical transition period in a physically and mentally exhausted state, typically dependent on an equally fatigued staff. These physical and psychological aspects require notice as well as the organizational matters that have been the subject of transition planning. In fact, how the new team manages the challenges during this stressful time may offer early signals as to the character and style of the presidency.

Table 1-2. Characteristics of Originated Presidencies, 1896–1992

President and year	Party change	Incumbent defeated	President's party in control of Congress	Prior executive service	Prior Washington service
McKinley (1896)	D to R	No	Yes	Governor	House
Taft (1908)	None	No	Yes	Secretary of War	Secretary of War
Wilson (1912)	R to D	Yes	Yes	Governor	None
Harding (1920)	D to R	No	Yes	Lieutenant Governor	Senate
Hoover (1928)	None	No	Yes	Secretary of Commerce	Secretary of Commerce
Roosevelt (1932)	R to D	Yes	Yes	Governor	Assistant Secretary of Navy
Eisenhower (1952)	D to R	No	Yes	Military commander	Army Chief of Staff
Kennedy (1960)	R to D	No	Yes	None	Senate
Nixon (1968)	D to R	No	No	Vice President	House and Senate
Carter (1976)	R to D	Yes	Yes	Governor	None
Reagan (1980)	D to R	Yes	Senate only	Governor	None
Bush (1988)	None	No	No	Vice President	House; CIA Director
Clinton (1992)	R to D	Yes	Yes	Governor	None

SOURCE: Compiled by the author.

Variations in Transitions

The most commonly referenced transition is that of the first-term, elected president who must create a new administration in the period between the election and the inaugural. There are, however, other types. Tables 1-2 to 1-4 show the variation as associated with the manner in which the president takes office. I identify three forms of transitions: *originated*—those associated with presidents elected for the first time, *regenerated*—those of reelected presidents and of takeover presidents who win election on their own, and *received*—those of vice presidents assuming the office. Attention here concentrates on four cases of originated presidencies, notably the four most recent instances of a party shift: Johnson to Nixon (1968), Ford to Carter (1976), Carter to Reagan (1980), and Bush to Clinton (1992). A useful purpose is served, however, by observing how these cases differ from other forms.

Note in tables 1-2 to 1-4 that the originated presidencies for first-time winners in this century are outnumbered by the other two types of transi-

Table 1-3. Characteristics of Regenerated Presidencies, 1896–1992

President and year	Change in margin or size of margin	President's party in control of Congress	Change in margin (Congress)
Reelected presidents			
McKinley (1900)	Small increase	Yes	Small increase
Wilson (1916)	Large decrease	Yes	Small decrease
Roosevelt (1936)	Increase	Yes	Small increase, House Large increase, Senate
Roosevelt (1940)	Decrease	Yes	Small increase, House Small decrease, Senate
Roosevelt (1944)	Decrease	Yes	Small increase, House
Eisenhower (1956)	Increase	No	No change
Nixon (1972)	Huge increase	No	Small increase, House Small decrease, Senate
Reagan (1984)	Increase	Senate only	Small increase, House Small decrease, Senate
Clinton (1996)	Increase	No	Small increase, House Small decrease, Senate
Elected takeover presidents			
Roosevelt (1904)	Large	Yes	Large increase, House No change, Senate
Coolidge (1924)	Large	Yes	Small increase
Truman (1948)	Narrow	Yes	Huge increase
Johnson (1964)	Landslide	Yes	Large increase, House Small increase, Senate

SOURCE: Compiled by the author.

Table 1-4. Characteristics of Received Presidencies, 1896–1992

President and year	Cause of takeover	Previous executive service	Previous Washington service
Roosevelt (1901)	Death	Governor	Assistant Secretary of Navy, Civil Service Commission
Coolidge (1921)	Death	Governor	None
Truman (1948)	Death	None	Senate
Johnson (1963)	Death	None	House, Senate
Ford (1974)	Resignation	None	House

SOURCE: Compiled by the author.

tions: thirteen versus eighteen (thirteen regenerated presidencies and five received presidencies). Observe also in table 1-2 the small number of cases among originated presidencies in which a new president succeeds one of the same political party—just three of thirteen. The importance of this fact is simply that a significant proportion of newly elected presidents enters office assuming strained or unfriendly relations with those they are replacing. Indeed, in half of the ten instances of party change (Wilson, Franklin Roosevelt, Carter, Reagan, and Clinton), the new team defeated the incumbent administration. Until 1968 it was common for the new president's party to have congressional majorities. Since then three of the five (Nixon, Reagan, and Bush) have had to manage with one or both houses of Congress in the hands of the opposition party. Transitions into split-party governments are bound to differ from those into single-party governments, given the need for Senate confirmation of major appointments and the requirement of cross-party coalitions to approve the president's program.[29]

Finally, most of these new presidents have had some executive service—six as governors. However, four, all governors, lacked any Washington experience. Only Kennedy completely lacked executive experience, though service as a lieutenant governor (Harding) barely qualifies and that as vice president (Nixon and Bush) depends greatly on how the president defines the position.

As shown in table 1-3, the regenerated presidencies are of two types: those reelected to a second term (or a third and fourth for Franklin D. Roosevelt) and those vice presidents serving out a term who were then elected on their own. Transitions for the first group should be relatively tranquil, requiring few adjustments in response to the election. There are exceptions, however. Woodrow Wilson won narrowly in 1916, and though the Democrats retained their majority in the Senate, they needed support from Progressives to organize the House. Democrats then lost their majorities in both chambers in 1918. After his narrow win in 1968, Richard Nixon won every state but Massachusetts (and the District of Columbia) in 1972, encouraging him to reform his government for the second term to suit his more imperial concept of the presidency. According to Stephen E. Ambrose, in the first meeting with the White House staff following his triumphal reelection, "Nixon gave perfunctory thanks . . . before announcing that the first order of business was to reorganize. 'There are no sacred cows,' he declared, then changed the metaphor: 'We will tear up the pea patch.'"[30] Other presidents in this group interpreted their reelections as public support for more of the same and thus made few changes.[31]

The second group of regenerated presidencies is better discussed following treatment of the received presidencies listed in table 1-4. These are the vice presidents who find themselves having to take over another person's government. Seldom have vice presidential candidates been selected as substitute presidents. More often they are chosen to suit political imperatives. Three of the five takeover presidents in this century had no previous executive experience. Further, there is no "day certain" when they will become president. Illness of the president or serious ethical problems (in the case of Nixon) may encourage them to prepare for assuming office. But public preparations would be unseemly. Succesfully managing these difficult transitions depends on the extent to which presidents equip their vice presidents to assume control by giving them important and relevant assignments and keeping them briefed on major issues.

Even when fully involved, however, the vice president inherits an administration organized to suit the operating style and policy preferences of another president. There is no emptying out of the White House and the appointive offices in the departments and agencies, as happens following an election. In fact, a takeover president may be under some pressure to retain many of his predecessor's appointments for continuity or because he is viewed as a custodian more than a president in his own right. An abrupt turnover in personnel would be interpreted as disloyalty.

Takeover presidents who then win election have an opportunity to regenerate an administration. They can make the case that election legitimizes their independence and therefore frees them to effect a transition not unlike those of first-time winners. What has been the experience with the four cases listed in table 1-3? Although Theodore Roosevelt made a number of cabinet changes in 1904 and 1905, mostly moving persons from one department to the next, his actions did not constitute a wholesale reorganization. Coolidge changed half of the cabinet following his election, but the changes were more a result of circumstances (scandal, death, resignation) than with the intent of establishing a new Coolidge administration.[32]

The Truman case is particularly interesting because he served nearly a full four-year term and succeeded a president with a contrasting style who had been in office more than twelve years. Many members of the cabinet were ready to leave; others were dismissed. As a result there was significant turnover in the first year. A second wave of changes came approximately two years later. There was no major reorganization following Truman's election in 1948 since by then he had already reshaped his government. Lyndon B. Johnson faced the highly sensitive political circumstances occasioned by the tragic death of his predecessor. However anxious he may have been to create his own presidency, Johnson had to protect the Kennedy legacy. He essentially managed for a time with two staffs and, according to Neustadt, "another circle, private, occasional, informal, wholly unofficial, and linked to the officials largely through himself . . . [that] included old Washington and Democratic hands."[33] He kept the cabinet in place. In fact, four of the Kennedy appointments stayed through Johnson's elected term, while another resigned only in the last year.

This rich variety of transitions illustrates yet again the vibrant nature of American national politics. Change is ever incorporated into government, as befits a democracy. But the methods by which change is absorbed differ substantially, even within one branch. I concentrate on a set of party-switching, originated presidencies. They offer a comparative base, so analysis of their experience should be helpful in the creation of future presidencies.

Transitions in a Separated System

The following chapters are organized to treat topics notably associated with the personal transition of a winning candidate to become president. I begin in chapter 2 by exploring the background of the candidate himself and its importance in determining how he is likely to fit into the job.[34] I pay particular attention to why the person wants to run for president and what is his concept of the office. What follows in chapter 3 is an analysis of the campaign experience for presidential candidates and the extent to which this experience enhances or modifies the candidate's political and policy motivations and conceptions. In this chapter I attempt to identify the candidate's campaign theme that provides an orientation for the subsequent presidency, showing that a theme may be more policy oriented (as with Reagan) or more stylistic (as with Clinton).

The transition itself is the subject of chapter 4. The analysis begins with those activities during the campaign that are designed to prepare for a takeover should the candidate win. It continues with the efforts between the election and inauguration to effect a transformation from campaigning to governing, with special emphasis on the president-elect. An important feature of this period is the extent to which an identifiable presidency is created, one that clearly moves the president-elect away from the campaign mode into a governing mode. Should this goal not be achieved, transition-type tasks then carry forward into the period of governing.

It is generally acknowledged that the press plays a potentially major role during the transition. Chapter 5 examines that role and its effect. The press itself experiences a transition during this time. National political reporters tend to have expectations arising from the campaign and from their coverage of other presidencies. What happens during this time can affect how a White House is then portrayed in the future and, consequently, how its press office may spend its time and resources.

A concluding chapter explores the importance of the transition for governing later and whether there is a "biggest mistake" that can be made during this time. As a part of that analysis, I try to identify certain realities characterizing this important phase of American politics and governing—realities that shape transition behavior and foretell its importance. Special attention is directed to the Clinton case because it may represent a transition in transitions. A final exercise considers how it is that presidents-elect bring change to the transition and how changes otherwise affect what they can accomplish. Special emphasis is placed on the significance of a change in governing style for future transitions.

Each election presumably settles an important question: Who will serve in the White House? It is the responsibility, then, of the winner to send clear signals as to how he will do the job. The transition period is an early opportunity to accomplish that purpose. Failure to take advantage of that opportunity almost certainly will result in problems later for the president. Richard E. Neustadt said it so well:

> Everywhere there is a sense of a page turning, a new chapter in the country's history, a new chance too. And with it, irresistibly, there comes the sense, "they" couldn't, wouldn't, didn't, but "we" will. We just have done the hardest thing there is to do in politics. Governing has got to be a pleasure by comparison: We won, so we can! The psychology is partly that of having climbed one mountain so the next looks easy, partly that of having had a run of luck that surely can't turn now!
>
> The arrogance that goes with this is native to contemporary nominations and campaigns, and to the young who man them.[35]

2

FUTURE PRESIDENTS AS CANDIDATES

WHY DO PERSONS want to become president? That question is asked for more reasons than to satisfy curiosity. It is of direct relevance to the subject at hand: the transition to power. In his brilliant treatment of politicians, Stimson Bullitt asked: "What are the rewards of this calling?" He answered: "It gives the pleasure of dealing with people, the fascination of work with ideas, the challenge of problems important to all the world, the excitement of sharing in the 'action and passion of the times,' and the satisfaction of helping to operate one of the great inventions of human kind." Bullitt explained that those with singular ambition have an advantage over those whose aspirations are more diffuse. "Politics is an all-or-nothing venture that does not easily fit into the scheme of a person who enters it to fulfill part of an aim that is wide rather than high."[1]

What is the purpose of the venture, apart from the pleasure it gives? That is where I begin an analysis of presidential transitions because I maintain that their shape and bearing are traceable to the ambitions of the candidates. There are personal, policy, organizational (to include personnel), and political reasons for seeking the office. Many, perhaps most, candidates run for all four types of reasons, though some factors may be weighted more heavily than others. Persons may decide to seek the presidency because they judge it to be a personally satisfying capstone to a career of public service. They believe their time has come. Or they may simply have harbored a longing to be the president. Most candidates also have a set of policy priorities, typically those they deem are not being sufficiently treated at present. Access to skilled campaign organizers and experience in using them effectively may contribute to the confidence that a candidate needs to take the plunge. And the decision also will be based on political or strategic considerations. In some cases it appears to be the opportune moment; political conditions are favorable. In other cases the fact that political conditions seem unfavorable for the party offers a chance to a candidate who might not otherwise be considered seriously. Someone has to be elected; why not me?

A fifth factor worthy of attention is that of acknowledged stature. Presidential candidates vary substantially in political background, proven executive capabilities, and national and foreign experience. Those who have established stature may expect to have an advantage in the transition. Those lacking such status are faced with having to achieve it to a level suiting the expectations of the presidency.[2]

Political appraisals may affect the decision by persons of stature to seek the presidency. The opportunity to win often attracts experienced and qualified candidates likely to have the advantages for the transition noted above. On the other hand, when such candidates decline to enter the race because they judge the politics to be unfavorable, then those of lesser national stature may win the nomination, beat the odds, and win. Should these unexpected winners be from out of town (as has been the case in recent years), they then face the task in the transition of familiarizing themselves with the inner workings of Washington while cultivating eminence. The problem for these persons of lesser esteem may be made more than ordinarily difficult because the exuberance of the postelection period can be mistaken for a grant of stature and a license for change. The pageantry of the inaugural may be misperceived as heralding the person rather than the office.[3]

These personal, policy, organizational, political, and stature factors are so basic to the "calling," as described by Bullitt, that, if probed early, they can be expected to offer a profile revealing of how a president-elect will manage the transition and launch his presidency.[4] They direct attention to the basics: What do candidates expect to get out of being president? What do they want to change once in office? Do they have a working concept of how to organize the White House and to manage the government? How have they played (or been played by) the politics of the time?

Four Presidents

Consider the four most recent presidents who represented a change in party control of the White House: Richard M. Nixon, Jimmy Carter, Ronald Reagan, and Bill Clinton. They differ in significant ways in regard to their reasons for seeking the office, based on the five criteria of personal goals, policy aims, organizational concepts, political opportunity, and acknowledged stature.

Richard M. Nixon, 1968

Nixon first ran in 1960 as heir apparent to the Eisenhower administration. As such he sought the nomination much as an incumbent would. He made no formal announcement in 1960. Rather "an aide confirmed that Nixon was indeed a candidate and that he had willingly agreed to let his name be entered in the primaries of New Hampshire, Ohio, and Oregon."[5] Nixon cruised to the nomination and lost to John F. Kennedy in one of the closest elections in history.

Nixon himself was unusually reflective on his candidacy. He offered the 1960 campaign as one of his *Six Crises*. He made reference to his competitive drive during his college and law school days, sustained by economic and personal factors.

> From an economic standpoint, I knew that I could not go on to college and to law school unless I was able to earn scholarships. . . .
>
> The personal factor was contributed by my father. Because of illness in his family he had had to leave school after only six years of formal education. Never a day went by when he did not tell me and my four brothers how fortunate we were to be able to go to school. I was determined not to let him down.[6]

This same competitive spirit carried Nixon into politics—first the House of Representatives, then the Senate, and, remarkably, given his age and experience, as Dwight D. Eisenhower's choice for vice president in 1952. By his account: "It was not until the spring of 1952 that the thought first seriously occurred to me that I might be a possible candidate for national office." He delivered a speech to the New York State Republican Committee on May 8, 1952. "When I concluded, the audience gave me a standing ovation. As I sat down, Governor Dewey grasped my hand and said: 'That was a terrific speech. Make me a promise: don't get fat; don't lose your zeal. And you can be President some day.' "[7]

Another major factor in shaping Nixon's ambition to serve as president was that of his emerging interest and expertise in foreign policy. In his review of the ups and downs of the years as vice president, Nixon cites the "ups" as his first round-the-world trip; the experience in Caracas, Venezuela, where his motorcade was attacked by an angry mob; and the "kitchen debate" with Nikita Khrushchev in 1959 (the latter two of which were included among the six crises).[8] Clearly his emergent interests in the presidency and in foreign policy ran parallel as he approached the race in 1960.

It is useful to speculate about what a transition would have looked like had Nixon won in 1960. As an heir apparent to an immensely popular president, he would have faced a situation very similar to that of George Bush in 1988–89. They shared strong interests in foreign and national security policy. But Nixon would have been a more conservative Republican following a moderate; Bush was the more moderate Republican following a conservative. Therefore, Nixon would have been freer to create his own presidency, whereas Bush was ever-sensitive to his status among the right wing of the party, which remained wary of his conservative credentials. Nixon was unlikely to have carried over any of Eisenhower's cabinet (though he did appoint Eisenhower's attorney general, William P. Rogers, as his secretary of state eight years later).[9] And Nixon expressed definite ideas about how Eisenhower managed his presidency, from which Nixon "seemed to have derived more negative lessons than positive ones."[10]

A President Nixon in 1961 would surely have been the first in this century to enter office facing an opposition party in both houses of Congress (he *was* the first in 1969). Republicans had a net gain of twenty-two House seats and two Senate seats in 1960. In 1958, however, their large losses left the Republicans at a serious disadvantage. Thus a narrow win for Nixon (and a switch of fewer than 15,000 votes, properly distributed, could have changed the result) was unlikely to have produced a different outcome for the 87th Congress, where Democrats had a 60 percent majority in the House and a 64 percent majority in the Senate. Again, the comparison with Bush is interesting. Democrats had exactly the same advantage in the House of the 101st Congress (60 percent) but a narrower advantage in the Senate (55 percent). There was, in brief, every expectation that a transition to a Nixon presidency in the final months of 1960 would have featured foreign policy themes and a conciliatory posture toward a Democratic Congress on domestic issues (not greatly different from that characterizing the transition in 1969).

According to biographer Stephen E. Ambrose, Nixon never stopped thinking about his quest to be the chief executive. Ambrose intimates that after his defeat for governor of California in 1962, Nixon thought about running against Kennedy in 1964.

> He had known no other life since 1946, and wanted no other, short of occupying the ultimate seat of power itself. . . . He couldn't imagine living without campaigning, and didn't try to. . . .
>
> But uncertainty about when Nixon would run again should not obscure the fact that he was running, and for nothing short of the Presidency. He was realistic enough to know that his fate rested to a large degree on chance, accident, and luck. . . . The point was to be ready to seize opportunities.[11]

Whether or not Ambrose is exactly correct regarding the thinking of Nixon during this time, there was little doubt that the former vice president would remain a major figure in the Republican party. Not even two defeats could somehow lower the national and international recognition of Nixon or automatically elevate some one else to greater prominence. All prospective candidates for 1964 and 1968 would want to know what Nixon was thinking before their own declaration.

In 1963, Nixon moved from his home political base in California to New York City, the base of his principal rival, Nelson A. Rockefeller. In fact, he moved into the same building in which Rockefeller had an apartment— Nixon on the sixth floor, Rockefeller on the eleventh. Nixon stated in his memoirs that "I was ruling myself out as an active political figure for the foreseeable future."[12] Yet as 1964 approached, Nixon recalls that he "was already getting calls and letters from friends and party leaders across the country urging me to run again for the presidency in 1964."[13] He believed, however, that he should not seek the nomination.

Nixon ran a noncandidate race in 1964, one in which he was available should the principal active candidates—Arizona Senator Barry Goldwater and Governor Rockefeller—deadlock at the convention. Nixon was encouraged in January by polls that showed him to be the strongest candidate, and he was personally persuaded that he would run the most effective race against Lyndon Johnson. In fact, he was preparing himself to do so, mostly on the basis of foreign policy.[14] As it happened, Nixon's availability remained just that. Goldwater won the crucial California primary on June 2, thereby securing the nomination on the first ballot at the Republican convention. In the end, that outcome was positive for Nixon since he surely would have lost a third straight election.

In moving to New York, Nixon came in contact with another set of campaign operatives who became important to his political future. According to Theodore H. White, his new associates in the law firm "offered him three things that were gradually to change his view of the world and of himself. They were, in order of ascending importance, the young and eager junior members of the firm [Leonard Garment, Tom Evans, and John Sears], the presence of John Mitchell, and a sense of having made it."[15] The New York contingent of political advisers was added to those from California to form a coast-to-coast team. Along with other friends, "Congress '66" was formed as an organization for Nixon to aid Republican congressional candidates in the midterm election. Nixon traveled 30,000 miles, visiting eighty-two congressional districts—an exercise he had grown used to as vice president during the Eisenhower administration.[16] And the Republicans realized substantial gains in both the House and Senate. "Congress '66" was judged to be a success electorally due to the expected gains and a success politically with the emergence of a potential organizational base for Nixon in 1968.

As with most ventures of this type, the "Congress '66" group completed its work with thoughts of a future campaign. They had worked effectively for a cause and with a leader many viewed as capable of filling the vacuum left by the devastating defeat of Goldwater in 1964.[17] It is not clear exactly when thinking developed from the 1966 campaign to a commitment for 1968, nor is it so important. For purposes of the eventual transition, the point is that an organization was emerging to take advantage of favorable political circumstances and in support of a nationally recognized leader with robust personal ambition.

By 1968 circumstances changed dramatically to favor a Nixon candidacy. The issues were his issues: the foreign and national security problems growing out of the Vietnam debacle. Nixon would not be a reluctant candidate in 1968. His active candidacy began in early January 1967. Meeting with several aides at the Waldorf Towers in New York City, he began plotting to win the nomination. "I'm not going to be coy with my oldest friends and closest advisers," Nixon said. "I want you to proceed with plans for winning the Republican presidential nomination next year."[18] According to William

Safire, one of those present, Nixon explained: "The purpose of this group is to begin planning now to win the nomination. . . . It is not the purpose of this group to help me on issues. On issues . . . I think we can assume that the Vietnam war will have been ended by the 1968 election. Other issues not so sure of solution . . . include inflation, race, and crime."[19]

Nixon had imposed on himself a six-month moratorium on political speeches two days before the 1966 elections as a means of preserving his options. He did not want to appear to be a candidate too early. "I wanted to run for President in 1968, but I wanted to leave open, until the last possible moment, the option of deciding *not* to run." To the group in New York City, however, he said: "But make no mistake, while I am lying back I want you to work your tails off getting the job done."[20]

Once his pre-announcement organization was in place and at work throughout the states, Nixon left on an extensive, worldwide fact-finding trip supported by the *Reader's Digest*, assigned as a special writer.[21] His purposes were "to learn, to see for himself, to be seen, to generate publicity both in the country he was visiting and back home, to be treated like an actual leader of the opposition or a potential President, to confer with foreign leaders in and out of power, and to project himself to the voters as the most knowledgeable man in America on foreign affairs."[22] He traveled to Europe and the Soviet Union, Asia, Africa, and Latin America in separate trips. Vietnam was among his stops. Nixon himself explained the trips prospectively in terms of his concept of the issues and his capacity to manage them.

> By undertaking these trips I was building on my political strong suit, my knowledge of foreign affairs. I also believed this was the best possible way to ensure that I would be able to frame foreign policy issues in a way that would be both effective and responsible, and, if I became President, to ensure that I could get a head start on what to me were the most important decisions a President faces.[23]

On the domestic front, Nixon was introduced to new thinking during this period of preparation. He encountered the analysis of Daniel Patrick Moynihan, then a professor at Harvard University. Nixon came to believe that a whole new concept was necessary in dealing with welfare issues, and he was attracted to the negative income tax. Nixon concluded: "Jobs is the gut issue. If you don't have jobs, you don't have housing and you don't get off welfare."[24] It is interesting, however, that in Nixon's own recounting of this period in his memoirs, he makes no mention of domestic issues, stressing foreign policy instead.

In regard to personnel and organization, Nixon relied on those with whom he had worked for years, supplemented by his new acquaintances in New York. This would be the seventh national election campaign in which he was heavily involved: two as a vice-presidential candidate, two as a presidential candidate, three in campaigning for congressional candidates in midterm elections.[25] He also worked actively for the Republican party between national campaigns. By his accounting: "Between the end of the 1964 debacle and the beginning of the 1966 campaign, I had logged 127,000 miles visiting forty states to speak before more than 400 groups. I helped to raise more than $4 million in contributions to the party." Not only did he know whom to call on in forming a campaign team, he knew most of the party operatives with whom the team would work at the state and local levels. During fall 1967, Nixon "visited most of the Republican governors and party leaders in their home states."[26] Few, if any, presidential candidates have known more about their party from the ground up than Richard Nixon. A close runner-up was Nixon's opponent in 1968, Hubert H. Humphrey.

Theodore H. White observed that as the 1960 election approached, Nixon and his aides were sensitive to "the principle of Legitimacy" (a concept related to what I refer to as stature). Nixon emphasized statesmanship, defined by his position as vice president and the foreign travel that it afforded in representing the United States. "His political phrasing of this principle in his campaign chant—Experience—was to prove, throughout the 1960 campaign, his soundest appeal."[27]

Stature was uppermost in Nixon's mind in the planning of his 1968 campaign as well. Foreign travel, again, was designed to portray experience and statesmanship. Nixon wished to be viewed as the leader of the opposition, as a person others could well imagine occupying the Oval Office. One problem to be faced was that, as the candidate himself put it, "Nixon can't win."[28] It was essential, therefore, that he enter the primaries and demonstrate that his perceived advantage in stature was bolstered by popular support within the party of which he remained the acknowledged leader. As he recalled: "I found [by early summer 1967] that sentiment was beginning to turn very decisively in my favor. But everyone was still asking the big question: after two defeats, could I shake my 'loser image'? It appeared more and more that the presidential primaries offered the only way to show that I could win."[29]

As it happened, Nixon's resolve and that of his organization were tested

several times during the nominating period. It was originally thought that
George Romney, the popular governor of Michigan, would be Nixon's most
serious opponent. Yet Romney's campaign was short-lived. Nixon's upstairs
neighbor originally decided not to run (Nixon, however, believed that
Rockefeller was behind George Romney's candidacy),[30] then announced his
candidacy in late April (winning only the Massachusetts primary in a low-
turnout contest in which all candidates were write-ins). The new governor of
California, Ronald Reagan, greatly worried the Nixon organization throughout. He was not an announced candidate but did control the California delegation (and actually garnered more total votes as his state's favorite son than
did Nixon in winning nine primaries).[31]

On the Democratic side, it was assumed that Nixon would be running
against Lyndon Johnson, but the president decided not to seek reelection.
Robert F. Kennedy was then judged by Nixon to be the probable opponent,
but he was assassinated. Meanwhile Governor George C. Wallace of Alabama
was also in the race as a third-party candidate, one who potentially could
cause difficulty for Nixon in the South. The eventual nominee, Vice President
Hubert H. Humphrey, was as representative of the traditional Democratic
party as Richard Nixon was of the Republican. He also served the Nixon
strategic purpose in that he had to speak for the Johnson administration in
regard to what was generally acknowledged to be a failed policy in Vietnam.

Nixon consistently signaled the type of transition to expect. Washington
insiders knew Richard Nixon well and he, in turn, knew a great deal about
them. That is not to say that either much liked the other. It is simply to suggest that the signs were clear in terms of his personal ambition and policy
interests, personnel and organizational preferences, political opportunity,
and source and degree of stature. In other words, a Nixon transition from
campaigning to governing was predictable from what was known in advance
about those crucial factors associated with seeking the office in the first
place. He wanted to be president and he knew why. He had clear priorities
and a concept of himself in the Oval Office. Therefore, one could expect an
orderly transition, one in which the president-elect played a major role, even
if he did not necessarily have a strong public presence.

Jimmy Carter, 1976

Democrats in 1976 had an extraordinary political opportunity because of
the historic collapse of the Nixon administration, and yet their candidate was

unlikely to be star quality and Washington-wise. As the surviving Kennedy brother, the one potential such leader, Massachusetts Senator Edward M. Kennedy, decided early not to run. Further, in the aftermath of Watergate and the unprecedented resignation of President Nixon, it was apparent to most political observers that a fresh face from out of town would have the best chance of winning. Therefore in 1976 circumstances virtually guaranteed that a Democratic president would face challenging transition problems as an outsider charged with making changes in a government with which he had not previously been intimately acquainted. The advantage for the dark-horse candidate afforded by Watergate could become a liability in assuming the job. Stature is virtually guaranteed to be an issue for an outsider.

In his account of the 1976 campaign, Martin Schram reports these reflections by Jimmy Carter on his early forays into Iowa in 1975:

> "The biggest problem I had was not campaign technique, or that I was from the South, or that I had not been in Washington, or that I didn't have any money, that I didn't have a good campaign organization—the problem I had was substantiality [sic] of campaign efforts in the minds of the people. Nobody thought I should be taken seriously."[32]

Carter's analysis of himself was confirmed in Jules Witcover's report of how he and other reporters reacted to his candidacy. "Carter from the very outset was hard to figure. The first question that came to mind about him was not what kind of President he would make or what he would do if he were President, but what on earth ever persuaded him that he was presidential material in the first place."[33]

The answer to "why not me" for Carter was simple. After all, what made George McGovern think he was presidential material? Or the several senators in 1976 whose names now are all but forgotten by most Americans (Fred R. Harris, Henry M. Jackson, Lloyd M. Bentsen Jr., Birch Bayh, Frank Church)? Or the representative (Morris K. Udall) who came to be Carter's principal opponent for the nomination? Further, it is worth recalling that the incumbent Republican was Gerald R. Ford, a former representative from Michigan brought to the White House by sheer circumstance, not election.[34]

In one sense it might be said that the 1976 Democratic nomination was an exercise in search of Jimmy Carter, or his clone. Burton I. Kaufman states it clearly: "For a revolt against Washington was what the election was all about."[35] Thus however much Senator Kennedy may have been the most visible and, for some, the most logical candidate, the Chappaquiddick scandal involving the death of a young woman would not have played well in the politics of character, post-Watergate. But there were other conditions, too, facilitating a Carter candidacy. Changes made in the nominating process encouraged outsiders and long shots to run. A conscious effort was made by the Democrats following their tumultuous 1968 convention to create a more plebiscitary nominating system. Grass-roots campaigning outside usual political party channels was promoted by the expansion in the number of primaries. Mood and method dovetailed nicely as advantages for Jimmy Carter. Kaufman sums it up:

> Disgruntled Americans sought new ideas, fresh faces, and a style of leadership predicated on openness, truthfulness, and public responsiveness. Indeed, morality was the emerging keynote of the campaign—a desire to restore a sense of purpose, trust, fairness, and civic responsibility to American life. Carter understood the national mood perfectly, and he attacked Washington in a positive way, emphasizing not so much what was wrong in the nation's capital as the power of the American people to set things right and appealing not to their cynicism but to their idealism.[36]

The challenge for Jimmy Carter, therefore, was very different from that of Richard Nixon. As the candidate from way out of town, the "man from Plains, Georgia," as he called himself, Carter had to establish national name, issue, and career identification. There was no doubt as to his personal ambition, confidence, and piety. By his own accounting, Carter began to think seriously about running for president following the 1972 presidential Democratic convention.[37] At that meeting Carter's aides engaged in an abortive effort to get the McGovern forces to consider their man as a running mate. Jerry Rafshoon, Carter's media adviser, recalled the experience as "degrading" as they sought an audience with McGovern's 22-year old pollster, Pat Caddell. After finally getting three minutes with Caddell, Rafshoon concluded that "he thought we were crazy."

> "We came out of there realizing that as much as we knew about Jimmy Carter and thought he had a good national image, the national politicians didn't take him seriously, and didn't take us serious-

ly," Rafshoon said. "I remember walking back from the convention the night McGovern was nominated and Hamilton [Jordan] and I are saying, 'Why can't Jimmy run for President?' "[38]

Dr. Peter Bourne, who headed the Georgia drug abuse program, wrote an early memorandum to explore the potential for a Carter candidacy. Bourne, Rafshoon, Jordan, and Landon Butler then met after the Democratic convention to discuss approaching Carter, which they did in late September. Carter reports that the meeting was a "frank assessment of my shortcomings. . . . We talked about politics, geography, character, education, experience, appearance, age, mannerisms, and lack of fame. In spite of these critical assessments, I decided to run."[39] The result of that meeting was a request of Jordan that he prepare a detailed memorandum analyzing the governor's chances and outlining a strategy for winning. The Jordan memo came to be famous as a shrewd appraisal of the politics of the time and a credible plan for winning the nomination and election. It reviewed potential candidates (notably Alabama Governor George Wallace and Massachusetts Senator Kennedy), set forth a scheme for running in the primaries, defined the problem of national recognition for his candidate and how it might be overcome, and suggested trade missions as a means of preparing Carter in foreign policy.

In analyzing the potential for a Kennedy candidacy in 1976, Jordan was prescient about politics in the post-Watergate era (written, it is important to recall, before the scope of the Watergate scandal was known):

Perhaps the strongest feeling in this country today is the general distrust of government and politicians at all levels. The desire and thirst for strong moral leadership in this nation was not satisfied with the election of Richard Nixon. It is my contention that this desire will grow in four more years of the Nixon administration. For this reason I believe it would be very difficult for Senator Kennedy to win a national election, as the unanswered questions of Chappaquiddick run contrary to this national desire for trust and morality in government.[40]

Whereas Nixon could be coy about his intended candidacy in 1968, Carter had to announce his intentions early and often if he was to overcome his lack of national recognition. He declared his candidacy on December 12, 1974, well over a year in advance of the first primary.[41] He spoke first at the

National Press Club in Washington, then flew to Atlanta for a rally. He stressed honesty, efficiency, and openness in government, citing his record in Georgia. He then touched on thirty issues to display his range of interests and the seriousness of his preparation.[42] The image that he portrayed was suited to the times: a serious and virtuous manager of public affairs willing to take on the difficult tasks of restoring confidence in government, almost as self-sacrifice. As he told his supporters in Atlanta: "I have to tell you with complete candor that being elected President of the United States is not the most important thing in my life." This statement was followed by the piety that came to be familiar during his presidency: "There are many other things that I would not do to be president. I would not tell a lie; I would not mislead the American people; I would not avoid taking a stand on a controversial issue which is important to our country or the world. And I would not betray your trust."[43] It was indicative of the post-Watergate public mood that such commonly accepted values needed emphasis.

In her evaluation of Carter's personality, Betty Glad concluded that, above all, the prospective president had confidence. She continued:

> There is a grandiose, a perfect quality to the claims Carter makes for himself. He claims to be able to love individuals he meets on assembly lines. He would never tell a lie. He has never experienced fear; death has no terror for him. He is not awed by the presidency, and he knew all along that he was going to make the White House.
>
> Beyond that, Carter seems convinced, at one psychological level, that he has obtained the perfection he seeks. The warmth, calm, and ease he showed on the campaign trail, and later in his "people-to-people" contacts and his dealings with small groups, suggest confidence. . . . He even finds it difficult, as one friend reports, to admit he gets ideas from other people. It's as if he thinks of everything good himself.[44]

In an August 1974 memo Hamilton Jordan expressed the "hope that your being the first to announce will result in your receiving a disproportionate amount of press coverage initially,"[45] a point reiterated in Carter's letter to supporters before his announcement.[46] As it happened, he was not the first candidate, but the announcement received adequate, if not disproportionate coverage. Of course, the hometown *Atlanta Constitution* gave it extensive front-page coverage under the banner headline: "It's Official, Carter Runs for President." The *Washington Post* article by veteran reporter David S. Broder led with Carter as the "New South" alternative to Alabama Governor George C. Wallace and stressed the relationship between the two governors.[47] The *New York Times* carried it on the front page, in the lower right-hand corner. The story stressed Carter's dark-horse status, mentioning among other things that Carter was not on a list of thirty-one persons mentioned in a recent Gallup survey, "a measure of the uphill battle he faces to gain recognition among voters outside the South."[48]

Carter prepared detailed policy recommendations on the issues. He had grand plans to restructure government as he had in Georgia, to tackle a legion of difficult policy issues, and to propose reforms. Well aware of the growing budget deficit, Carter believed that it was time to reduce programs and make government more effective. He took his campaign proposals seriously enough to bind them into a book of promises that eventually was to overload the lawmaking process.

The primary process was unusual in that once Carter was established as the front-runner, he continued to draw challengers. He got off to a fast start in the early contests, winning all but one. When his front-runner status became clear, with Udall consistently running second, others decided to enter the race (notably Idaho Senator Frank Church and California Governor Jerry Brown). The result was uncommon, with Carter actually running second in five of the final twelve primaries. Yet no alternative candidate emerged as a serious challenger to Carter. Still, the results of these late primaries demonstrated voter uncertainty about his candidacy that concerned him and his aides. Further, this pattern indicated a problem that would face Carter during the transition, namely how to come in from the outside and create an organization for managing insiders who harbored doubts about the new president.

In regard to personnel, it was astonishing that the group of provincial aides who had gone, hats in hand, to McGovern's staff just four years earlier was managing the Democratic Convention. These were young men, for the most part, who had worked for Governor Carter. They had little or no Washington experience, nor did they judge that lack to be a disadvantage. Rather they offered the freshness of their youth and the fact that they were untainted by what had transpired in Washington during the Nixon scandals. The asset of distance during the campaign came to be a liability in forming a government.

The candidate himself emphasized exactly these "beyond the Beltway" themes in accepting the nomination. Two sentences were of special relevance for signaling issues for Carter's transition. The first illustrated the stature problem that dogged the candidate throughout as a former, little-known governor of Georgia. The first words he spoke to the Democratic convention were: "My name is Jimmy Carter, and I'm running for President." However satisfying it may have been for Carter to remind the delegates of his achievement, the time was approaching when he had to abandon the obscurity gambit, at least in his own mind, in favor of accepting the need for a sophisticated understanding of Washington ways. The second line defined his position within the Democratic party and therefore identified problems he would face in building an administration: "I have never met a Democratic president, but I've always been a Democrat." The fact that Jimmy Carter was an outsider, even within his own party, no doubt aided him immeasurably in winning the nomination in the first post-Watergate election. But that status was of little or no help in designing an effective transition.

It is a fair reading that President Ford won the general election campaign while losing the election itself. Starting over thirty points behind in the polls, Ford lost by just 2 percent in the popular vote and by the narrowest margin in the Electoral College since Woodrow Wilson's twenty-three-vote margin in 1916. A switch of a few thousand votes in Ohio and Hawaii would have returned Ford to the Oval Office. Thus in the first post-Watergate election, a year of great opportunity for the Democrats, the outsider won narrowly over an appointed vice president serving out the term of a disgraced president (who had been pardoned by his successor). At the very least, these results defined the challenge for Jimmy Carter and his aides for accomplishing an effective transition atop the executive branch of government.

Carter wanted a broad-based win. According to Witcover, "He underlined that 'the mandate that's crucial to me' to carry out his campaign pledges could come only 'from a wide-ranging success among the electorate' that would impress a recalcitrant Congress."[49] His victory, however, was regional, coming primarily from the South and Northeast, with added support from three midwestern states.[50] Meanwhile the "recalcitrant Congress" was Democratic by huge margins: 67 percent in the House, 61 percent in the Senate. Incumbent return in the House was 96 percent, among the highest rates in the post–World War II period. Most Democrats returned believing correctly that they had won on their own, well aware that the president-elect did not receive the broad base that he sought. This fact presented the new administration with special challenges in effecting a transition—a president having to orient himself to his own party in Congress, a party against which he had campaigned in winning the nomination.

Review of the personal, personnel, political, organizational, and stature factors for the Nixon and Carter presidencies provides most interesting contrasts. I have described the Nixon case as illustrative of how analysis of pre-campaign and campaign motives and activities presage the nature of the transition. The Carter case also provides innumerable signals regarding the transition, notably by accenting the problems to be overcome during that period. To be sure, presidents-elect have in the past lacked extensive Washington-based experience (though most have had that seasoning). It was unusual, however, for a president-elect to approach the new job by preserving an outsider's status. To do so generated special problems in forming a presidency with ambitions to reform Washington-based government and politics. The president-elect had to establish credibility in a government he didn't much like in order to have it reform itself to suit his true preferences. It was a familiar conundrum to students of reform, if not to reformers themselves, and a special challenge for those lacking experience, who nevertheless raised expectations about their performance. Such presidents-elect need help, but they and their staffs may have promised themselves that they wouldn't seek it.

Ronald Reagan, 1980

Ronald Reagan first actively sought the presidency in 1976, having tried in 1968 to be available should Nelson Rockefeller derail Nixon's candidacy at the convention.[51] According to one biographer, Lou Cannon, Reagan rejected the option of running for the Senate in 1974 (challenging Alan Cranston) because he was more interested in running for president. " 'There's nothing I can do in the Senate for what I believe in that I won't be able to do anyway,' Reagan said to a close supporter."[52] Ronald Reagan was not a lawmaker, he was a performer. Describing Reagan in his role as governor of California, former campaign aide John Sears explained: "He is an endorser. Reagan sat with his California cabinet more as an equal than as its leader. Once consensus was derived or conflict resolved, he emerged as the spokesman, as the performer." Michael K. Deaver, Reagan's long-time public relations aide, doubted that "Reagan himself would quarrel with that statement. . . . He saw the presidency as Teddy Roosevelt did, as a bully pulpit."[53] Cannon pointed out that as a "creature of habit," Reagan carried this style over to the White House. Cannon further explained: "He thought his staff would tell him anything he ought to know and invested most of his energy and interest in the public performances of the presidency."[54]

There was no doubt that Reagan thought of himself as an actor-performer and was perfectly comfortable in that role. "I'm an actor, not a politician," is what Ronald Reagan responded when people urged him to run for governor of California during his tour of the state in 1965. Thus was the stature issue defined early in Reagan's political career (though late in his life). According to Reagan, the incumbent governor, Edmund G. "Pat" Brown Sr., asked the question: "What is an actor doing seeking an important job like the governorship of California?" Reagan's response was to present himself as "an ordinary citizen who wanted to start unraveling the mess politicians were making of our government. 'Sure,' I said, 'the man who has the job has more experience than anyone else . . . that's why I'm running.' "[55] The actor beat the governor by a margin of 16 percent.

By his own recollections and those of his aides, Reagan justified his political career by an almost Boy Scout sense of duty, a strong competitive edge once in the race, and a Western-movie-script oversimplification of good and bad in social and political life. In May 1974 former Nixon aide Sears offered persuasive analysis that Reagan could and should run for president in 1976. He judged that Nixon would not serve out his term and Ford would not be effective as a replacement. Even if Nixon survived, the race to succeed him would be open in 1976. Further fueling the positive strategic situation was the stimulus of Ford's selection of Nelson Rockefeller as his vice-presidential appointee, a move judged by Reagan and his team "as a slap in the face." According to Cannon, "Reagan wanted to run . . . so much that Ford's lapses became magnified into crises of presidential leadership."[56] Cannon describes the work of Reagan's advisers following the 1974 midterm losses for the Republicans even while Reagan preserved the option of not running. "As always, he drifted in the direction of what he really wanted to do."[57]

Deaver, who ought to know, relates this story of Reagan's decision to run. In January 1975 Reagan and Deaver were flying from San Francisco to Los Angeles when a woman stopped and urged Reagan to run for president.

> After the woman had left, [Reagan] turned to [Deaver] and said, "You know, she's right. Jerry Ford can't win and if I don't run I'm going to be like the guy who always sat on the bench and never got in the game. . . ."
>
> Then, as I had grown accustomed to his doing, he dug into his inventory of Hollywood anecdotes. "I remember in the movie *Santa Fe Trail*, I played George Custer as a young lieutenant. The captain

said, 'You have got to take over.' And my line was 'I can't.' And the captain said, 'But it's your duty.'

"And that's the way I feel about this. I'm going to run."

I was amazed at how he had formed this titanic decision.[58]

Reagan's bid to wrest the nomination from an incumbent president was unsuccessful, but the effort itself was revealing of his personal style, as well as providing national campaign experience for his aides. After a narrow loss to Ford in New Hampshire, Reagan lost the next four primaries, including crucial defeats in Florida and Illinois. In a dispirited meeting in LaCrosse, Wisconsin, on the day of the North Carolina primary, the Reagan team, low on funds, had to decide whether to continue. Sears "broached a new idea." A supporter from Texas had offered to lend the campaign $100,000. Sears suggested that they use the money to run a speech by Reagan critical of President Ford and Secretary of State Henry Kissinger on national defense issues.

Reagan was quiet—the whole room was quiet, for what seemed liked endless minutes—before he spoke. "OK, we'll do it. Borrow the $100,000. And run the national defense piece on national television. I'm taking this all the way to the convention in Kansas City, and I'm going even if I lose every damn primary between now and then."[59]

Martin Anderson, who related this story, explained the importance of Reagan's decision for his team. It was a case of "going to the mat . . . a quality especially admired by politicians, and particularly prized by their supporters. . . . Politics is riddled by enough uncertainty. It is critical to have someone you can count on."[60]

Reagan won the North Carolina primary in an upset, went on to win nine of the remaining twenty primaries, and lost the nomination at the convention by a margin of just 117 delegates (1,187 to 1,070). By Reagan's own account:

After Gerald Ford won the nomination in Kansas City, I met with the members of the California delegation and said: "Nancy and I are not going back and sit on our rocking chairs and say, 'That's all for us. . . .' " I think we both knew it wouldn't—couldn't—end in Kansas City. . . .

After Ford's loss, I knew some of my supporters would begin
knocking on my door and urge me to run in 1980, and they did. I
told them I wasn't going to make a decision yet.

I wasn't the reluctant candidate I'd been in 1965 and 1976.[61]

Reagan's personal ambition has always been muted by a patina of self-
lessness, as associated with duty. This point is illustrated by this statement in
his autobiography: "I wanted to be president. But I really believed that what
happened next wasn't up to me, it was up to the people: If there was a real
people's movement to get me to run, then I said I'd do it, but I was going to
wait and see."[62] In other words, he wanted the job but wanted to make certain that he would get it—that the support was there. He appeared to understand, instinctively perhaps, that legitimacy, and therefore stature, is rooted
in public endorsement.

As in acting, Reagan consistently viewed himself in politics as requiring
a supporting cast and careful staging. He was not accustomed to managing
on his own or attracted to doing it all himself.[63] As governor, he expressed
his method of governing as commonsensical:

> First, I had to select the best people I could find for my administra-
> tion—people whom I could rely on and trust. . . .
>
> Then, I had to set policies and goals I wanted these people to
> accomplish and to do whatever I could to help them achieve these
> goals. It seemed like simple, basic, sound management policy to
> me. . . .
>
> I've been criticized for what some people call a "hands off"
> management style. But I think the criticism has come from people
> who don't understand how we operated.
>
> I don't believe a chief executive should supervise every detail
> of what goes on in his organization. The chief executive should set
> broad policy and general ground rules, tell people what he or she
> wants them to do, then let them do it; . . . As long as they are doing
> what you have in mind, don't interfere, but if somebody drops the
> ball, intervene and make a change.[64]

Perhaps no president or presidential candidate in recent times has been so
clearly associated with a specific policy message. He repeated a basic conception of the role of government: active in defense, limited in the domestic

sphere. In his announcement of his candidacy, November 13, 1979, Reagan emphasized these very themes, concluding that the federal government has "overspent, overestimated and overregulated."[65] He made his announcement in New York City so as to appear less the regional candidate and spoke of foreign and defense policy, calling for a North American accord, so as to dispel his image as interested only in domestic policy. He was the last of ten Republican candidates to announce for the good reason that he was the odds-on front-runner. The announcement itself was unique: a half-hour television presentation purchased from over eighty individual stations since the major networks would not sell the time to the Reagan campaign. Reagan then appeared at a fund-raiser in New York on the same evening.

Organizationally Reagan had the distinct advantage of a team that had been tested in 1976 and had been successful beyond the odds. Naturally the Californians made up the core of the team. Theodore H. White and Lou Cannon identified Nancy Reagan as the future president's closest adviser. According to White, "Nancy Reagan was, and is, a woman of politics. . . . The central Reagan command meets in bed at night."[66] The California team included long-time associates like Michael Deaver, Edwin Meese, Lyn Nofziger, Richard Wirthlin, and Martin Anderson. They were joined by easterners Sears and William Casey, among others, and by a Californian who had worked for Ford in 1976, Stuart Spencer. All along there were several wealthy supporters who formed an important advisory group. That they were tested does not mean this group worked smoothly together. Sears alienated several of the Californians, some of whom—Nofziger, Deaver, and Anderson—actually withdrew from the campaign. "What Sears wanted, and made no bones about, was total control of the revolution he foresaw."[67] A surprise loss to George Bush in the Iowa caucuses (after Sears had assured Reagan that he was ahead), the "morale problem" and "bickering" (Reagan's own account) within the organization, and the large expenditures early in the campaign convinced the candidate that Sears should be fired. By Reagan's telling, it was exactly the "total control" by Sears that led to his removal.

> I thought Sears was smart and talented, but he became angry if I spoke to anyone but him about campaign affairs and he kept pressing me to fire Ed Meese and other people on the staff whom I thought highly of. . . .
>
> A change was necessary at the top of the campaign staff. I knew

I had to do it before the results were in from New Hampshire because if I lost and then fired Sears, people could say I was trying to make him the scapegoat for my loss, and I didn't want that to happen.[68]

William Casey took over as the campaign director, with Meese in charge of the day-to-day operations. Nofziger, Deaver, and Anderson rejoined the campaign, and Stuart Spencer joined at the urging of Nancy Reagan. Unfortunately internal staff conflict continued with Casey and Meese paired competitively against Deaver and Spencer. "The rival teams managed to work together in uneasy coexistence."[69] The rivalry carried over into the transition period.

Beyond the New Hampshire primary, which Reagan won handily, the Republican race was barely a contest. Reagan's principal opponent, George Bush, won but five primaries. His other strongest rival, John Anderson, actually bolted the party to run as an independent candidate. Former President Ford was a potential rival but only as a "statesman-in-waiting" should the active candidates fail to command sufficient support for the nomination. Polls taken in 1979 showed Ford to be the strongest potential rival to Reagan, as well as a stronger challenger to President Carter. The effect of Ford's noncandidacy was to prevent other challengers from gaining strength and raising sufficient money. Thus Ford gave his 1976 rival the advantage of blocking up the middle for him in 1980.[70]

The political opportunity for the Republican candidate in 1980 was apparent in the challenge to President Carter's renomination from Senator Edward Kennedy, a deteriorating economy, a prolonged hostage crisis in Iran, and declining approval ratings for the president. Leadership problems for Carter within the Democratic party preceded the most serious economic problems and the hostage crisis (the latter of which actually boosted the president's approval rating in the short term). As expected, Carter's difficulties encouraged several serious Republican candidates to enter the race in 1979. In all, nine announced between August 1978 and mid-November 1979. Of these, two withdrew before the first primary. Of the others, five were credible candidates, judged by their political status: John Connally, George Bush, Robert Dole, Howard Baker, and Ronald Reagan. John Anderson, a ten-term member of the House of Representatives from Illinois, came to be a serious candidate as a favorite among the media, and Gerald Ford conducted the classic noncandidate campaign—that is, like Nixon in 1964, prepared to run should a deadlock develop.

The relevance of the political opportunity is that it provides the context within which a transition takes place. A politically handicapped incumbent seeking reelection understandably draws nationally prominent opponents who are then more likely to manage predictable and effective transitions. Related to this advantage is the experience for the challenger of campaigning against serious opponents within his own party, which then aids him in defining the spectrum of interests and issues within the party, an essential exercise too for the transition.

The matter of stature was not fully resolved by Reagan's two terms as governor of California. He was still viewed by many as an actor, charming on the campaign trail but lacking real substance and relevant Washington experience. The Democrats were said to favor Reagan as their opponent precisely because he was judged to be a conservative ideologue, one too old for the job. Respected columnist James Reston explained early in the campaign that in Ronald Reagan the Republicans were about to give Carter his "favorite opponent." "Seldom in the history of American politics," Reston said, "has a party out of power shown so much generosity to a President in such deep difficulty."[71] Many pundits and politicians agreed with this analysis, believing that Gerald Ford, George Bush, or Howard Baker would be the stronger candidates.

In part because of the stature problem, the Reagan team developed what I have called a *trifocal* campaign. As I noted in 1981, that campaign concentrated "on creating party unity and winning the general election during the nomination phase."[72] In pursuing this strategy, Reagan invoked the so-called Eleventh Commandment: "Thou shalt not speak ill of other Republicans." He retained a moderate, Bill Brock, as party chairman against the advice of some of his more conservative advisers; expanded his staff to include aides of his opponents (most notably James A. Baker III); held a fund-raising dinner for his opponents to help with their campaign debts; and met with Republican candidates for other offices as well as party leaders from Congress and the states.[73]

Ronald Reagan had become a virtual icon within the Republican party. Missing his chance for the nomination in 1976, he and his team prepared carefully for the 1980 election. Mounting problems for President Carter created the opportunity for Republicans to recapture the White House. Reagan's personal ambition and policy message were entwined. He wanted to be president for a purpose. Yet he was able to adorn these aims with the motive of reacting to what the people wanted him to do, confident that the support would be forthcoming. Reagan was also secure with himself. He did not overreact to criticism. He had a concept of how he might best serve as an executive, and that image helped him overcome the stature problem by never really acknowledging it in classic terms. Further, though hardly a student of organization, he did believe strongly in delegation and reliance on staff. Thus he appointed experienced hands to manage the several phases of dismantling his campaign and organizing his administration; then he left town to spend time in the more relaxing atmosphere of his ranch in California. As with Nixon, though for different reasons, one might expect a purposeful and well-developed transition.

Bill Clinton, 1992

Ambition is an important ingredient for achieving political success. Bill Clinton is certainly ambitious. But he is more. He finds great satisfaction in personal relationships. He likes talking with, listening to, touching, and being touched by people of all walks of life. He is a man of many jackets, as David Maraniss points out:

> Within hours in one day, he could eat pork ribs and listen to the Delta Blues music at Sim's Bar-B-Que in the lowlands of Little Rock's predominantly black south side; then drive up to the Heights for a round of golf at the Country Club of Little Rock, an elite hideaway with manicured fairways and no black members; then, on the way home, he might pop in his favorite tape of white Pentecostal gospel music from the Alexandria Sanctuary Chorale. Clinton could go from a meeting with deer hunters in Scott County, furious because the state Game and Fish Commission would not let them run their dogs in December, to an education summit in Charlottesville staying up all night crafting an agenda of education goals for the fifty governors and the Bush administration, to a West Coast fund-raising dinner at Norman Lear's house where he mixed with the Hollywood glitterati. . . . No single world could keep him content for long.[74]

Besides showing Clinton's "contrasts and contradictions," Maraniss provides an account of a person comfortable in a wide range of settings. Further, those whom Bill Clinton touched were fulfilled. He was "blessed with a gift for making instant connection with people. He could dominate a whole room with his raw physical presence . . . or win voters singly with a word, a touch, a grin, and a steady, attentive gaze. It seemed not to matter that, as one of his most loyal troopers put it, his attentions were a mile wide and an inch deep. For those few moments he rationed to you, friend or stranger, he made you feel as if you were the most important person in his world."[75]

It was by no means remarkable then that many of Clinton's closest associates thought he should seek the presidency. "The expectation was always there. . . . Wherever it came from, it was always there, not a matter of pre-destination but of expectation and will, and it had built up year by year, decade by decade."[76] He first thought about running in 1988 but was warned not to by his aide, Betsey Wright, primarily because of potential revelations about philandering (Gary Hart having withdrawn in 1987 for precisely those reasons). Clinton went as far as to call a meeting of his closest friends for a luncheon preceding an announcement. In the end, however, he decided against running, citing personal and family reasons, notably the effects on his daughter, Chelsea.[77]

Clinton did have a major speaking role at the 1988 Democratic National Convention. He delivered the principal nominating speech for Michael S. Dukakis. It was a chance before the nation and the Democratic party to display his talents for a future campaign. The hall was noisy, the house lights were not turned down, and the speech was too long and inaudible to most people.[78] There he stood, one of the fine orators of the modern age, a distant and unheard voice droning on for thirty-two minutes. Two of the networks cut away. It was a miserable experience for the young governor, hardly suited to his expectation or to his abilities. Only humor could partially save the situation and Clinton did his best to salvage it on that basis, afterward appearing on the "Tonight Show" with Johnny Carson.

The defeat of Dukakis meant that the nomination would once again be open on the Democratic side in 1992. Clinton's national ambitions survived the humiliation of the 1988 convention. There were, however, the matters of timing and opportunity. In 1990 he would have to decide whether or not to seek reelection as governor. Two significant problems faced Clinton. First and foremost, it was by no means certain, by Clinton's own review, that he could be reelected. In discussing the situation with media consultant Frank Greer, Clinton reportedly said: "I think I'm in terrible trouble. I'm at 46 per-cent, and I'm dropping like a rock."[79] Also important was Clinton's attitude, which was, according to political consultant Dick Morris, "dithering and depressed."

Clinton's dilemma, as Morris viewed it, was that he was temporarily without a crusade, such as education reform or economic development, and that he was incapable of being a caretaker chief executive. He had to be engaged in "some important, valiant fight for the good of the world to lend coherence and structure to his life, and when he didn't have those fights he would turn on himself, he would eat away at himself, he would become depressed, paranoid, surly and, one suspects, escapist." Clinton was an activist, Morris concluded, "because it was the only way he could maintain any reasonable degree of psychological coherence."[80]

Greer and Stanley Greenberg, a Yale political science professor turned pollster, came to Arkansas to help him resolve his dilemma. "With his art and his handlers' artifice, Clinton cobbled up a plan for the future and managed somehow to reposition himself as the agent of change."[81] He won with 57 percent of the vote, a substantial victory, yet a decrease of 7 percent from his win in 1986.

A second matter related to a change in Arkansas that was implemented in 1986, extending the term for governor from two to four years. In a debate with his opponent in 1990, Clinton was asked he if would serve out his term as governor. He responded: "You bet."[82] With that response, Clinton would either have to sit out the 1992 election or renege on his promise.

During this time, Clinton continued to receive national recognition within the Democratic party for his activities with the Democratic Leadership Council. He delivered a well-received speech in Cleveland, May 6, 1991, that was bound to stir talk of his candidacy in 1992, particularly given the search for a credible candidate to run against President Bush. Bothered by his promise to serve the full four years as governor, Clinton was urged by Greer and others to tour the state to judge whether the voters were likely to be bothered by his running for president. In what was dubbed "The Secret Tour," Clinton got the answer he wanted. "Everywhere he went, people told him to run."[83]

In many ways, timing is opportunity. Presidential candidates have to prepare themselves, seek financial support, and develop an organization well in advance of an election year. Yet the spring of 1991 was not an encouraging time for Democrats. In the blush of the spectacular success of Desert Storm, President Bush was riding high in the polls—still enjoying more than 70 percent approval ratings into the summer. Further, no elected Republican president in the post–World War II period had been defeated for reelection, and two Democratic presidents from the South had not fared well: Johnson withdrew under pressure from the race in 1968 and Carter was badly beaten by Reagan. Yet it was precisely the lack of perceived opportunity that gave Clinton his chance. "If Al Gore . . . had shown signs of interest, Clinton would have stood aside," given that Gore was also a prospective Democratic Leadership Council candidate and had been tested in the 1988 campaign.[84]

Those Democrats judged to have the best chance of defeating Bush— Gore, Senator Bill Bradley of New Jersey, and Governor Mario Cuomo of New York—either decided against running or, in Cuomo's case, could not decide. Consequently, newcomers like Bill Clinton were encouraged to run. By the end of the year, with the exception of former Governor Jerry Brown of California, the Democratic field had to be introduced to the country: former one-term Senator Paul E. Tsongas of Massachusetts, Senator Robert J. Kerrey of Nebraska, Senator Tom Harkin of Iowa, and Governor L. Douglas Wilder of Virginia. Bill Clinton was bound to stand out in this competition. And so the lack of opportunity for Democrats had allowed the five-term governor of Arkansas to have his shot. As with Carter, the circumstances of recruitment aid in explaining the character of the transition from campaigning to governing. Conditions that give outsiders a chance likewise challenge them at the point of effecting the passage from candidate to president. Also an outsider, Reagan showed how these conditions could be managed by turning to experienced aides. Carter and Clinton were much less successful in this regard.

There was evidence of trouble ahead for President Bush even at the height of his popularity. The high approval ratings were based primarily on the success of the Gulf War. On the specific question of Bush's handling of the economy, the disapproval score exceeded that of approval in three of four readings during the first six months of 1991. His mean scores on these four tests were approval 44 percent, disapproval 52 percent.[85] By September, the comparison was stark between Bush's approval rating for handling foreign affairs (73 percent) and the nation's economy (42 percent).[86] In early April 1991, when President Bush's approval rating was at 80 percent or better, responses to an ABC News/*Washington Post* survey showed troubling signs: 42 percent said the country was "headed in the right direction," while 51 percent said the country was "on the wrong track."[87] In brief, it was apparent that once the blush of victory over Iraq had passed, President Bush was highly vulnerable on economic and personal security issues.

Post–Gulf War domestic issues, then, were bound to serve as the agenda for Bill Clinton, who, by reason of experience, would be seen as a domestically oriented candidate. Thus it was that the agenda facilitated a Clinton-style campaign. Clinton had been actively planning to run since the late spring. His announcement came on October 3. He was preceded by Tsongas (April 30), Wilder (September 13), Harkin (September 15), and Kerrey (September 30). Brown announced his candidacy on October 21. Several others decided not to run, including unknowns like Representative David McCurdy of Oklahoma (October 18) and well-knowns like Jesse Jackson (November 2) and Cuomo (December 20). The overall obscurity of the group of candidates was revealed in an NBC News/*Wall Street Journal* poll of registered Democrats in fall 1991. Cuomo and Jackson were the choice of 29 and 20 percent respectively; Brown was named by 6 percent; the other five, including Clinton, were named by 4 percent or less.[88]

There was little doubt that Clinton and his aides had noted the disquiet among Americans as evidenced by the polls. In his announcement in Little Rock on October 3, Clinton stressed the need to "fight for the forgotten middle class." He concluded that "the country is heading in the wrong direction fast, slipping behind, losing our way." Later the political director for Clinton's campaign, James Carville, placed these reminders on a post near his desk:

Change vs. more of the same
The economy, stupid
Don't forget health care[89]

It could be said that the purpose of these prompts was to recall what was said in Clinton's announcement and revealed in the polling on issues. The campaign stayed "on message," as the phrase has it.[90]

Coverage of the announcement was what one might expect, given that Clinton's national visibility was no greater than that of his competitors for the nomination. The *Washington Post* placed the story on the front page, lower right-hand corner. The story stressed his economic themes and mentioned that Clinton was best known "for his long-winded speech nominating Michael S. Dukakis." Also noted was the fact that "he broke a pledge . . . to serve out his four-year term" as governor.[91] The announcement apparently did not merit a front-page story in the *New York Times*; it was on page 10. The story identified Clinton as a representative of the New South and stressed his emphasis on programs that work for the middle class.[92]

Given his "Gary Hart" problem, there was, understandably, discussion within the Clinton camp as to how to handle the expected questions about his marriage. Reportedly Clinton's inclination was to refuse to answer "have you ever" questions. His wife doubted that this approach would work, arguing that he had to be forthright. Clinton attended one of the famous breakfasts hosted by Godfrey Sperling Jr. (of the *Christian Science Monitor*) in mid-September and was convinced by his wife to meet the issue head on. When asked about his marriage he stated, with Hillary Clinton at his side: "Like nearly anybody who has been together for twenty years, our relationship has not been perfect or free from difficulties, but we feel good about where we are and we believe in our obligation to each other, and we intend to be together thirty or forty years from now, whether I run for president or not."[93] It was very much the approach taken on Super Bowl Sunday 1992, when the couple had to face the revelations by Gennifer Flowers of a long-standing affair with the governor. Whatever the nature of the relationship between the Clintons, they were seemingly joined in a common political endeavor. As was observed in one account: "The two of them seemed consumed by a common flame."[94]

And so the Clintons began another campaign, the most ambitious ever. Remarkably, they had undertaken eighteen elections in eighteen years: eight primaries, two runoffs, and eight generals. They won sixteen and lost two. The campaign for the nomination would be number nineteen; the successful fall campaign would make it an even twenty. This experience made Bill Clinton a specialist in campaigning, an important factor in predicting how he would then organize and manage the White House. Perhaps he would not effect a complete transition from candidate to president; possibly he would show that it was not needed.

The emerging Clinton team was a mixture of the bright, the savvy, and the loyal—all three characteristics showing up in the same person many times. Foremost was his wife, Hillary Rodham. A professional woman and an active policy advocate, the governor's wife was a constant presence in all decisions that interested her. James Carville, the political director for the campaign, took her measure early.

> I decided the first time I met her that I was going to take five minutes and do nothing but watch Hillary.
>
> You didn't have to be a genius in room dynamics to figure out the drift of her place in the campaign. You got it from her body lan-

guage, from the deference with which people spoke to her, from the way she was referred to in the conversations that were breaking out around her. She has a way about her.[95]

But Bill Clinton had many long-lasting relationships with interesting and able people. He collected and nurtured friends from his college and law school days at Georgetown, Oxford, and Yale Universities. Like the "old gang," these people were more or less "on call" for the person around whom the group orbited. They included a number of his Rhodes scholar colleagues, some of whom showed up later in the Clinton cabinet and subcabinet, all of whom were consulted at one time or another. Others worked into the campaign staff were those who served with him as governor and leader of the Democratic Leadership Council (for example, Bruce Lindsey) and those added to enhance the professionalism needed for a national campaign (for example, Frank Greer, Stan Greenberg, George Stephanopoulos, Carville, and Paul Begala).

In addition to intelligence, the team shared another feature, but one less likely to serve them well. No one of them had been tested in any important way in a national campaign. Had they been up against more serious opposition, this lack of experience might have made more of a difference. As it was, however, they were no more the neophytes than were the advisers to the other campaigns. More serious was their candidate's management and decisionmaking style of conducting a kind of continuous seminar and his heavy involvement in the early days of the campaign. The description of the Clintons' choice of David Wilhelm as the campaign manager reveals the practice.

> His inexperience at national politics seemed to suit Clinton fine, since it guaranteed real control to Hillary and himself. Deep into autumn [1991], the candidate was serving de facto as his own manager, scheduler, and political director, and the resulting organizational problems only got worse as the campaign grew in size. No one was really in charge. The Clintons, by chance or design, had seen to that.[96]

Carville's "patience with crowded rooms and extended discussion was notoriously short. . . . The diffusion of power and the competition for Clinton's ear sent him into a sulk that would last intermittently into spring and would finally end only when a palace coup put him clearly in charge."[97] Interestingly, Carville was one of the few on Clinton's campaign staff who understood that the transition was about ending a campaign and starting a government. As a campaign operative, he wanted no official position in the Clinton administration, though he continued to perform as a political consultant.

By the time of the Democratic convention in July, the Clinton team had matured and was working well. They had been baptized by fire during the campaign for the nomination. In addition to the usual problems associated with a multicandidate nomination race, the campaign staff had to manage a threat from the independent, unpredictable candidacy of H. Ross Perot and a seemingly endless series of embarrassing personal matters associated with their candidate: the accusations by Gennifer Flowers, Clinton's effort to avoid military service, his antiwar activism while a student at Oxford, a pot-smoking incident, and Whitewater and the association with James McDougal, owner of a failed savings and loan. At one point, David Wilhelm was reported to have said: "You can't take all these hits and survive. Story after story after story. It is very hard."[98] But they did survive to accomplish what had escaped most postwar Democratic presidential candidates: a nominating convention featuring party unity.

It goes without saying that a young governor from a small state has a stature problem in seeking the presidency. Bill Clinton had no significant Washington political experience and therefore would be found wanting by the test of Theodore H. White's legitimacy principle. Little occurred during the long campaign to confer eminence; much occurred to detract from that quality. The many personal issues raised during the campaign were managed but not put to rest. Those associated with his lack of military experience and the financial arrangements in the Whitewater venture carried over into his presidency. In addition, the Clintons were from the postwar "baby boom" generation, as were his closest aides. They naturally represented a very different life-style than had been typical in the White House. A period of adjustment was, therefore, to be expected since the Clintons were the first professional couple to serve. The point is that Bill Clinton had, from the start, a serious stature problem that begged to be addressed at some point.[99]

It is said that there is no such thing as luck. Perhaps so. There are circumstances, however, that favor one candidate over another. The Clintons and their close associates prepared themselves to take advantage of a series of breaks: a weak field of candidates; an economy recovering slowly;

Perot's withdrawal during the Democratic convention; Pat Buchanan's stronger than expected challenge to Bush's renomination; the apparent failure of President Bush to control the Republican convention; and the reentry of Perot as a candidate.

Bill Clinton's personal drive to win the presidency seldom flagged from his first entry into politics. Less clear was how that ambition was augmented by a clear policy purpose. No one doubted his broad interest in issues. What was lacking was a centralizing theme comparable to that of Ronald Reagan, for example. The lack of Washington-based executive experience among Clinton's advisers was not automatically compensated for by the energy of their youth—another factor to be accounted for during the transition. Finally, the president-elect's own stature was more a liability to be overcome than an asset to bank on in forming his administration. As with the other presidents-elect in this set, therefore, even a cursory review of Clinton's background reveals a predictable set of relevant issues for the transition from candidate to president.

Signals along the Way

Transitions begin with the initial stirrings that prompt a person to consider running for president. The personal quest for power is further shaped by the current agenda, that quest then to be realized by taking advantage of political opportunity with the help of a coterie of ambitious, satellite-like aides orbiting the star. Would-be presidents vary substantially in regard to their innate organizational abilities and their national and institutional stature. Where circumstances favor the outsider, as they have in several recent elections, the president-elect is then challenged to bolster his legitimacy during the transition and thereafter. Since stature itself is not so easily defined, designing a strategy for enhancing it is no simple matter.

The four cases presented in this chapter offer contrasts for understanding differences in the transition experience. The signals are there in the prenomination and nomination periods as to what problems face a president-elect during the transition. Nixon was a familiar figure with ample Washington experience and acquaintance with other seasoned political hands. One could predict a relatively smooth, conventional transition, though no definitive resolution to the problems of trust that plagued him throughout his career. The other presidents-elect were outsiders, though that was about all they had in common. Carter's candidacy itself foretold a special set of problems for the transition, given that he campaigned against the politics of the government he was elected to manage. Viewing himself as an agent of change, Carter resisted meeting standard expectations from the first and therefore denied himself the help he needed. Reagan, too, crusaded against Washington, focusing more on national-level programs than on politics. However, as shown in his campaign organization, Reagan was perfectly willing to rely heavily on savvy Washington insiders, thus portending a willingness to adjust to political realities in creating an administration. Clinton portrayed an even more flexible posture but, somewhat like Carter, was a candidate of circumstance. His background and acquaintances signaled exactly the set of problems to be overcome during the transition, as well as the conditions that interfered with finding solutions. Further, his lack of stature and bearing meant that he had to find other sources of support in his struggle to create and maintain his presidency.

3

BEYOND THE CAMPAIGN PSYCHOLOGY

A REAGAN AIDE, experienced in both campaigning and governing, expressed this view:

> Part of [the problem] is a campaign psychology. It's us versus them. It's Republican versus Democrat. That's not the same as governing. . . . There aren't many Hail Mary passes in governing. It's chewing things up five and ten yards at a time and making people play on your side of the turf.

A presidential campaign is an experience unique to the American political system. It is lengthy, intense, and strenuous. An elaborate, temporary national organization is created around a person, who becomes an inescapable presence. One presidential adviser referred to it as a "one-ring circus" as contrasted to the "thousand-ring circus" of government. Another explained that the campaign is cocoon-like. "In the campaign you can pretty much determine what you're going to do during the day and stick to it. External events . . . do not have to intrude upon you unduly." Legions of workers commit their time and energy to the candidate, generating a dedication and identification otherwise reserved for saints long past. This extraordinarily self-centered apparatus propels itself at a frenzied pace to a day certain: the first Tuesday after the first Monday in November once every four years. And then it is over and the winner is charged with forming a government. A candidate the day before, the winner is president-elect the day after. "It's like flicking a light switch. The next day, it's different." One former cabinet secretary, with substantial campaign experience, thought about the complications of this transition in this way:

> Running for office is a very, very selfish thing to do. You have to be selfish. You have to steal time from your family, you have to steal diligence from your friends, you beg and plead for money. . . . Serving, if you serve well, is selfless. And there aren't a lot of politicians who are able to make the shift from selfish to selfless in a short period of time.

This chapter draws heavily on the recollections and analyses of a number of persons with experience in campaigns and transitions. It focuses on the effect of the campaign and the set of issues associated with the abrupt ending of one activity and the start-up of another. Campaigning is not governing. But campaigning has lessons for governing if candidates and their aides are prepared to learn them. A theme can act as a bridge from the campaign to governing, as can preelection planning if it is integrated into the campaign structure. I do not tell the story of each campaign; rather I treat the abovementioned topics, with illustrations from each of the four presidents' experiences and attention to developments leading to a more campaign-oriented style of governing.

No two candidates or campaigns are exactly alike. Yet in the set of four, there were similarities between the two Republicans as party insiders and between the two Democrats as Washington outsiders. Nixon and Reagan relied more on experienced political operatives than did Carter and Clinton. Nixon's political career was based in Washington, D.C., and so his reliance on contacts developed during that time was to be expected. Reagan served as governor of the largest state and had been involved in a national campaign for the nomination in 1976. In addition, he was a popular fund-raiser for the party. As an outsider to Washington, he was very much an insider to the party. Carter and Clinton, on the other hand, were not major figures on the national political scene.[1] They were dark horses at the start, with few pundits giving them much of a chance for the nomination. Each won the nomination in a field of candidates with limited stature, then defeated an incumbent president in an intense campaign emphasizing change. Neither had coattails.

Whereas expectations ran high (both also entered with Democratic Congresses), political resources were limited, thus heightening the need for a proficient transition.

Campaigning Is Not Governing

By the conventional standards of the presidential transition, campaigning is not governing. Transition aides and reporters have typically measured incoming administrations by these standards. As one said, "Campaigning is so addictive and such a high that it's very different from the kind of solidness that one needs in governing." Therefore the transition is conventionally viewed as a passage from one type of politics to another. Skills are not readily transferable. Those with campaigning talents and limited Washington-based governing experience may well find it necessary to hire a new team and learn a new trade.

The Clinton experience, however, insinuates the need for altered standards. Like his predecessors, Clinton had to form his presidency so as to govern in the conventional manner, but campaigning for policy had become a more common exercise. This trend toward a campaigning overlay to classic governing suited Bill Clinton's talents and style but was unlikely to find favor with traditionalists, some of whom dubbed his transition in 1992 the worst. Viewed in the context of developments in contemporary styles of governing, however, the Clinton experience should have been judged by revised criteria. As it happened, these revised standards did not exist in 1992. Consequently, the Clinton team was bound to do poorly, failing to meet the conventional expectations; they were unprepared to identify and meet altered expectations.

Following is a sample of how three seasoned veterans of transitions see the differences between campaigning and governing—differences that, by their estimates, must be managed following the election.

> Campaigning is about sharpening differences and making promises. And governing is about fulfilling promises and making the system work. These are very, very different goals. . . . Campaigning, you are talking about themes. You're talking about fairly simple solutions [to problems] that are much more complex. There are many more nuances in governing. And finally, in campaigning you

can be elected by being against somebody. "I'm not so-and-so." But when you get into office, that . . . certainly won't carry you for four years.

*   *   *

If you make a mistake campaigning . . . it can be corrected the next day by a good speech or a good appearance. . . . So it's kind of transitory—a series of transitory events. Governing, once you make a mistake, that sticks with you because you've done something that has implications and ramifications for the real world. . . . Every decision the president makes has consequences.

*   *   *

In a campaign you make promises to everybody, and you don't really have to make choices [among these promises]. . . . You make all sorts of promises to [a special interest] that you're going to support these little programs that everybody else thinks are a waste of money but they think are the end of the earth. And then, at the same time, your campaign is putting millions of dollars into advertising to say that you're for [something else]. . . . But [when] you're governing, and the budget comes up, you've got to make a choice. The point is, in a campaign you can avoid choices. You can fudge choices. When you govern, and the rubber hits the road, you can't fudge those choices anymore.

That campaigning and governing are different is not to suggest they are unrelated. The challenge in the conventional transition is to be aware of the distinction so as to avoid mistakes and, even more important, to take advantage of what is relevant in the campaign experience for governing. Meeting that challenge is complicated by the nature of the campaign experience, which, among other consequences, leaves one exhausted for the trying task of creating a new administration.

The freneticism of the campaign [is very real], where you get up every day, you read the newspapers, you see what the polls say and you take a course that day depending on [what you find] because you're trying to change something. That doesn't work in governing [where] you've got to have long-range plans, and you've got to stick with things, to reach that long-range goal.

*   *   *

Internally [campaigns are] a nightmare. I've worked in a number of them. I despise transitions. One, you're tired. You come off of a campaign that is, in the last ten weeks, extremely intense. No sleep, no rest, yanked from cover to post, nits blown out of all proportion, that whole rigmarole. And instantly, the next morning, you're president-elect.

These familiar characteristics of a campaign underscore the importance of thinking about the transition, using standard criteria, well in advance of the election. To delay is to be tempted to rely heavily on the recent campaign experience for creating a presidency. To delay is to engage in a nongoverning event, the campaign, lacking a framework for extracting lessons about governing. To delay is to expend precious transition time identifying and correcting weaknesses that should have been attended to earlier. In brief, the only way to learn governing lessons from the campaign is to prepare oneself in advance to do so. As it is, however, some candidates and their aides find they have neither the understanding nor the time for advanced strategic thinking.

Expectations of the president-elect are very different from those of that person as candidate. Having just succeeded in one arduous task, the winner is now faced with having to acquaint himself with a new job—one defined by the anticipations of others who have a clear stake in their definitions. When there is a party change, as with the four candidates receiving attention here, a challenger to the incumbent party (and to an incumbent president in three of the cases) is transformed from a candidate to the next chief executive. He moves from being a pretender or claimant to being the certain successor. Whatever had been formulated during the campaign now must be tempered by the complex set of anticipations of power holders and presidency watchers. For just as the campaign differs from governing for the candidate and his aides, so too are the two activities viewed separately by other power holders, including analysts in the media. Identifying these perceptions is important for the winner, even if he is bent on changing them.

One respondent was particularly expressive on this point, stressing accountability as a prime difference in expectations between campaigning and governing.

When you're governing, you know that performance counts, and that if performance is good, a year down the pike, the story will be good. When you're campaigning, you want to get on the nightly news every night. When you're governing, getting on the nightly news every night may or may not be the best thing to do. . . . The concentration on daily spin makes it hard to have a clear direction because . . . you don't notice that sometimes you're . . . seeming to zig and zag in ways that make people think you don't govern with a steady hand.

The only thing that really matters in the campaign is what happens on the airplane. . . . If somebody [in the campaign headquarters] does something stupid during the campaign, [the candidate] can say: "It's just a campaign worker, it doesn't mean anything. The real story is what I'm doing. I'm the candidate."

When you're president, it doesn't work that way. [A cabinet secretary] . . . does [something] and it's stupid. The president gets blamed . . . and he might not know anything about it until he reads about it on the front page of the *Washington Post*.

So that's the big difference. You need to have systems of accountability and control in place to govern that you don't when you're a candidate.

Expectations may well be influenced by the election outcome. Landslide winners are given latitude in creating their presidencies, while still being held accountable for what is done in their name. Note, however, that there was but one landslide winner in the four most recent cases of party turnover: Reagan in 1980. The point is that presidents-elect, even those with the political resources to assume office in their own way, are expected to work within the generally accepted rules for forming a government.

Lessons from the Campaign for Governing

Are there lessons in the campaign for governing? Absolutely, according to those actively involved. Campaigns involve selling ideas, dealing with the press, organizing and managing staff, and interacting with established party organizations. For the most part, however, the lessons are internalized, and they become part of what amounts to training for coping with issues and dealing with people later on. There is, in fact, little or no time for reflective thinking about governing during the campaign, and special arrangements for preelection transition planning can lead to conflict among staff. Thus, in spite of the fact that most respondents identified a number of lessons from the campaign that carry over to governing, few thought there was time or that they had the capacity to absorb these lessons along the way. Indeed, most believed with this Democratic aide that "a lot of people in our administration and campaign had an aversion, almost a superstition, about [thinking ahead] too much."[2] An aide to a Republican candidate agreed: "First of all, [the candidate] was so superstitious that he wouldn't allow himself [to think ahead]. Some of us did . . . [but] even then it was two different organizations."

What lessons from the campaign then carry over? Several of those identified were valuable only if the candidate and his aides understood at the time of the campaign how different governing would be. For example, the "crisis mentality" of the campaign is, in many instances, self-generated so as to maintain enthusiasm and effort within the organization and as a means for accommodating press coverage. Therefore, if this purpose is understood by the candidate and his closest advisers, then they know that in governing they need to "take the temperature down as much as [they] possibly can, and try to translate that . . . campaign/crisis mentality to a longer mind-set, to a calmer environment."

One respondent gave an example that essentially reversed the relationship—that is, a lesson from governing for campaigning. He noted an instance in which the presidential candidate attacked his opponent in the primaries on a proposal that later emerged as important in his own presidency. Though the president shifted positions on other issues, he refused in this case. "We couldn't budge him. We just literally couldn't budge him." The lesson is that those experienced in governing are cautious about campaign positions that may later cause problems in governing. As another aide pointed out: "Certainly you want to try not to paint yourself into corners . . . [to] be alert to not limit . . . options when [you] get in." Perhaps the outstanding example in recent administrations is the "no new taxes" pledge of George Bush in the 1988 campaign.

The most frequently mentioned lessons from the campaign with relevance to governing concerned the related topics of the media, issues, and the importance of words. In regard to the media, the points made reflected changes in communication. "We get [exposed to] about a hundred times more [miscellaneous] information in a day than our parents got in a lifetime," and therefore, according to this aide, "you have to say it over and over and over and over again. George Bush, in a campaign, would say something and if you missed it, forget it. You'd never hear it again. With Bill Clinton in the campaign . . . if you missed it, don't worry. You're going to hear it the next day and the next day and the next day." Equally important is the training the candidate and his aides receive in contemporary news cycles. One aide noted that "the ability to react in minutes, not in hours or days . . . [is] important in campaigns and . . . in governance." Another said, "Responding in the same news cycle is critically important, which is now taking place in the White House." One adviser was expansive on this point:

> Campaigns today . . . are making everyone who's in government acutely aware of the media cycles. . . . The new technologies can be used by presidents and others. There's a whole element of direct satellite activity . . . of trying to understand what it means to have worldwide . . . coverage of particular events, and how you as a public figure have to either react or . . . try to shape some of that.

This particular aide expressed concern that the right lessons be learned from the campaign, which was his way of illustrating again the differences between campaigning and governing. In other words, simply understanding technological developments is no guarantee that knowledge is then competently translated to the governing mode. Rather, a White House may simply continue to manage campaigns, interested more in public response than in institutional reactions within the government.

In regard to issues, several aspects were stressed. The candidate and his aides learn about what the people are thinking: "You get their reactions to ideas, particularly if you're campaigning genuinely on the same . . . objectives and goals that you intend to use in governing. . . . You also get an idea of what the opposition to your ideas is." Another aide also mentioned the importance of the message component, stressing that "a successful campaign has to have great discipline in its message and a successful presidency has to have . . . discipline in its message [to provide] direction." He mentioned Reagan as an example of such discipline, citing an instance of where he repeated a tax reform speech seven times in a row, and Bush as a counterexample.

Issue exploration and discussion during the campaign also affect the candidate. One respondent observed, "If you don't have a good sense of what people are thinking after two years, eighteen months or whatever, of slugging it out through all the primaries and then going through the general election, then you just are politically tone deaf. . . . You have a pretty good sense

of how far you can push down below what the public will accept." The associated effect should be that "the candidate . . . builds up in the public mind
what he is all about," which all contributes to the president-elect's personal
comprehension of who he is and what are his advantages in leadership. An
unambiguous cast to a candidate's leadership contributes to "the capacity to
govern, particularly if he carries over the leadership positions he has projected, the sense of who he is then into governing."

Related to these lessons of leadership is the management of issues.
Campaigns teach that "the politics of issues is often . . . more important than
the substantive debates around them." However right one may be in regard
to an issue, even when measured by public support, the cause may be lost if
the politics is poorly managed. A balance has to be achieved.

> The dilemma is that the lesson that often gets learned is that the pol-
> itics of managing the issue becomes the issue. And the key . . . is the
> ability to find people who are going to staff these sensitive posi-
> tions, who understand that it's not a pure exercise of making public
> policy. It's not a Kennedy School graduate who's learned whatever
> the analytic techniques are, but it's equally dangerous to staff these
> jobs with people who are simply going to worry about the politics
> of it all.

This former Democratic aide gave the early Clinton administration as
an example of erring on the side of politics and the Carter administration
as an example of erring on the side of policy.

The lessons associated with the use and meaning of words are intimately
affiliated with the set of issues just discussed. The use of words is also a case
of where prior governing experience at the national level may have something to teach the campaigner since it involves an understanding of the distinction between the two activities—campaigning and governing. "The
words of a president are scrutinized with much greater intent than the words
of a candidate." Two variations of this theme were offered. In the first, candidates were advised that words will be taken down even if they are not scrutinized to the same degree as for presidents, a version of the don't-paint-
yourself-into-a-corner lesson.

> You should not be making speeches and pronouncements to the
> American people of things you're going to do if you don't sincerely

intend to try to follow through on them. So those words do matter, and they do come back to haunt you. I can remember . . . watching Clinton's first press conference in Little Rock. [He was] sitting there telling reporters: "Well, I never said that." And I'm sitting there [thinking]: "Honey, this is just beginning. You did say it. They know you said it. You can't . . . say 'I never said that.' " It's just not how it works. So, yes, it matters what you say.

Another aide had obviously thought a fair amount about this subject, particularly as it relates to the difference between campaigning and governing. For him, words *are* the action in the campaign, whereas they are but a part of the job in the White House.

The premium in campaigns is on words. Especially when you are a challenger all that matters is what you say, not so much what you do. What you say is your action. So that's not perfectly transferable. As president words are also actions but they're not enough. You must govern. You are responsible for actual operations. The campaign doesn't particularly prepare you for that.

This aide identified a time horizon difference as well that had to be acknowledged by the candidate. Others, too, discussed the frenetic pace of the campaign compared with that of governing. But he offered a subtle component to dissuade candidates from being misled by the urgency of the campaign:

You certainly now . . . need to manage big governing issues as you would manage a campaign. But you can't get locked into the mindset . . . of simply worrying about the daily win or loss. When you are governing you not only will lose some days but you have to lose some days in order to achieve your goals. In a campaign you really can't afford [to lose a day]. It sounds simplistic but it is true: our job every day was to win the day. That's different from running a presidency.

The time horizon is not the only critical difference for the new president. There are relationships in governing that are markedly dissimilar or simply do not show up to any substantial degree in the campaign. In the words of one respondent, "Press relationships are totally different in a governing mode than they are in a campaign mode. Congressional relationships are almost nonexistent in a campaign. Constituent relationships . . . are almost nonexistent in a campaign mode and they become very high in a governing mode." Comparing Clinton and Bush, this aide concluded that a balance is required: "Clinton is faulted for trying to govern as if he were campaigning; [Bush] can be just as faulted for trying to campaign as if he were governing."

The Matter of a Theme

"The transition is such a people-oriented thing. You can pass briefing books back and forth. You can produce papers endlessly. . . . But the fact is that the people are 90 percent of the transition." This assessment in response to a question about a theme for the transition aptly emphasizes the extent to which appointments and staffing dominate the creation of a new administration. But, of course, people do not come to Washington as blank slates, particularly following an intense campaign in which they have sought to convince the voters that they know more about managing government than their opponents do. An important element to any transition from candidate to president-elect to president is, therefore, to identify what it all means. Can the winning team identify a theme or purpose that has developed during the campaign to orient the transition? Should they do so? The responses varied but, when consolidated, reveal differing experiences and expectations between the Democrats (Carter and Clinton) and the Republicans (Nixon and Reagan), that, again, may be more related to their outsider-insider status and styles than to their party affiliations.

The Democratic respondents emphasized a more organizational or process-oriented theme, suggesting that the campaign itself had not necessarily produced integration among people, organization, and ideas, and that the candidate and his team were not automatically prepared to manage the new role on the day after the election. One Clinton aide lamented that "maybe the theme should be on resting, reflecting, and getting ready." This person expressed the view that such a posture would demonstrate "respect for the office" and "for the man or woman who still inhabits the office." Other Clinton and Carter respondents painted corresponding portraits— essentially of campaign-weary organizations turning their attention to the task of creating a leadership structure to reassure voters that they had made the right choice. There was a strikingly less confident tone in these comments, no doubt explained by the fact that these two presidents-elect, Carter and Clinton, won narrowly, had no Washington experience, and governed relatively small states then dominated by the Democratic party. As a consequence these aides stressed the need to develop and display confidence as a means of engendering stature:

> I don't know if there should be [a theme]. I think it is a futile exercise. I think if you are looking at it from the president-elect's point of view, what should he want? What he wants, I think, is to communicate a sense of crisp assumption of responsibility and command . . . and that he's going to assume command of the process and have in place people who are going to take command of the process.
>
> * * *
>
> I don't think there needs to be a theme. It is a procedural exercise, which is supposed to get people ready to go.
>
> * * *
>
> I'm not sure the substantive themes should tip anyone off, or give them any suggestion about the timing of issues, because the truth is, you want to get some people together and start talking it through. . . . I don't know whether it's really right for the president, right after he's elected to announce the themes and then to move right into it. I really think you need to have a lot of conversations with people.

Note that this third respondent (a Clinton appointee) acknowledged the probability of a substantive theme, simply advising that it should not be put forward early since it could presumably then act as a constraint. Rather the president-elect and his team should engage in policy conversations. This perspective was similar to that of a Carter aide:

> So, yes . . . the president does need to have some broadly stated themes for his presidency, and try very hard from the very beginning of his administration, and indeed through his administration, to be pursuing and expressing and reflecting by his actions and his directions those themes. He must also, however, have the flexibility to respond and to deal with subjects that need dealing with that don't necessarily come under his thematic blanket.

Discussions of this topic by Republican respondents were exceptionally consistent, particularly those by Reagan aides and appointees. Thematic continuity from the campaign into the transition was embodied in the candidate himself. For them, Reagan had projected a strong and clear message that served as a basis for structuring a transition organization and making appointments. Several stressed the extent to which people, organization, and policy were integrated through the clarity of purpose of the candidate. None of them believed that further conversation was necessary as a means of translating a theme into recommendations for appointments, nor did they mention the importance of flexibility. "I don't think you should run for president unless you've got some fairly well conceived notion of what it is you want to talk to the country about," was the view of one Republican aide. Yet he acknowledged that it could happen—that the candidate and his organization could work through a campaign and election without knowing in the end what it was all about.[3] Presumably in such cases further conversation would be required.

In fact, most of these respondents doubted that it was necessary to announce a theme during the transition since it would have (or should have) developed during the campaign. Therefore the importance of the theme was less as a public relations gimmick (called "hokum" by one respondent) than as a campaign outcome to guide appointments and set the agenda for the first 100 days. "Really, in my view," said one, "it's hands-on management in operation. It's not so thematic and it's not so visionary except the crafting of the 100-day plan. . . . What was it that you said during the campaign? And how does that fit with your 100-day plan?"

The Reagan advisers were not in the least puzzled about the messages from the campaign and election. They had the advantage of a seriously weakened economy that provided an obvious agenda for action and a candidate who fastened on a limited number of issues.[4] Various Reagan aides and appointees produced a remarkably coherent composite sketch of the effect of the campaign for creating an administration:

> *On campaign issues:* You have to remember back to 1981 when inflation was what it was, and interest rates were in the double digits and all that. . . . It was clear that the first priority was trying to get the economy back on track. And so it was fairly easy. The theme was kind of there for us. If we didn't solve that, we weren't going to be able to do anything anyway.

On thematic continuity in the candidate: I think you can come in with a theme; Ronald Reagan did because he ran on the tax cutting theme and a very definite four-point program. And he wanted his transition to reflect it, appointments and everything. . . . President Bush didn't have a strong theme in his campaign, didn't have a strong theme in his transition.

* * *

[Part of the problem for the Clinton staff, compared with Reagan's, was that] they don't have the luxury that we had, and that there wasn't any real confusion about where we were going and what the priorities were with Reagan.

On the importance of theme as a bridge to governing: The transition should not be hyped as a big separate thing, as much as the bridge between the campaign and governing. And so . . . you utilize that to translate what was said in the campaign . . . into how we're going to now make this the undergirding of the governing period. . . . Our whole idea was to build up to the inaugural day as the big event of the transition. . . . That's why the president stayed out of the limelight. . . . He wanted to . . . if you could, freeze the day that he won the election, and then carry that forward two and a half months later with the inaugural.

On effective bridging as reassurance: You want to reassure the public at large that they've made the right decision. A lot of them . . . take a flyer on you when they vote for you, and you want to offer immediate assurance that they did not cast an incorrect vote.

* * *

You were elected to do certain things. So I think the transition leading up to governing should be a continuation or reinforcement of this. You're going to follow through with what you said you were going to do when you've been campaigning. . . . I think people know why they voted for you. And if you all of a sudden changed horses and said: "Well, by the way I'm really not going to do the following," I don't think it would work.

Clearly, the Reagan operatives were well aware of their political and organizational advantages. The election was, in many ways, a model for bridging the gap between campaigning and governing. No one of the other three—Nixon, Carter, or Clinton—had so many benefits, though Nixon had direct experience in previous transitions, as well as contacts with Washington-savvy personnel.

Preelection Transition Planning

Most political advisers believe that developing plans for governing while campaigning must be done cautiously, even furtively. First, as mentioned previously, there is the suspicion most candidates have about appearing to be confident about winning, a hesitation derived from the classic upset by Harry S. Truman in 1948. Edwin Meese III reflected on these concerns in his book:

> We had learned from the experience of other candidates how "dividing up the White House offices" had detracted from the election campaign. Besides, planning to govern before being elected would smack of smugness and have a negative effect on the electorate. People don't like someone who thinks he has the election "in the bag." Reagan, particularly, had always campaigned down to the wire; he constantly worried about being a latter-day Thomas Dewey. Nevertheless, I knew that we had to prepare at least in part for the transition before election day.[5]

Why would it not be impressive to the public to have a presidential candidate display an understanding of the office and announce preparations to take over? After all, even if the candidate and his immediate advisers are fearful of projecting confidence, they surely don't want to cast an image as a loser. Yet, however rational a positive posture might seem, no respondent advocated it. I observed to some respondents that in 1994 Newt Gingrich not only planned ahead but announced in advance that he would become Speaker of the House of Representatives against all the odds. The response was that however important the speakership, the presidency is "an order of magnitude" larger and, in any event, the Speaker as a member of the House of Representatives runs for election initially within one congressional district, then among his 434 peers.[6] Presidents run nationwide. "And so I think it's a very dangerous thing for a president [to announce transition plans] because this idea of overconfidence, ever since the days of President Dewey, [makes them superstitious]."

Additionally, according to one respondent, the rhythm of the campaign works against thinking ahead toward governing. First is that the pace simply does not permit categorizing time in that way. Second is the worry that any such attention by aides may take them out of the immediate action of the campaign.

> There is a kind of crazed atmosphere that takes over, and the "who's up/who's down" that you see in government is a very pale imitation of the "who's up/who's down" in the campaign. . . . If you step aside [as a staff aide] to try to think for half a day about government, your policy enemies will point out that you weren't at the meeting on what the president should say in Detroit. And the power has to be . . . retained from moment to moment. And it must always be building or it is eroding. It's a really brutal psychological environment. And I think this is uniformly true. . . . In other words, you may become marginalized if you think ahead.

All four of the presidential candidates included in this study formed pre-election planning structures, but they differed in notable respects. Nixon and Reagan integrated the planning effort into the campaign apparatus, with top advisers working with those charged with looking ahead to the transition. Carter and Clinton organized rather impressive planning exercises, but both were more independent of the campaign organization, came to be viewed as competitive with that organization, and after the election were promptly marginalized or dissolved.

The Integrated Approach: Nixon and Reagan

Of the four candidates, Nixon clearly had the advantage of knowing Washington and the White House so well that integration between campaigning and planning to govern could be embodied in the candidate himself. One of his aides explained:

> We were working for a man who already had concepts, who had studied the presidency as vice president for eight years, and had been president of the Senate and a congressman. So he had a pretty good grasp of the whole thing. And he had some very strong opinions of what he wanted to do and how he wanted to do it that didn't really necessitate or even permit on a reasonable basis our spending

a lot of time doing a lot of independent staff planning, because basically we were going to do what he wanted done. But . . . he himself
did not get into that area, planning for the takeover, really at all, until
after the election. Then the day after, he got intensively into it.

The planning that was done was under the tight control of two of Nixon's
closest advisers, H. R. Haldeman and John Ehrlichman. Six or seven weeks
before the election, two researchers on loan to the campaign from business-
man H. Ross Perot were assigned "to help plan what we should do to effect
an orderly transition from Lyndon Johnson to Richard Nixon."[7]

We'd go out and campaign during the week. And we'd come into
New York in the weekends. [We'd] sit down with these two fellows,
and listen to what they had to tell us, and then send them off on
assignments to do that week. Then we would take what they had
come up with on the previous weekend and as we rode around in
the airplane from stop to stop, we would talk about how this thing
ought to shape up.

The strong role of Nixon's experience was invariably emphasized.
Nixon's aides studied the Johnson and Kennedy transitions, but "knowing
Richard Nixon, we knew that it had to be a more formal process than they
had had. . . . Nixon went back to Eisenhower and Sherman Adams and a
rather GI kind of structure as his sort of base point. . . . He liked the idea that
there was a process [with Eisenhower]."
Reagan did not have Nixon's Washington service to orient his staff planning, but he had himself experienced a transition into the second largest elected chief executive position in the country as governor of California, and he
believed strongly in delegating responsibility to those with experience. Carl
M. Brauer observes that more than Eisenhower, Kennedy, Nixon, and Carter,
"Reagan deliberately set out to exploit and build upon the momentum that
was generated by the election itself, to use his mandate, ambiguous or not."[8]
It was all of a piece, as conceived by Reagan's advisers. The strongly ideological campaign message was to direct the planning and management from
the campaign to governing. For organizational purposes before the election,
this orientation meant that the planning could be integrated into the campaign,
advised by the caveat that the advance work not seem to presume a win.
According to Meese's account, Pendleton James, a professional head-

hunter with personnel experience in the Nixon administration, asked late in 1979 if he could be of help to Reagan. Meese responded that James could prepare "a plan for the presidential personnel operation—just in case we won."[9] Planning was "quietly" begun in James's Los Angeles office. In September 1980 he was moved to an office in Alexandria, Virginia, "where he assembled a small staff who were not involved in the campaign itself." Meese describes how it all worked:

> In two months this group . . . had compiled the necessary data on some three thousand appointments that would have to be made. They also developed a system for recruiting qualified candidates and handling the thousands of expected recommendations and applications.
>
> All of this was done in such a quiet way that no one in the campaign—or the news media—learned of it. Even my own contacts with the personnel planning group did not interfere with my campaign responsibilities. I would sometimes meet with Pen James at 6:30 in the morning at a restaurant near campaign headquarters and then attend evening briefings, from 9:00 to midnight, at his Alexandria office. When the President-elect appointed me director of the transition on election day, we were ready to go with Pen's operation.[10]

The James group did not entirely escape press notice. Adam Clymer wrote an article for the *New York Times* shortly after the Alexandria office was established in which he quoted Meese as stating, "We're not looking for high visibility," and assuring Clymer that the operation was not interfering with the campaign effort. Meese declined to identify those working on the transition "both because he did not want them flooded with job applications and because the campaign wanted to avoid 'setting up a whole separate shop. . . . We're trying to learn from the Carter experience.' "[11] Brauer noted that "the story attracted little attention,"[12] no doubt because it evidenced no competition with the campaign effort or between campaign staff and transition planning staff. The Carter and Clinton experiences were very different.

There was a second transition-related preelection operation that was managed from the campaign office itself. Meese wrote that there were almost fifty groups and more than 450 advisers.[13] Brooks Jackson reported in the *Wall Street Journal* that there were twenty-three advisory teams and 329 "domestic advisers."[14] Whatever the exact count, this huge enterprise, coordinated by Darrell Trent, generated a large number of policy proposals designed both for possible campaign use and for governing should Reagan win. Meanwhile the Heritage Foundation, a conservative think tank formed in 1973, had been active since the fall of 1979 in preparing an agenda. "Our premise was that conservatives must be prepared to answer the question, 'What is the conservative agenda, particularly for the first 100 days?' "[15] The product, a 1,100-page book, was organized by cabinet departments and other agencies, with detailed reviews of jurisdictions and hundreds of policy recommendations.

One of Reagan's campaign and transition aides reported one advantage: "We had a lot of people who didn't want jobs in government. Therefore they were willing to stay with us for a short period of time, along with others who were interested if there were opportunities to go into government." Another feature of the Reagan operation during the campaign and after was a distance maintained by the candidate and president-elect. Perhaps because of his acting background, Reagan tended to think in terms of roles, scripts, and institutions rather than personalities. "You had to generate as staff a very structured kind of support system for him to do that," was the view of another aide who compared Reagan with Bush in this regard.

> President Reagan . . . did not bring very many people from the campaign into the White House. He treated them as separate entities [befitting his structured, segmented perspective]. And he signaled that really by hiring Jim Baker as his chief of staff. . . .
>
> President Bush was the opposite. He personalized all relationships. . . . He liked people in the White House who had been involved in the campaign—liked people he knew and was familiar with.

The advantage for preelection planning of the integrated approach is in the clear signals sent by the candidate, relatively unaffected by personalities. A structure could be generated that was unlikely to be foiled by the candidate due to closeness to one person over another. The trick was to develop devotion and loyalty among staff who could weather being ignored or passed over. Associated with this accomplishment was a two-track structure after the election, with Meese managing the transition and Baker, designated as chief of staff, in charge of creating a White House. Seemingly Reagan was successful in achieving what one aide referred to as "vertical loyalty," a quality engendering allegiance to the leader as a constraint on personal ambition.

One should not get the impression that the integrated approach, as labeled and described here, is unerringly smooth. It is, after all, a method for coping with one of the least well-formed or patterned activities in politics—that of being propelled from the frenetic pace of a campaign to the creation of executive leadership in a separated system of government. Thus, for all of the more positive reviews of the Reagan effort, the following appraisal by one of his aides is no doubt warranted:

> I've just never seen one [transition organization] work very well, and maybe it's too much to expect that you could ever go from campaigning to transition to governing, and have that a smooth process. I've just never seen one that really works. I think the best you can say [is] that some are less chaotic than others.

According to this aide, the "boxes of résumés" that poured into Pendleton James's unit were cleared by the political and policy people but "people . . . tell me that they basically started all over come January 21 anyway."

Another aide raised questions about the extent to which various interests, including think tanks like the Heritage Foundation, aid the campaign and transition. "Some conservative interests would be watching the process, and if they didn't quite like what they understood to be coming out of some element of the transition, they'd weigh it in the public press and try to influence the course of the transition process." The issue of campaign allies wanting a payoff for commitment raises a problem probably best treated by the integrated approach with its clear policy signals from the candidate become president-elect. The more certain the policy direction, the more likely it is that the staff will have working criteria for judging which way to bend under pressure of their supporting groups, or whether not to bend at all.

The Dissociated Approach: Carter and Clinton

The Carter and Clinton campaigns share several characteristics, as might be expected given that both candidates lacked Washington experience and had served as governors in medium-sized and small southern states, respectively. Still, each was sensitive to the need for preelection planning, with his concepts of presidential leadership evolving during the campaign and transition. Preelection transition planning was likely to be exploratory, that is, to be part of their development rather than being integrated into a more purposeful pursuit of structure and policy. While it was logical enough to have some staff thinking beyond election day, a campaign organization of limited Washington-based experience and one uncertain about results was bound to focus primarily on winning, not governing.

The feature that came to dominate judgments about Jimmy Carter's presidency—his lack of an overarching theme—was evident in the campaign. He won, yet nearly lost, as the candidate from outside Washington. Said one respondent, "Carter never came up with a single unifying slogan or framework to encapsulate his administration."[16] The contrast with Reagan could hardly have been more stark. James Fallows, who resigned early in the administration as Carter's chief speechwriter, observed, "Jimmy Carter is an engineer without deep philosophic roots, and that explains a lot."[17] Shortly after he resigned, Fallows wrote a critical article in *The Atlantic*. At some length, he questioned Carter's sophistication about how government in Washington works. Even more to the point regarding preelection planning, Fallows observed that "Carter did not really know *what* he wanted to do" on various topics on which he had campaigned. "After taking office, he commissioned panels of experts to tell him what to do."

> No one could carry out the Carter program, because Carter has resisted providing the overall guidelines that might explain what his program is.
>
> I came to think that Carter believes fifty things, but no one thing. He holds explicit, thorough positions on every issue under the sun, but he has no large view of the relations between them, no line indicating which goals . . . will take precedence over which . . . when the goals conflict. . . .
>
> Carter thinks in lists, not arguments; as long as the items are there, their order does not matter, nor does the hierarchy among them.[18]

The message of "let's do it all, in no particular order" lacks the crispness that staff often require. As a result, the chaos, confusion, and mixed signals identified with a campaign lurching forward to governing are intensified in the face of inexplicit marching orders. Still, candidate Carter was an experienced executive with an orderly, if list-oriented, manner. Therefore he arranged for preelection planning, committing precious campaign funds to the effort.[19]

Following the Pennsylvania primary on April 27, Jack H. Watson Jr., a young lawyer who was a partner in a firm with Carter's close friend and confidant, Charles Kirbo, began to have conversations with Jule Sugarman, administrative officer for the city of Atlanta with experience in the federal government. The subject was "the categorical areas of work that will face the transition team when it begins in November to try to get the president-elect ready for the assumption of office." Watson wrote a memorandum regarding transition planning to his partner, Kirbo. With Carter's approval, Watson and Sugarman continued to formulate memoranda in a process of refining the priorities for acting once the election was over. These subsequent memoranda, too, were directed to Kirbo, a good friend of Carter but not a campaign operative. The emerging structure was, therefore, independent of the campaign organization. According to one aide, "Planning a transition, isolated like that from the hierarchy and the ongoing of a campaign, is absolute disaster." Watson suggested that a major national figure, such as John Gardiner, former president of Common Cause, direct the transition planning group. Carter chose the person he knew, Jack Watson, meeting with him in June to discuss the planning effort. Watson then hired a group of young people to work in Atlanta on the set of issues to be dealt with following the election.[20]

The Watson group quite naturally developed enthusiasm related to the presumed importance of their work—preparing the president to govern. What was less obvious to them was the extent to which their work would be viewed later as threatening to the campaign organization. Harrison Wellford, one of Watson's aides, noted, "The people that are out on the campaign have been there sometimes for two or three years, with no pay, no sleep, eating terrible food. The last thing that they really want to be told is that there is a group of pros sitting back in some comfortable office in Washington . . . basically planning who's going to get the spoils of the victory."[21] Another member of the Watson group observed:

> There was a lot of resentment in the campaign. They were slaving away, you know, twenty-four hours a day having to respond to issues. And there we are, given the luxury of thinking and sitting back and watching. So there was a lot of friction between us and Stu [Eizenstat's] staff, the campaign staff, the campaign policy people,

because they were the ones . . . at 2:00 a.m. having to put together
a statement for the candidate, and we weren't doing shit. And there
was a feeling that, "Oh, they're going to plan to take over the government while we're doing all the work?"

Jack [Watson] didn't want to bother Hamilton [Jordan] and the
others during the campaign, particularly when he got all the plans
done; it was like ten days, two weeks before. What is he going to
do? Here's the election slipping away from us [Carter's poll numbers were decreasing], he's going to bother them with what's going
to happen [after the election]?

As with any campaign, a part of the difficulty was traceable to unresolved
personality conflicts. According to the observer quoted above, Jordan and
Jody Powell resented Watson's privileged financial status. They were "the
country mouse versus Jack was the city mouse, Harvard educated versus the
bumpkins. These guys [Jordan and Powell] had never made more than
$15,000 in their lives versus guys who made six figures." Additionally, the
Watson group naturally made contact with those in Washington who knew
something about transitions—mostly people whom "Hamilton and Jody
despised . . . I don't mean personally, but. . . . " After all, Carter had campaigned against the whole Washington establishment, not just Republicans.
The idea that the Watson group would then work with Washington insiders—
"the people they ran against, the Kennedy people"—to form a government
for the candidate from outside Washington was a lot to digest.[22] As this same
aide asked, "These are the people who helped Jack [Watson] design how the
White House was going to be?"[23]

There was the further problem of beginning a process of selecting
appointees in advance of full political clearance by the campaign staff, who
were preoccupied with the election itself.

Jule [Sugarman] had this notion that we should serve up finalists to
the president in mid-October, and actually have Cabinet selections
done before the election, maybe a few weeks before the election.
And the campaign people thought that was an absolutely wretched
idea, I mean, a terrible idea, and they pounced all over Jule and Jack
about that.

With no coordination between the planners and the campaigners, conflict was predictable. In fact, one aide speculated that the Carter decision to permit cabinet secretaries to select subcabinet appointees was a consequence of Watson's program for identifying potential talent: "No way he's [Watson] going to decide who's going to be subcabinet."

For his part, Jack Watson pursued his mission as he understood that mission. After all, he had been detailed by candidate Carter to prepare for the transition. He might logically expect, therefore, that he and his group would be responsible for organizing activities following the election. "Jack's motives were the purest in the world. . . . He did what the [candidate] asked him to do," said one Carter aide. That is not to suggest that he was lacking in ambition. As one Carter adviser explained, "I think Jack is the man that you never can give him enough to do. He thinks he's getting left out, and you have to load him down. He was wanting to have a big role in the White House, which I thought was good." For this adviser, a large part of the conflict was a result of staff anxiety about getting a job.

> People began to realize they may have an opportunity to have a job in the White House, and then they began to look around, and it's just a normal thing that I think will happen, and it's more apt to happen with strong people like Jack and Hamilton who are ambitious and they . . . want to do good, but they have to get in a position to do it.

Press coverage of Watson's operations surely contributed to angst among campaign staff.[24] The effort was typically depicted as the most comprehensive and ambitious exercise ever for taking over the government. Watson was referred to as a "closet figure" for an "undercover" operation. A senior campaign aide was quoted as stating, "Most people here [at campaign headquarters] don't even know what Jack Watson looks like. He is entirely apart from the campaign."[25] Watson's early meeting with Clark M. Clifford, the dean of counselors to Democratic presidents, was reported approvingly in the press. The clear message was that the group was planning to take charge the day after the election. Watson was quoted as saying: "It's something that a responsible man would do. It has nothing to do with confidence or presumption about the election. . . . The range of responsibilities of the president is so great and complex he needs some in-depth analysis. Our job is to gather information and ideas and assess their values so that we can present informed options to the governor."[26] The responsibilities were identified as the budget, reorganizations, foreign and domestic policy issues, and talent recruitment.

Shortly before the election itself, Hobart Rowen of the *Washington Post* provided details of the budget preparation by the planning group and explained that "Watson is also in charge of the massive effort to screen possibilities for the critical jobs in a Carter administration. There are 20 to 25 jobs considered to be of first rank, including the Cabinet, and a group of 50 to 60 immediately below them. Finally, there are perhaps 1,300 or 1,400 persons in lesser but key jobs in the various agencies."[27] A campaign worker reading this article could be excused for believing that the "closet" operation in Atlanta was to be a vital center for decisionmaking about his or her political future with the new president.[28] And it was, understandably, the intention of the Atlanta-based group to serve precisely in that way. As Bruce Adams and Kathryn Kavanagh-Baran described, "Two days after the election, the Atlanta TIP [Talent Inventory Program] group loaded up a rented truck with thousands of résumés and drove north to Washington, assuming that they were the team about to assist Carter in his appointment selections."[29]

Further contributing to this view was a *Time* magazine article published shortly after the election that touted Watson's team and their planning effort. The article was based on reporting by Robert Ajemian, who spent a week with Watson before the election and "was allowed to study some of the documents that were prepared for Carter's reading." The article ended with a paragraph bound to rankle Carter's senior campaign staff.

> Thus it was almost natural last May that Carter would ask Watson to direct his ambitious plans for the transfer of power. When Watson sent his first memorandum, Carter wrote across the top of it: "Proceed and be bold." Watson really liked that. And Carter knew his man. As the President-elect's principal in Washington for the next ten weeks—and probably a lot longer—the bold Jack Watson will certainly take the boss's advice.[30]

Resentment and jealousy of Watson's operation were predictable, though seemingly not at the time to the candidate, as explained by a Carter aide familiar with the planning effort and the resulting strife.

> I mean, I think it's not terribly wise for the planning chief on the eve of the election to be giving interviews to *Time* magazine. But that in fact was what was happening. And it made it look as if, to the people out there in the trenches fighting the war, that there was this

pointy-headed group of intellectuals ready to take over the spoils of victory. Well, that's just destructive as hell, as you can imagine.

How might this situation have been avoided? This same aide offered advice: "If there could be more integration, I mean, maybe you want to have the campaign chief also in charge of the planning, even though he's going to give planning short shrift, at least there would not appear to be this organizational division." The Reagan team accepted this advice four years later.

As with Carter, there was sufficient reason for candidate Clinton to engage in preelection planning. If victorious, he would face the special problem of organizing his place in government with limited experience in Washington or in managing an immense organization. There was the further problem of the time frame—the Democrats having been out of office for twelve years. One adviser identified both of these factors this way:

> Let's suppose that the person making the transition happens to be Hubert Humphrey moving from vice president to president. That I suspect is a much different transition in many areas than an unknown governor from Georgia making a transition. . . . [Further,] one of the problems the Democrats ran into this time going around, I think, in '92, was that when you went to look for those natural people who would be assistant secretaries or secretaries or undersecretaries . . . there really wasn't a government in waiting. We hadn't been able to build up the Democratic side of this thing, kind of a cadre of naturals, if you want to call them that.

Sensitive to this need, Clinton appointed a six-member preelection transition board to begin thinking about organizing a government in advance of the election.[31] The group was chaired by Mickey Kantor, who also served as the national campaign chairman.[32] Kantor put a number of experienced Washington hands to work on preparing briefing books on various issues, especially in regard to the budget, the economy, and national security. Several of those doing the work had experience during the Carter transition.

With Kantor in charge, could it not be expected that the Clinton operation would look more like that of Reagan than that of Carter? One might have thought so. But Mickey Kantor was no Ed Meese in regard to the campaign or his association with the candidate, and Clinton was no Reagan in terms of delegation of power. Whereas Kantor had known Clinton for a long time, he was not as close as Meese was to Reagan, nor had he served Clinton as a senior staff aide. In fact, as one adviser observed, "Mickey was theoretically the chairman of the campaign, but as far as I could tell, had very little to do with the campaign effort." The *Washington Post* reported that Kantor had been moved sideways in the campaign because of difficulties with other aides.

> Kantor has tangled with such other trusted Clinton aides as communications director George Stephanopoulos, and was directed to oversee presidential debate preparation and then the pre-transition effort in part to give him an area to direct separate from other campaign aides. . . .
> Press secretary Dee Dee Myers said that reports of dissension between Kantor and other staff workers are "grossly exaggerated." But another aide confirmed that there had been bitterness for months about Kantor and said the California lawyer "went out of his way to alienate people."[33]

It was repeatedly said that the Clinton team wanted to avoid being compared with Carter's. Yet in regard to this vital matter of organizing the transition, they produced nearly a carbon copy of the dissociation between pre-election planning and the day-to-day operation of the campaign. As with Carter, unresolved personal conflicts among senior aides complicated the issue. The effect was to negate much of the positive work that was done before the election, greatly disappointing those staff aides who had made an effort to correct the mistakes of the Carter transition. One of those aides, who was also involved in Carter's planning, Harrison Wellford, observed that he had witnessed "two train wrecks in preelection planning, where everyone knew exactly what to avoid, and yet they step right in it all over again."[34]

Adding to the disconnection was the decision to manage the transition from Little Rock so as to avoid a Washington orientation. One Washington participant summarized the results this way:

> What happened in the Clinton transition is that somebody decided that they should stay in Little Rock and do the transition in Little Rock to send some kind of a signal about . . . not being captured by Washington. And the result was that the people who were at the heads of the transition sat down in Little Rock and agonized with

the President over who should get what job. There was no White House transition. And the people here in Washington went through this exhaustive personnel exercise which was not productive, and everybody else was sort of flailing around and creating a lot of material, none of which was ever used. I mean, most of the work that was essential for the Clinton transition was done before he was elected. And almost all of that was ignored, as well.

QUESTION: How do you explain that?

RESPONSE: I can't explain it. It was outrageous and stupid. And it was, in my judgment, after having looked at a lot of transitions, the worst transition in history. And I think it was principally responsible for the chaos inside. . . . All I am saying is that they didn't basically use the work that was done.

Another respondent had distinct memories of the Carter experience and expressed dismay in observing a repeat performance of the influence of personality clashes.

In both cases [1976 and 1992] the fruits of that effort were tainted by the campaign staff, [who were] suspicious of what was going on and the efforts to kill the sponsor, in the first place Watson and in the second place Kantor. . . . It happens in like 48 hours. And there is nothing that the people working on it can do much about. You would say, "Well . . . you were there in the Carter thing. Why couldn't you have prevented this?" I tried. I mean, I was perfectly aware that everything that we were doing on this economic planning group, trying to put together an outline of the budget to give the president. We knew the economy issue was going to be the number one issue and we thought we could do a lot of work before the election that would give Clinton a good start.

We attempted to be sure that the people at the top of the campaign both knew and blessed what was going on. But . . . I don't think any of us appreciated the degree of distrust that had developed between Mickey Kantor and [George] Stephanopoulos and that crowd. [Warren] Christopher was on the board of this group and was getting copies of everything we did. He was saying nice things about it. We had friends in the campaign who we tried to keep informed about it. But all that was sideshow because what was

going on between Kantor and Stephanopoulos and company was at
a level of intensity way beyond anything we could do about it.
QUESTION: Was it personal, therefore leading to the matter of who
is going to control appointments, or was it . . . about ideas, or both?
RESPONSE: I don't think it was ideas. I think it was more who is
going to get what.

The Carter and Clinton preelection efforts are textbook cases of having
the right instincts but failing to acknowledge the importance of designing
means by which real gain may be realized from good work. It is perfectly
normal to have disputes, dislikes, and jealousies among staff—even a fair
measure of paranoia, given the depth and intensity of the commitment by
aides and the stakes involved. Resolving those problems so as to use the transition period most effectively depends ultimately on who the candidate is,
including what his prior experience is in Washington or in large-scale management. In Clinton's case, one aide observed that "it was very hard to
engage [Clinton] in discussion about what was going to happen after the
election, especially when all the evidence was that the vote was narrowing.
So it was hard to get direction . . . at crucial times." Even so, he judged that
it would have been possible to be ready with a plan had Clinton, like Reagan,
been able to rely on a cadre of people with Washington experience and in
whom he had confidence.

> One of the problems with Bill Clinton is [his] having come from a
> small state without people terribly well versed in how the govern-
> ment operates, with the Democrats having been out of power other
> than the brief interregnum with Jimmy Carter. It was not a universe
> of people he could have turned to with confidence to present to him
> a plan the day after the election.

Many of those working with Kantor did have Washington-based experience. Further, as with Reagan and the Heritage Foundation, Clinton had the
advantage of having access to policy research done by the Progressive Policy
Institute, a think tank affiliated with the Democratic Leadership Council. But
the planners did not enjoy the same close association to Clinton as did the
campaigners. Yet their work was bound to affect the future of the campaigners and, accordingly, was not accepted as the basis for the transition. Can
these staff anxieties and potential conflicts be managed and resolved? While

acknowledging the complexity involved, one aide believed it could be done.

> That's what leadership is all about. . . . If a leader takes it seriously
> enough and has the time to reflect on it and can give this responsi-
> bility [of planning] to a group of people who . . . know his idiosyn-
> cracies, how he gets and digests information, know enough about
> the campaign and what was the underlying rationale for it and know
> how government operates, you can clearly put something in place
> that can work.

Unfortunately, this formula for leadership is based on assumptions less applicable to Clinton. Staff had worked for Clinton long enough to be cognizant of his idiosyncrasies, as well as his gargantuan capacity for digesting information. Substantially less clear was an "underlying rationale" for the campaign that would then serve as direction for operating the government. Planning begins with setting goals. It produces options for achieving those goals. Clinton's more cerebral style favors continuous weighing of goals and options, with talk as a process of policy and political exploration. This style is less accommodating to accepting "something in place that can work."

A great deal must go right to achieve integration between the campaign and preelection planning. Even where an effort is made, there is no guarantee that all will go smoothly. Thus, for example, if that balance is not struck in a manner well suited to the candidate's known preferences or if the candidate is unsure of his preferences, then it will be difficult to put a plan into effect. It is clearly not only a matter of the availability of seasoned advisers. It also requires the capacity of the candidate to receive that advice and put it to good use, as well as to know enough about who can be of assistance once the campaign is over.

Summary

The system of choosing a president calls for uncommon organizational, political, personnel, and policy skills among those seeking the office. Three affiliated yet distinct processes—the campaign, the transition, and assuming office—take place, each requiring sufficient foresight to prepare the person to transform successively, and in a short period of time, from one complex role to another and yet to a third. However difficult it may be for the individual involved, it is made vastly more burdensome given that the candidate comes with a coterie of "vertically loyal" aides, each of whom, in his or her own mind, comes to represent a part of the president-elect's transformation to leadership. Therefore the first metamorphosis from campaign to transition is perhaps the most dramatic and emotional since not all of those who aided in his playing the role of the candidate are useful in this second performance. And others must themselves adapt to different roles associated with the new job of the leader they serve.

This chapter has shown that the manner in which the campaign ends and the transition begins depends to a substantial degree on who the candidate is, including what his political background and experience are, and what he wants to accomplish. The organizational, political, personnel, and policy challenges of advance preparation alone may very nearly overcome some candidates, as they did Carter and Clinton. Those who need help most are sometimes wary of relying on experienced people whom they do not know.

Future candidates can draw lessons from the distinction between campaigning and governing, the campaign itself, the utility of a theme, and the alternative forms of preelection planning. To profit from these lessons, the candidate as president-elect needs help from those with experience and savvy.

Finally, the discussion throughout this chapter has been based on a conventional distinction between campaigning and governing, with the Clinton transition judged to be the least effective. It is well worth considering, however, that an altered type of transition is upon us. The standard shift is from campaigning to governing, whereas the emerging progression may be from campaigning for office to campaigning for policy and status. The latter style of governing calls for a White House staff to organize and function differently as it seeks to influence and manage opinion in establishing its place in government. The transition is from campaigning to governing in both instances, but with modified standards, skills, and strategies for the emerging form of campaigning as governing. Equally vital is an understanding that the character of governance too is changing in a manner that invites a more campaign-oriented style.

4

PREPARING TO GOVERN

JOHN F. KENNEDY's transition to the presidency in 1960, according to Richard E. Neustadt, was "a brilliant piece of work."

> Part of the brilliance was that those people could not wait to start governing. They were so glad the campaign was over. Within three hours they were getting ready to do what they wanted to do. The Tuesday after the election I was asked to go down and see Ted Sorensen, who had been designated as special counsel. . . . He was literally thinking his way into the role he was going to play. The next weekend I was hauled down to Palm Beach to see the successful candidate, and his belief was the same. He [had] said: "I've had 24 hours to celebrate, now let's get to work." Somebody said: "How bipartisan do you think you can afford to be to your opponents?" "Well, in another day or so, we'll celebrate over the Republicans and then we'll get down to it." In the week after, they did get down to it. . . . The season for governing was real for those people. I don't think, alas, from what I have been told . . . it was real for Mr. Clinton in the same time period. I don't know if it has ever become real for those people.[1]

Surely Neustadt is correct in identifying the generally accepted task to be accomplished following the election: preparing to govern. And he chose an

83

interesting case since Kennedy won by one of the narrowest margins in history. As Roger B. Porter observed (also referring to the Kennedy postelection period): "Wisely managed, they [transitions] can help create an environment for transforming a narrow election victory into a capacity to govern."[2] A Nixon aide explained the challenge this way: "There is no White House organization. It's what you make when you get there. There's no prescription. There are very few laws to restrict how you can organize. It's almost entirely left up to the president. So we started out with a clean piece of paper." Essentially confirming Neustadt's observations, a Kennedy aide identified the tasks of the conversion from candidate to president and the effects of a failure to so act:

> I think it's important that the president get off to a running start. That means that he should have people in place before the end of the year, and in all the key positions. It means he should have his priorities for legislation and for executive action, and for foreign policy action clearly in mind. He should go to the country and the Congress early in the first month of his presidency with these initiatives. He should not permit a vacuum which Congress and the pressure groups and others will fill while he's trying to figure out which way to go.

Accomplishing these organizational and governing goals first requires that they be acknowledged as important. As I have sought to establish, that recognition is facilitated if the *intent* to govern has been incorporated into the nomination and campaign phases of a president's political life. By this view, "winning" is assuredly not the only thing for presidents. Yet having just won, and being surrounded by those taking credit for that achievement, presidents-elect and those around them need judgment and long-range perspective to switch roles and rejoice that the campaign is over and the season of governing is nigh.

What if a president-elect and his aides lack that judgment and long-range perspective, as Neustadt suggests is the case with Clinton? Even more, what if their preference is less for governing than for campaigning—essentially lacking that eagerness to start governing? Even more intriguing, what if their talent and penchant for campaigning, along with developments in polling and political advertising, encourage governing by campaigning? And what if governance too is undergoing changes that invite a more campaign-oriented approach?

Surely such preferences, talents, and trends influence the purpose and methods of a transition, as does the agenda. Presidents-elect in these times are expected to meet the demands of the conventional transition, while preparing themselves for more public, campaign-oriented government as well. The Clinton experience is particularly instructive in this regard, though the Reagan approach signaled what was to come.

The Agenda

Campaigns are essentially about agendas. Presidential elections function as a time of national stocktaking, providing voters with an opportunity to listen to at least two candidates identify the major issues and evaluate their opponent's capacity for resolving them. Elections happen by the calendar, not by policy crises. Still, issueless elections are rare (the one in 1988 between Bush and Dukakis is said to be one such). Certainly the four elections included here did not lack for issues, each winner having ousted the incumbent party and defeated an incumbent president in three cases (Carter over Ford, Reagan over Carter, Clinton over Bush), the incumbent vice president in the fourth (Nixon over Humphrey). The challenge then in each case for the new team was to ensure that preparations during the eleven-week transition period were oriented to the dominant agenda so as to meet the expectations associated with their win.

Nixon and Reagan had perhaps the greatest agenda advantages for their respective transitions. For Nixon there was little doubt that Vietnam was the major issue, thus playing to the president-elect's policy strength. Though he won narrowly, there was little question as to the postelection policy expectation: an honorable withdrawal from Vietnam. Stephen E. Ambrose explains:

> Peace in Vietnam was his number-one priority, a clear-cut goal. . . . Nixon's model was Korea, 1953. He would get peace not through victory, or withdrawal, or surrender, but through an armistice. . . . Peace in Vietnam would solve many of his other problems and lessen all of them. Most obviously and most immediately, peace in Vietnam would bring peace to the campuses and an end to the antiwar movement. The generation gap, if not bridged, would at least be narrowed. No more violence in Vietnam would mean much less violence at home.[3]

Likewise, Reagan had an agenda that had been clearly etched during the campaign, one much more domestic in nature. With the country experiencing double-digit inflation, unemployment, and interest rates, he was expected to act aggressively to improve the economy. He had the added advantages of an Electoral College landslide, a Republican majority in the Senate, and a substantial increase in the number of House Republicans. It appeared to be a victory with a message. The campaign and election produced a policy direction and political momentum that permitted, comparatively, an orderly and poised transition—one with established purpose and demonstrated support. As with Neustadt's characterization of Kennedy's transition, the Reagan team was goal oriented and anxious to govern.

Carter and Clinton could also identify agenda rationales to aid in structuring the transition. But the issues were somewhat less clear cut and the election results less crisply determinative. For Carter, the principal campaign message was related to his outsider status at a time when Washington politics was in bad odor. Not surprisingly, then, much of his agenda was reform oriented. The one specific issue requiring early attention was that of energy supply and demand, but it was difficult to interpret the election as having conveyed a message on that issue that was greatly different for Carter than if Ford had won. And though Carter expressed a desire for a broadly based mandate, in fact he won by a surprisingly narrow margin while his party retained substantial majorities in the House and Senate. He could not rely on the election results as having provided an unambiguous, orienting agenda for building a government during the transition.

For Clinton it was the much ballyhooed "It's the economy, stupid," along with welfare and health care reform. While undoubtedly important, the economic issue was not as dominant as in 1980, certainly not to the extent of yielding such a commanding orientation as to preclude distractions. Further, Clinton fashioned a conference in Little Rock at the midpoint of the transition to aid him in defining the problems and deciding what should be done, suggesting that the election had not settled those issues for him. And in any event, though commanding a large majority in the Electoral College, he won just 43 percent of the popular vote, and the Democrats had a net loss of seats in the House and no gain in the Senate—hardly the components of a mandate.[4]

Clearly the agenda can aid in effecting a smooth and orderly conventional transition, especially if the president-elect is resourceful enough to realize this advantage. The classic day-after question—"Now what do we do?"—

can be most effectively answered if the campaign and election defined an agenda and projected a policy direction so compellingly that the winner felt instructed thereby. A strong showing in the election by the winner and his party in Congress may also grant the new president latitude in organizing his administration; a narrow win may constrain those options. Of the four presidents-elect, Reagan had the greatest edge in these regards.

The Preferred Sequence

Is there a preferred sequence of activities and appointments for the conventional transition from campaigning to governing? In discussing this matter, respondents offered various forms of advice that, taken together, suggest a recommended order. Several mentioned the importance of taking time to rest following the election, yet they acknowledged the problem in doing so given what has to be accomplished, the time limits, and the psychological barriers to relaxing after such an intense experience and under the circumstances of reveling in the newly won status. H. R. Haldeman may have spoken for most presidents-elect, but surely for his own, and very likely for Bill Clinton too, when he said in December 1968:

> What do we do with him [Nixon]? . . . He knows he needs to relax, so he comes down to Florida. He likes to swim, so he swims for ten minutes. Then that's over. He doesn't paint, he doesn't horseback-ride, he doesn't have a hobby. His best relaxation is talking shop, but he knows he should not be doing that, because that doesn't seem to be relaxing. So what do we do with him?[5]

Some respondents also advised that sequence depends on the president-elect: who he is, how he won, and what he wants. This view was well summarized by a Carter aide: "The order and pacing that Carter followed was, in fact, an accurate reflection of what he wanted and what he got, which was a cabinet that was relatively independent of the White House staff."[6] A Reagan aide judged that Bush too wanted a strong cabinet—"stronger . . . than he did a White House staff." These exceptions aside, and acknowledging the need for rest, however well managed, respondents substantially agreed on issues of signal sending, order, and pacing.

Appointments Should Make a Statement

In a sense, this point is related to that regarding the differences among presidents. The appointments and staffing should be consistent with the campaign themes. They will be viewed as signaling presidential priorities and decisionmaking. A Carter aide said, "What are the principal focuses or the principal themes . . . of his presidency that he wants to start illuminating? . . . The appointments process is a way to do that." A Reagan aide: "I think people want to know with respect to a new president who the key movers and shakers are going to be because they influence his decisions. And they make a lot of the decisions themselves." Few placements by recent presidents sent stronger signals than that of Hillary Rodham Clinton to oversee one of the president's principal domestic priorities. Elizabeth Drew reports: "There were . . . long discussions in Little Rock among the Clintons, their friends, and their advisers about what, actually, Mrs. Clinton's role was to be." It was finally decided that a specific policy area was better than being designated as a "quasi Chief of Staff role" and so "she decided to do health care." This designation served to announce that the Office of the First Lady would be an active center of power in the Clinton White House.[7]

Act Fast

Hamilton Jordan's advice to the incoming Clinton team was: "Be as speedy as you can in filling jobs. Get it over with."[8] It is important to move quickly for several reasons: to establish policy and political direction, to allow cabinet secretaries as much time as possible for their transition, to prevent agency or department transition teams from assuming too much control, to create a sense of momentum, and to resolve potential disputes among those expecting appointments. Much depends, of course, on whether the president-elect has thought in advance about important positions. As one respondent said, "I think most of the time you've got a pretty good idea already who you're going to put in. And I think you ought to move fairly rapidly on those, just because those people need all the time they can get."

Select White House Staff Early

In their famous memorandums to Kennedy on managing a transition, Clark M. Clifford and Richard E. Neustadt wrote first of the designation of White House aides. The Neustadt memo argued:

> After Election Day the President-elect will need a *small personal staff* to operate through the transition period and to take office with him. A few staff aides are immediately necessary; their names and jobs should be announced at once, so that importunate office-seekers, idea-peddlers, pressmen, legislators, diplomats, and cabinet-designees know who and what they are.[9]

The transition aides I interviewed uniformly agreed with this analysis and recommendation. One emphasized that presidents-elect typically know in advance how they want to organize, and they tend to follow a style of decisionmaking long since established. Thus, for example, "Jimmy Carter knew he wanted to be his own chief of staff at the start. . . . I think that Bill Clinton still wanted to be his own chief of staff right at the beginning." In Reagan's case, the "top-level staffers . . . almost kind of fell out of the campaign and out of the president's prior experience with them."

As identified by Neustadt, the reasoning for resolving these organizational matters early is straightforward and compelling. Designating who will fill the top positions in the White House staff aids in clarifying who will represent and act for the president. Thus, for example, the appointment of James Baker as chief of staff for Reagan sent a strong signal that the so-called California Reaganauts would not be in total control.[10] Further, to establish a high-level staff early then allows the president-elect to employ that structure for processing other appointments and making connections to the permanent government. Delay can only cause problems, as noted by a Carter aide: "The channels of communication aren't clear. So another lesson . . . is: name your White House staff and delineate the responsibilities as early in the transition as possible." A Reagan aide summarized the argument as follows:

> I think I would put the White House staff in place first because [they're] . . . the ones that are going to make it all work. The chief of staff, the press secretary, and probably the counsel, would be the ones that I would put in and announce them early on; maybe national security [adviser]. Because these people can then go take care of all kinds of things once everybody understands who's in charge. And then you can begin working on getting the cabinet choices. The country will run without the rest of those people. [But] your transition won't run without those White House people being appointed.

Find Out How the White House Works

Related to early designation of key White House aides is the need to acquaint them with working in the White House. Much of this lore is house-keeping or office management in nature. Those presidents-elect and their aides, like Nixon, who have served hardly need an orientation. Those who have only visited the White House, and rarely at that, need to know how to go to work in the morning and how to get through the day. Harrison Wellford describes the problems encountered by the Clinton team, partially the result of a failure to designate staff aides early on:

> Without an established pecking order of who's going to do what in the White House, it was very difficult to get the planning work done for the actual takeover of that institution after the inauguration. So you had this interesting phenomenon, that on the day after the inauguration, Pennsylvania Avenue had a strange event. Standing outside of the northwest gate was a long line of senior White House people trying to get in. But their White House passes had been screwed up, so they couldn't actually get into the place to do the work that they had been elected to do. People didn't understand how to park. They didn't understand how to use the telephones. The computers didn't have hard drives. The White House switchboard was absolute chaos. There was a whole series of totally avoidable events that created an impression that the transition was in disarray.[11]

Quickly Settle the Futures of Close Advisers

A corollary to early appointment of top-level White House staff is that of taking care of the president's closest advisers. If not resolved, questions will persist, as will speculation as to their placement. One person described the Bush transition: "When Bush named James Baker Secretary of State the next day, it was done, I'm sure, to keep the first question . . . from then on until he did it [being] 'What are you going to do with Baker?'" Particularly important is the resolution of potential or real conflicts among immediate and devoted campaign aides.

Of course, acting quickly in this manner does depend on the president-elect's confidence about how he wants to organize the White House and cabinet, itself a major variable among those treated here. Thus, for example, a

Clinton adviser pointed out that, as governor, Clinton "didn't have a staff that was significant in terms of his identity or his governance. He knew about cabinets [being a former governor]. But he didn't know very much about a White House staff." Accordingly, most of the White House staff was appointed last, and its chief, Thomas "Mack" McLarty, was a person essentially new to Washington. Four years later, in his second transition, Clinton acknowledged that it was a mistake on his part to devote more time to picking the cabinet over picking his White House staff, "which turned out to play a much more critical role than he expected."[12] That admission is itself revealing of Clinton's modus operandi in the first transition, which appeared to be stylized to suit the president-elect's active involvement in all phases and idiosyncratic use of staff. Advice was available. A memo from Neustadt to a Clinton associate in summer 1992 led with this "lesson":

> Organize the core of the White House staff by or before Thanksgiving Day and set them to superintend the preparatory work on things the President-elect himself has to do or approve first. They desperately need to gain experience before January 20 in working with him *and* with each other in the new roles they are all assuming.[13]

Fill the "Inner-Cabinet" Posts Early

There is a more or less standard view regarding the cabinet posts to appoint first. It is generally acknowledged that the national security–foreign policy team should be put in place early to send reassuring (or warning) signals throughout the international community. The economic team too is important for both domestic and international clienteles. Therefore the standard list of first appointments includes State, Defense, and Treasury, with Justice typically added for reasons associated with domestic concerns, most notably the enduring crime issue. Also consequential for the same reasons are early designations of the White House advisers for these policy areas: the national security adviser, director of the Central Intelligence Agency, and top economic aides (to include the director of the Office of Management and Budget).

Let Appointments Speak for Policy

Several aides mentioned the importance of not appearing to act as the president before inauguration. The appointments themselves send a mes-

sage, as do announcements regarding the agenda and general policy orientation. But taking positions regarding pending decisions for the incumbent
president was judged by many respondents to be highly questionable. A
notable example of bad form in this regard were the statements by President-
elect Clinton in regard to the Haitian refugees.[14] Among other effects, pre-
mature signals may result in the president-elect having to reverse himself
once full information is available. The recommended postelection policy
stance is to convey an impression of hard work on an agenda for the first 100
days but to avoid pronouncements on pending issues.[15]

Separate Important Transition Tasks

Two crucial organizational tasks during the transition are best managed
separately: building an administration and disassembling a campaign. The
two activities are related through appointments. But not all campaign staff
can expect to get jobs, and yet many may deserve or otherwise expect interim assignments. Managing this disassembly and reorientation requires spe-
cialized talents, just as does that of creating a White House staff and making
high-level appointments (most of which will not be filled by campaign operatives). The model for this separation was the division of labor between
Baker and Edwin Meese in 1980. With Meese taking charge of the transition,
Baker was freed to prepare for January 20. Consultation was frequent but
functioning was properly separate.

Feed the Press

Press relations during the transition are treated in a subsequent chapter.
Suffice it here to point out that the media are the major carriers of the
sequence of events during this period, as well as interpreters and evaluators
of how it is going. Increasingly, it seems, the president-elect and his transition officials must be attentive immediately to how announcements, appointments, and other actions will be treated, and how this treatment differs from
that during the campaign. For example, the pacing of news is a consideration. A Reagan aide explained, "Because there's nothing else to write about
at the time, the press is going to write all kind of crystal balling into it."
Another Reagan aide expanded on this point:

You have to meet the press's professional need to produce a story. And a lot of this is competitive from one publication to the next, and from one time period to the next. So the worst thing is to have three really big stories, and then nothing for three weeks, because if nothing happens, they have to write something anyway. And so they'll write that nothing is happening, they're slowed down. Then they'll descend to the level where they start talking about infighting. So what you need is a series of substantive decisions to deflect them from infighting [stories], to feed them professionally, and to communicate a kind of steady activity level.

Of course, it may well be the case that "infighting" is a story, one that prevents orderly sequencing and pacing. As will become evident, effective management during the transition period depends heavily on clarity and unity of purpose as understood and communicated by savvy advisers and the president-elect they are serving.

The Practice: Four Cases

To what extent were these recommendations followed in regard to the Nixon, Carter, Reagan, and Clinton presidencies? Again, there were differences between the Republicans as party insiders and the Democrats as Washington outsiders. The Nixon and Reagan aides seemingly were satisfied with how they proceeded, whereas the Carter and Clinton aides discussed how they might have done it differently. In making comparisons, one Carter respondent, who watched her boss come in and leave, was very impressed with how Reagan entered:

By the time Reagan got elected, they were really well organized. And they had a really good sense of the kinds of people they wanted to appoint. I was stunned. I'll never forget this as long as I live. When the advance people came into the White House to work on the first Reagan visit to the Carter White House, they came in . . . when they were flying Reagan from California to Washington, and we were going to send the plane for him, they came in and they asked *for the plane numbers*. They had all been Ford and Nixon

Figure 4-1. Sequence of Presidential Appointments by Nixon, Carter, Reagan, and Clinton

Nixon
1st week: congressional liaison
2d week: chief of staff, press secretary, counsel
3d week: none
4th week: chairman of Council of Economic Advisers, head of National Security Agency
5th week: none
6th week: entire cabinet, director of Bureau of the Budget
7th week: ambassador to United Nations
8th week: none
9th week: none
10th week: none
11th week: director of Central Intelligence Agency

Carter
1st week: none
2d week: press secretary
3d week: none
4th week: none
5th week: secretary of state, director of Office of Management and Budget
6th week: secretaries of treasury, transportation
7th week: secretaries of interior, commerce, agriculture, defense, labor, housing and urban development, and attorney general, head of National Security Agency, ambassador to United Nations, and chairman of Council of Economic Advisers
8th week: secretaries of health, education, and welfare and energy and director of Central Intelligence Agency
9th week: none
10th week: none
11th week: congressional liaison, counsel, domestic policy

advance people. They knew the numbers of the planes they wanted to fly him [Reagan]. Pretty good, right? I mean, these [Clinton] people, they knew nothing. Half of them still don't.

Another Carter aide reacted this way to the Reagan transition team: "They're very competent. They're no strangers to Washington. They're experienced. They know their way around and they know what they want. They're more relaxed than we were four years ago."[16]

The differences among presidents are illustrated less impressionistically by reviewing the timing of appointments. Figure 4-1 shows the sequence of major presidential appointments: White House staff, cabinet secretaries, and other major appointments, including budget director, chair of the Council of Economic Advisers (CEA), director of the Central Intelligence Agency

Figure 4-1 (continued)

Reagan

1st week: none

2d week: chief of staff, counsel

3d week: none

4th week: none

5th week: none

6th week: secretaries of commerce, treasury, transportation, health and human services, defense, state, labor, and attorney general, director of Office of Management and Budget, and director of Central Intelligence Agency

7th week: congressional liaison, domestic policy, secretaries of interior, energy, housing and urban development, and agriculture, head of National Security Agency, and ambassador to United Nations

8th week: none

9th week: press secretary

10th week: secretary of education

11th week: none

Clinton

1st week: none

2d week: none

3d week: none

4th week: none

5th week: none

6th week: chief of staff, secretaries of treasury, labor, health and human services, and commerce, director of Office of Management and Budget, and chairman of Council of Economic Advisers

7th week: secretaries of housing and urban development, veterans affairs, education, energy, defense, and state, director of Central Intelligence Agency, ambassador to United Nations, and head of National Security Agency

8th week: secretaries of interior, agriculture, and transportation, and attorney general (appointment later withdrawn)

9th week: none

10th week: none

11th week: congressional liaison, press secretary, domestic policy, counsel

SOURCE: Compiled by author.

(CIA), ambassador to the United Nations, and national security adviser. Perhaps the most striking difference is in the timing of the appointment of the White House staff and close advisers. As shown, Nixon and Reagan designated the chief of staff and counsel positions in the second week, with Nixon also choosing other key posts (congressional liaison and press aide) shortly after the election. In each case this action resolved potential personal conflicts between close advisers. Carter and Clinton, on the other hand, first dealt with the carryover issue of transition management and postponed most White House staff appointments until the final week of the transition (though Carter designated his press secretary in the second week, Clinton his chief of staff in the sixth week).

Figure 4-2 shows the sequence of cabinet secretarial appointments. Nixon announced his entire cabinet on December 11, the earliest of the four presidents, thus facilitating judgments about the appointments as a unit rather than encouraging a concentration on each designee. Also promoted by this process was the early identification of the administration and its purpose.[17] The other three presidents spread their appointments over several days: twenty for Carter, twelve for Reagan (with an outlier appointment for secretary of education on January 7),[18] and fourteen for Clinton. As shown in figure 4-2, there were variations among these three presidents. Carter appointed singly and in groups on different days as follows: 1-2-1-3-3-2; Reagan: 6-2-3-1-1; Clinton: 1-2-1-2-2-2-4. Of the three, Reagan's pattern was most like that of Nixon in permitting judgments about the group as a unit. He made an initial six appointments on December 11, two more five days later. Carter was somewhat slower but did make seven appointments in four days (December 18–21). Clinton's appointments were the most strung out, with the largest number of appointments coming last, on the day before Christmas.

Clinton's pattern, in particular, encouraged attention to each position. His early declaration that "my Cabinet will look more like America than previous administrations" invited representational tests.[19] Upon reflection, several Clinton advisers observed that the emphasis on diversity came to be the message or theme during the transition, superseding the more substantive, programmatic themes and seeming to displace the policy experience and expertise of several fine appointments in their own right. The diversity focus also had a scorekeeping effect within the media and among groups, which in turn contributed to heavy concentration on the qualities and group identity of each nominee.[20] Additionally, the withdrawal of Zoe Baird for the important position of attorney general raised questions about the vetting process and had the unfortunate effect in January of media concentration on one appointment rather than on the quality of the cabinet as a unit.

Figures 4-1 and 4-2 also show the variation among presidents in regard to the early designation of the national security and economic teams, along with the attorney general. Again, Nixon placed everyone at the same time, though he designated Henry Kissinger as national security adviser in advance of the rest of the cabinet, the only president to do so. This decision was widely interpreted as an indication that major foreign policy decisions would be made in the White House. Only the CIA director was named later

Figure 4-2. Sequence of Cabinet Secretary Appointments by Nixon, Carter, Reagan, and Clinton

Nixon
12/11/68: entire cabinet appointed; confirmed 1/20/69[a]

Carter
12/3/76: Cyrus Vance (State) appointed; confirmed 1/20/77
12/14/76: Brock Adams (Transportation) appointed; confirmed 1/20/77
 Michael Blumenthal (Treasury) appointed 12/14/76; confirmed 1/20/77
12/18/76: Cecil Andrus (Interior) appointed; confirmed 1/20/77
12/20/76: Griffin Bell (Justice) appointed; confirmed 1/25/77
 Robert Bergland (Agriculture) appointed; confirmed 1/20/77
 Juanita Kreps (Commerce) appointed; confirmed 1/20/77
12/21/76: Harold Brown (Defense) appointed; confirmed 1/20/77
 Patricia Harris (Housing and Urban Development) appointed; confirmed 1/20/77
 Ray Marshall (Labor) appointed; confirmed 1/26/77
12/23/76: Joseph Califano (Health, Education and Welfare) appointed; confirmed 1/24/77
 James Schlesinger (Energy) appointed; confirmed 9/1/77[b]

Reagan
12/11/80: Malcolm Baldrige (Commerce) appointed; confirmed 1/22/81
 Drew Lewis (Transportation) appointed; confirmed 1/22/81
 Donald Regan (Treasury) appointed; confirmed 1/21/81
 Richard Schweiker (Health and Human Services) appointed; confirmed 1/21/81
 William Smith (Justice) appointed; confirmed 1/22/81
 Caspar Weinberger (Defense) appointed; confirmed 1/20/81
12/16/80: Raymond Donovan (Labor) appointed; confirmed 2/3/81
 Alexander Haig (State) appointed; confirmed 1/21/81
12/22/80: James Edwards (Energy) appointed; confirmed 1/22/81
 Samuel Pierce (Housing and Urban Development) appointed; confirmed 1/22/81
 James Watt (Interior) appointed; confirmed 1/22/81
12/23/80: John Block (Agriculture) appointed; confirmed 1/22/81
1/7/81: Terrel Bell (Education) appointed; confirmed 1/22/81

Clinton
12/10/92: Lloyd Bentsen (Treasury) appointed; confirmed 1/20/93
12/11/92: Robert Reich (Labor) appointed; confirmed 1/21/93
 Donna Shalala (Health and Human Services) appointed; confirmed 1/21/93
12/12/92: Ronald Brown (Commerce) appointed; confirmed 1/21/93
12/17/92: Jesse Brown (Veterans Affairs) appointed; confirmed 1/21/93
 Henry Cisneros (Housing and Urban Development) appointed; confirmed 1/21/93
12/21/92: Hazel O'Leary (Energy) appointed; confirmed 1/21/93
 Richard Riley (Education) appointed; confirmed 1/21/93
12/22/92: Les Aspin (Defense) appointed; confirmed 1/20/93
 Warren Christopher (State) appointed; confirmed 1/20/93
12/24/92: Bruce Babbitt (Interior) appointed; confirmed 1/21/93
 Zoe Baird (Justice) appointed; appointment withdrawn[c]
 Mike Espy (Agriculture) appointed; confirmed 1/21/93
 Frederico Pena (Transportation) appointed; confirmed 1/21/93

SOURCE: Compiled by author.
 a. William Rogers (State); David Kennedy (Treasury); Melvin Laird (Defense); John Mitchell (Justice); Winton Bount (Post Office); Walter Hickel (Interior); Clifford Hardin (Agriculture); Maurice Stans (Commerce); George Shultz (Labor); Robert Finch (Health, Education and Welfare); George Romney (Housing and Urban Development); and John Volpe (Transportation).
 b. Schlesinger was designated as Carter's choice before the Department of Energy was established.
 c. Baird withdrew her name, as did a second candidate, Kimba Wood. Janet Reno was appointed on February 11, 1993, and confirmed on March 11, 1993.

by Nixon, and that was a reappointment of the incumbent, Richard Helms. Reagan, too, fit the recommended model in appointing the major cabinet positions—State, Defense, Treasury, and Justice—in the first round, along with the budget and CIA directors. The national security adviser and United Nations ambassador were designated in the second round.

Carter appointed his secretary of state the earliest of these four presidents, on December 3, along with his budget director. His selection of Cyrus Vance as secretary of state, and two weeks later Zbigniew Brzezinski as national security adviser, were of special note since his chief campaign adviser, Hamilton Jordan, had earlier stated that he would quit if such establishment figures were appointed. "If after the inauguration you find a Cy Vance as secretary of state and Zbigniew Brzezinski as head of national security, then I would say we failed. . . . And I'd quit. But that's not going to happen. You're going to see new faces, new ideas. The government is going to be run by people you never heard of."[21] The treasury secretary was appointed in the second round and the rest of the national security and economic teams were appointed in the third round. Clinton appointed his entire economic team first, as suited to his having set the economy as his major priority. The designation of the team was made just before his conference on the economy in Little Rock in mid-December. The national security team was selected in the next to last round—all on December 22.

The variation in sequences among these four presidents reveals a great deal about the pace of adjustment in political roles from candidate to president-elect, as well as the shift in activity from campaigning to governing. Nixon and Reagan moved deliberately and confidently to prepare organizationally and programmatically to assume office on January 20. Carter and Clinton made many of the prescribed moves in planning the transition, but time and energy were directed during the immediate postelection period to resolving personal conflicts and alleviating anxieties. They had the most to accomplish, given their outsider status and the manner in which they won office.

The Role of the President-Elect

According to transition aides, what exactly should be the role of the president-elect during the transition? How actively should he be involved? How public should his role be? There is substantial variation in the answers to these questions for the four cases, again with differences between the insider-Republicans and outsider-Democrats.[22]

Several aides identified organizational and psychological issues associated with the transition period and as affecting the role of the president-elect. A Reagan adviser believed that one consequence of the campaign is that: "People are sick of him. . . . During the transition, you don't want to be on television every night, but you do want to reemerge from time to time in a sympathetic setting with a sympathetic audience enunciating a specific theme that you want to emphasize."

Two Clinton aides had exactly opposite views in regard to the president-elect's visibility. One noted that when there is "a change in the party on top of the change in leadership, I think it's important that [the president-elect's] role be a highly visible role." Another advised the president-elect to make appointments and prepare "a long-term and a short-term plan, and stay out of sight." This second aide concluded that an "out-of-sight" strategy might enhance the status of a "devalued" office:

> One of the things I think has happened to the presidency, and I think it was happening before we came in, although we get a lot of blame for it, is a kind of devaluing of the office. And I think this kind of a strategy that I'm talking about might help pump the office back up. . . . If the . . . president-elect starts to show this sort of awe for the office, then when he or she inhabits it they get more of that elevation. Rather than making the office an extension of their campaign they sort of have a break . . . that says: "You know, I'm now preparing to assume this office." Now the trick is doing that without appearing to lose touch with the people.

This advice was not given at the time by this aide, nor did Clinton employ it. Clinton was anything but "out of sight" following the election. He was a continual public presence during the weeks of the transition.

How should the winner prepare to govern? A Reagan aide summarized the recommended process as "getting himself mentally geared up for the job of being president" (to include getting his private affairs in order) and "thinking of his concept of the presidency, a part of which is developing his inaugural address." In elaborating on these themes, this aide expressed similar views to those of Neustadt in describing the motivations of the Kennedy team: "The campaign was a means to an end, not an end in itself." Therefore, the president-elect had to engage in forward thinking. He continued:

> In the army we talk about a commander's concept of the situation.

... And that's his idea of what's going to happen. They now talk about visualization of things from start to finish ... how runners, if they can visualize the race, will do a better job. ... Well, a president[-elect] has ... got to do that. He's got to think about how he's going to be president. ... And if he's tied up in the nuts and bolts of the transition, he's doing the wrong thing. ... So I think the president needs to stay out of it.

However rational this posture may be, postelection forces do not easily accommodate a reflective and distant pretense for the president-elect. After all, the postelection orientation surrounds him as the star attraction. The personal futures of hundreds are in his hands. It is humbling, exhilarating, and rather overwhelming. Respondents discussed this situation, offering various perspectives that, taken together, portray the special organizational features of this period.

A first advisory has been mentioned before: don't become the president during the transition. Neustadt put it this way in a preelection memo to the Clinton campaign: "Don't prematurely announce actions the President-elect can't actually take before 12 noon on January 20. Remember Carter's $50 tax cut: announced in December, withdrawn after the inaugural!"[23] "Be deferential to the outgoing president" was the advice of one aide. Quite apart from the bad form of the affectation associated with jumping the gun is that "incredible pressures rush in [and] you don't want that."[24] A Clinton aide agreed for much the same reason: "[The president-elect's role] is not to go out there and start immediately either extending your campaign or starting your presidency. ... There is so much attention once you're in there you can afford the downtime."

Associated with this temptation to assume an office won but not yet conferred are the organizational issues with which the president-elect must deal. It is relevant that the organizational skills of presidential candidates are virtually never cited as an asset in the campaign. Neither is it assumed that the winner really knows how to organize and manage large endeavors. Yet on the day after the election, substantial organizational talents are required to manage the transition and direct it toward identifiable purposes of the new administration. One respondent viewed the transition mostly as "mechanical" and therefore not a subject for in-depth involvement by the president-elect: "It's basically mechanical and ministerial except for the appointment of people and the creation of your first 100 or 150 days. ... It's the mechanics of taking over control of the government, the levers of power. . . . It's important for [the president-elect] to be briefed up . . . but not hands-on management of the transition."

Another respondent with a most orderly concept of the transition viewed the president-elect's role in three phases, each successive phase requiring less active participation. First is the preelection phase discussed earlier, in which the candidate selects the planners and supports their work (preferably integrating their effort into the campaign organization in some way). Next is the early transition by the "people that are basically in charge of things until the White House staff comes . . . who are going to go with him into the government." Third is the "core leadership" that replaces the transition people and handles the mechanics referred to above.

One interesting perspective is that these developments in phased staffing create a buffer between the president-elect and those seeking influence, including campaign staff. In the conventional transition the president-elect needs to have an organization emerge that begins the process of distancing him from the campaign so as to advance toward the newly won responsibility. The preelection structure, done right, is a reminder that the campaign is a means to an end; the transition organization, properly set, serves as an inventory of the new tasks; and the White House staff, selected early, symbolizes the new, governing orientation to be absorbed by all who want to be a part of the new administration. Establishing a two-track structure to manage the transition out of the campaign and into governing (with the creation of a White House staff) can contribute to achieving these ends. If all of this works effectively, the president-elect is protected to the extent of his being able "to get up at 7:00 o'clock in the morning . . . and sit down with a couple of people, and decide, 'What do I have to do today to help me become a good president?' and then deliberately do it."[25]

Can a winning candidate, anointed president-elect, accomplish these organizational goals? Perhaps. But it is by no means guaranteed given the variation in experience and personal attributes of those few in this position. Generalized good sense may not suit specific styles of decisionmaking. In fact, one Bush aide explained that most politicians typically eschew staff support, or "care and feeding," as he put it.

If you were to go to President Bush or now President Clinton, they would say: "I don't want anybody, I don't want advance men, I don't want to be told when I have to go where. . . . I just want to be

able to get on the plane and go. I don't want a lot of speech writers. . . ."
So you have to kind of build the care and feeding responsibility into
the solution through trickery. You almost have to say, well, we will
also have a lot of people who will be helping you. "Well, keep those
numbers down; I don't want a lot of people helping me."

Thus it may well be that the impediment to erecting a buffer is the president-elect himself for several reasons: he may not yet be comfortable having
others act for him; he may not as yet have developed confidence in a staff
hierarchy; he may lack the discipline to permit it to work; he may not comprehend the organizational demands of the presidency; or he may not think
in standard organizational or managerial terms. A Carter aide judged that this
tendency to want to be overly involved in management was particularly a
problem for newly elected, first-term presidents, much like that for newly
nominated candidates.

They always want to run their own campaigns and they think they
can run the government down to the deputy assistant secretary level.
The notion that they have assumed a job that requires all of their
energy and intellectual capabilities at the policy direction level
doesn't sink in for months and months, sometimes too late. [The
exception is] Reagan, who by virtue of his personal style and taste,
had delegated. You never read a news article about Reagan arguing
over whether he was going to get command of the details of the
campaign, let alone the transition, let alone the government. Carter
was into it. Clinton's been into it. Nixon was notoriously into it, but
episodically.

Parallel to the organizational considerations are those of defining the
purposes of the new administration through appointments, the inaugural,
and the first 100 days. It is all really of a piece in the standard transition,
according to many respondents, since it is fundamentally a matter of setting the course for governing. "What does he want these people to do in
his behalf?" A "baseline guidance" is required, or those at work in the
transition will waste a great deal of time and effort. Without such clear
guidance, one respondent said, an energized transition team will try to do
everything: "There is the taking command of the policy agenda from the
campaign . . . and translating that now into what we're going to try and do

in the first several months." Similar sentiments were expressed by other respondents. A Clinton adviser: "His role in the transition ought to be to lay out priorities and encourage his team to get him ready to get out onto a fast start on the things that are most important, get well versed on those issues, and be ready to go himself."[26] A Reagan adviser proposed a role that integrated the appointments and policy agenda, then described how it worked:

> I think obviously he's got to be involved in the key personnel choices, and I think he's got to get his inaugural address, which should set . . . the agenda for everybody, the marching orders. And I think he needs to get involved in some kind of a review and approval of the first hundred days. . . . We spent a lot of time, some of us, on what the first hundred days are. Then we sat down with Reagan and went through all that. . . . Reagan signed off on it, and we went to work.

Making Appointments

The making of appointments is obviously an important task for a president-elect. For one Democratic aide: "It's important as president-elect . . . to focus, and during the transition his focus should be on the appointments process." How it is done is a matter of some difference in views. As discussed earlier, nearly all respondents believe that key White House staff should be selected early. Yet it is not unlike choosing favorites among your children. And since they will all still be around doing whatever you tell them, it is tempting to postpone decisions. An adviser to both the Carter and Clinton transitions explained it this way:

> You've . . . got to decide what is the structure of your own White House family. It is one thing to choose a cabinet. It's another to have a functioning White House. Presidents don't like to do that because they have to make choices among friends and they'd love to put it off—love, love, love to put it off. It's very frustrating for somebody like me who sees all the things I think they ought to be doing and they don't do it. But that's kind of a natural part of the process, I guess.

A Republican with ample experience himself in selecting people had these reflections on the importance of appointments:

> I look back now to my own time in government and [one] of the most important things I ever did was to pick people. And if you do that well, then virtually anything's possible. If, on the other hand, you blow it, you don't get good people on board . . . then it doesn't matter how hard you work or how smart you are; you're not going to have a successful administration.

A Carter aide agreed wholeheartedly: "If you pick the wrong people . . . you will never recover. You could recover from a bad policy move . . . people will forget a bad policy move. You will not recover from bad appointments unless you get rid of them all."

No one can imagine the appointment process to be trouble-free, even apart from having to choose from among friends. It requires sophisticated knowledge of the president's role in the government before the experience of serving, managing pressures from diverse interests, being familiar with the capabilities of persons who typically have not previously served in the position, and being able to estimate the effects of personal interactions on achieving the administration's goals (among other things, as Neustadt advises, "compensating for the mismatches in the styles of others").[27] Additionally, the process must go on in the spotlight of media coverage, in a relatively short period of time, and in the context of interest group anxieties about being represented properly.

It is in large part because of the sensitivity and complexity of this exercise that many respondents advise that the president-elect get help by appointing White House staff as soon as possible (as well as to create the buffer referred to earlier). It was for these reasons that a Reagan and Bush adviser stressed the need for the president-elect to focus his attention on the White House, to the exclusion even of the cabinet (noted mostly, I believe, to make his point).

> I have never understood why presidents-elect are so enamored of this idea that cabinet officers matter. They don't matter. You can run a damn cabinet for months without a cabinet officer and nobody will ever know the difference. That's the least crucial item that should be on a presidential agenda. Instead, because of the symbolic value they spend enormous amounts of time on it. They spend

very little time on the staff or how the White House works. It always amazes me that presidents don't understand—even those that have been governors—how much of the real power and decisionmaking in government is in the White House operation.

It was this respondent's view that the problem in part was a combination of a lack of understanding of staff operations and the phenomenon mentioned above: a refusal to believe that they really need that much help. He emphasized that staff relationships are "never explored until they get there, and then they've got to work it out on the fly." The most crucial relationship is that with the chief of staff.

[Presidents] always treat chiefs of staff incorrectly. They . . . think of chiefs of staff as nothing more than foremen, hired hands basically. Whereas chiefs of staff and everybody else think of [them] as exalted kinds of rulers with great power. So I think presidents need to think more about staff functions—how the White House operates, how it's going to operate, and the kind of people they choose to be around them. They don't seem to have that sense of history about them. It's like staff history is below them.

The Clinton appointments received the most criticism, even among those respondents who were involved in his transition. Most of what has been presented here by way of advice was breached or ignored. Here is one summary:

Bill Clinton spent far too much time trying to make up his mind who should be in his cabinet, and far too much time worrying about diversity, and far too much time making ad hoc decisions at the last minute. All this juggling around at the last minute. . . . I think competence is going to take a much larger role than diversity the next time around. . . . It's made people quite angry.

The Clinton experience illustrates how important it is for the candidate quickly to achieve a transformation in job analysis. The appointments will be critical in defining his presidency. If they are made primarily to satisfy campaign goals, past or future, rather than obviously suited to governing purposes, the transition will be prolonged as those designated adjust to their new assignments along with the president and his aides.

In winning a second term, President Clinton apparently concluded that he had made a mistake in concentrating too heavily on selecting the cabinet over building a competent White House staff. Accordingly, he appointed his new chief of staff, Erskine Bowles, first so that he might in turn make changes to suit his (that is, Bowles's) operating style. However, diversity once again came to eclipse substantive criteria in cabinet selection, with the "bean counters" encouraged to tote up the score.[28]

Choosing from among Campaign Aides

One of the lessons from Jeffrey H. Birnbaum's book, *Madhouse: The Private Turmoil of Working for the President*, is that a surprise winner attracts aides with little direct experience in big-time Washington politics. For example, in describing the background of Dee Dee Myers, who served as the press secretary in the Clinton White House, Birnbaum points out:

> When she joined the [Clinton] campaign, no one believed George Bush could be beaten. And even when it became clear that Clinton would win, Myers could never quite get her mind around it. She had not wanted to leave California, certainly not to set down roots in Washington. She had never given much thought to governing; politics was her profession.[29]

As Birnbaum describes it, Myers was one among several young White House staff who, to their surprise, found themselves at the presumed center of governing for the nation. Observers were understandably critical of having young campaign staff assuming critical positions, especially if they had experienced friends who did not get jobs. "Working in the White House should not be your first job," was the reaction of one such Democrat in commenting on Clinton's staff. Or as one respondent reported in regard to the Carter administration: "Someone once told me that the problem with the Carter administration was that there [were] too many people . . . for whom it was the best job they ever had. And that probably is true here [in the Clinton administration] too." But, of course, it is the nature of underdog campaigns that those in from the start may well be the candidate's young friends and the even younger ambitious volunteers with time on their hands. Thus it is that the bonds between the candidate and the loyalists are first formed. And it is this group that then becomes the "keepers of the flame"—those whose campaign experience invests them with the right, in their minds, to influence policy once their candidate is in office.

Winning candidates arrive in Washington having become larger than themselves through an organization styled to suit their personal, political, policy, and management preferences. However competent on the campaign trail, their aides have been selected for a purpose that is weakly related to governing, if related at all. Yet they are loyal, having pledged themselves to this person, folding their future into his. "You've got hundreds of people who have literally disrupted their lives, committed themselves to this enterprise for upwards of two and sometimes three years. And, at a moment, it's over. And now they're suddenly worrying about: 'Am I going to have a job? Where am I going to fit into the constellation?'" Understandably these aides come to believe that they, too, have won, and they look forward to the benefits of their having sacrificed for the candidate. The immediate reaction may be that of having won a prize—the White House—not that of assuming a responsibility.

As one respondent said, "So the tugging begins immediately. There's no moment of reflection. It just happens. It's the natural course of the beast." The president-elect is, therefore, faced with unusual managerial quandaries: How can he capitalize on the strengths and circumvent the weaknesses of his top-level campaign aides? How can he discern governing talent of staff who have never governed? How can he meld his campaign specialists with those who know how to govern? How does he prevent a campaigning style of governing?

One solution to these problems is simply to acknowledge that campaigning and governing are different undertakings and therefore require different specialists. One aide explained that a candidate for whom he worked clarified the relationship at the start of the campaign: "[He] said to us (campaign manager and myself and a couple of other people), 'I want you to know that I strongly and really appreciate all the work that you're doing. But if we happen to win this thing [they did not], do not expect that you guys are going to move into the Oval Office.' " Whether the candidate as president-elect would have followed through is problematic given the nature of the campaign experience (including fund-raising) and the potential effect of alienating staff intimately involved. More likely, however, is that the bonds of loyalty would have overcome any such early exhortation.

However rational on managerial grounds, abandoning campaign staff the day after the election is impractical. The reality is that the candidate and his closest aides virtually become one. The description by this Carter aide is typical:

> One thing you just can't . . . lose sight of—academics have a tendency to do this—is that people who have ever been . . . personally on the line with a candidate for president don't ever forget [it] and don't ever misunderstand it or underestimate it. And the "it" in that sentence is the bonds of common experience and loyalty that are created in a campaign. Generally it's a campaign that starts years earlier. Generally speaking there are people who are involved with the candidate, whether he's governor or congressman or senator . . . for a long period of time. And it's just not realistic in the least to expect the president once he's the candidate, once he's elected, to say: "Thank you" to all these people and say "I am now going to form a new team." That is just so totally contradictory of everything we know about life and human nature that it's silly to think about that happening.

Another Carter and Clinton adviser stressed that "campaigns generate alliances . . . and alliances don't stop at Little Rock. . . . I don't think that you can just rule in or rule out any particular types." Thus the problem as described must be engaged. It cannot be finessed. The issues are those of choosing from among the campaign staff and placing them in the right position. Given the universality of these issues, it is not surprising that all respondents had unequivocal views on the topic. The issue becomes that of achieving balance between the campaigning and governing orientations of staff.

Who Should Serve?

For one Clinton aide, the transition is the first decision point. His advice was: "Don't keep them around for the transition if you're not going to keep them around for the White House." A Carter aide believed the criterion for carrying over campaign staff to the transition and White House staff "has less to do with campaign versus noncampaign."

> In my opinion, it has to do with the people who are sufficiently knowledgeable of the president's political interests, concerns, sensitivities, and his substantive priorities. . . . The president ought to have around him, both in the transition and as he moves into the

> White House, a core of senior people, maybe widely divergent in their backgrounds, and may hate each other's guts, and may back-stab and fight for bureaucratic and political advantage among themselves. But . . . at root, the senior group . . . understand this guy's history, his needs, his priorities, what he's going to be sensitive to, what in the tight spots he's not going to want to decide himself.

This same aide warned that if the transition is staffed by "worker bees out of the campaign," the president-elect will lose a strategic edge since these people have a regional or group politics mind-set. "They're not thinking nationally . . . in terms of the president's strategic level."

It was uniformly agreed that "hired guns" should not be carried forward. Some were adamant on this point: "I think the damn pollsters should be put out to pasture. You don't need to have somebody take a new pulse every two days in transition. You've already won the thing. You ought to be thinking about longer-term stuff, not the instant temperature testing of reaction to the new regime." The term *hired guns* refers to "people that don't have . . . a long history of involvement with the president [and] have not expressed any interest in policy." Most often these are the public relations consultants and pollsters working under contract to the campaign. Lee Atwater for the Republicans and James Carville for the Democrats were most often cited as the classic hired guns. As was pointed out, neither wanted to be a part of the transition or the new government because they understood that their own expertise was substantially more electoral- than policy-oriented.

The conventional advice to cut the White House off from the campaign professionals fails to acknowledge, and is typically disdainful of, contemporary developments. Most recent presidents have followed the polls assiduously and incorporated those with public relations training into White House staff operations (for example, Haldeman with Nixon, Michael K. Deaver with Reagan). Promoting the president is a time-honored function of the White House. What was to change in the Clinton case, and was accelerated following the disastrous 1994 midterm election, was the greater use of consultants to campaign for policy and to restore presidential status.

The Right Placement

Making placements is itself a tricky venture for a newcomer to the White House. But it is critical given the attention paid to a new administration during its early months in office and the intricacy of making connections with the permanent government. A Reagan aide explained that almost all of the campaign staff could be used in the transition; he would not automatically rule out anybody. Knowing the needs of the new administration, the president-elect then must make the proper assignments (a target more easily achieved if most campaign staff have governing experience).

> I think everybody has a role of some kind. The trick is defining that [role]. . . . You could take the operatives, for example, the Carvilles, the Rollinses and . . . say there's not much of a role in a governing sense. . . . But in truth I think there is a role for them in terms of defining how politics is going to relate to the governing process. Where does it fit in in the decisionmaking process, in the chief of staff operations, etc.? How does the president want to use that information? My two experiences were that Ronald Reagan integrated his political people into the decisionmaking process . . . but was very compartmentalized. . . . The patronage people, there's a role for them. The personnel people. I think everybody has a role. The trick is to get them in the right place.

Essentially this respondent was explaining that the usefulness of any campaign staff person is directly related to having clearly defined purposes for the transition. To know the right place for the right person depends heavily on having a personnel or staff matrix that is oriented to the policy and political goals of the administration. Much depends on the president-elect's definition of those goals and his awareness of the skills of his aides. A Carter aide explained that the president-elect is not going to say that "I don't have any further need for your services."

> But what he does have to say, if he's going to be a successful president, is: "Here's what I want you to do because I think this fits. I think this really fits your talents best, and I think this is where you can continue to help me the most." And making those judgments is very hard . . . because generally speaking there are going to be three people or six or more who want to do this particular job.

The inventory of talents may vary. A Reagan aide explained that some aides were primarily campaign oriented, others were primarily interested in governing, and still others "have both talents." Further, some wanted jobs in the new administration, others "wanted to go back to whatever they were doing, and they were not interested in being either in the transition or in the government." Again, the task for the president-elect and his close advisers is in using their talents purposefully. "If a person is primarily a politically oriented guy . . . you may want that person as an adviser on the sidelines in the transition, but you don't want that person making decisions because . . . for them the political saliency of a candidate becomes more important than their ability to do the job in government."

Keepers of the Flame—and Other Problems

Certain advisers discussed the staffing problem in terms of the changes that occur in the basic mission of the transition versus that of the campaign. If those changes are well understood, then the president-elect is in the position to make meaningful assignments. A Republican viewed it this way: the policy people from the campaign should move directly into the transition staff, and the media and scheduling people should continue to do what they did in the campaign (while acknowledging the changing circumstances). Then "there's a small number of people who are kind of the keepers of the flame that move over to work with the transition staff." A Democrat had much the same view in identifying various levels of campaign people. The hired guns would continue to have a role because "they brought him there and candidates learn to trust and work with these folks." However, a strong executive will say at that point: "Okay. Now I'm entering . . . a new stage. What we've got to do, and the skills that you've brought me now are important and I need to tap into them. But they're no longer the ones that should guide all of my thinking. So what I have to do is balance what you've got over here with what other parts of it can do." For the rest—field folks, legislative people, liaison to various groups—they can be placed in the transition teams or assigned to the inaugural activities. "You've got to do something with these folks." And, of course, the provision of funds makes it possible to give them jobs—a sort of mustering-out pay.[30]

Several respondents dealt with this matter of the role to be played by dominant campaign personnel in the transition period. It was precisely that issue that Carter and Clinton had to resolve before they could proceed since the campaign directors were not about to relinquish control. A Democrat stated the case:

The campaign people, of course, lay claim to being the keepers of
the truth. There is this sense in the transition that the campaign people want the rest of the apparatus as it starts to emerge to understand: "We're the ones that know what the American people wanted. We're the ones who were out there. You folks [in Washington]
live in, wherever, your law firms and wherever you've been. You
weren't out there. . . ."

So there's a truth-telling and a truth-holding kind of process,
and claim, that gets asserted. You've got the campaign workers [ver-
sus] all the sophisti-kids and the people who've been living the
fancy lives and waiting for the election; now they're coming in,
right? The silk stocking guys, now they're going to walk in and take
over the corner office. And it's almost a we/they kind of mentality—
not almost, it *is*.

A Republican aide observed that this self-protective, perhaps even defen-
sive, strife carries over to relationships between the White House staff and
the cabinet and other major departmental or agency appointments. Actually,
the point was made as an argument for appointing major White House staff
positions early enough that they can be a part of the process of selecting the
cabinet, that is, as a means for lessening the potential for conflict. If it is not
averted, the keepers of the flame will protect their turf, with unfortunate
results.

The attack by White House staff on cabinet is a source of bad government. And it is extremely pervasive. There is mutual contempt,
but it is much stronger . . . contempt felt by White House staff for
cabinet than vice versa.
QUESTION: Why, do you think?
RESPONSE: Two reasons. One is the White House staff, by virtue
of physical proximity, feels closer to the president. All White House
staffs feel embattled and form deep kinds of bonds, an us-against-
them mentality, even in good times, much stronger in bad times.
And secondly, the cabinet has something to do that is serious and
real with a direct and serious effect on the outside world. The White
House staff can only influence those decisions through threat, oil-
ing, offers of reward.

Table 4-1. Transition Period Press Conferences and Appearances of Presidents-Elect Nixon, Carter, Reagan, and Clinton

President-elect	Press conferences	Appearances[a]
Nixon	5	1[b]
Carter	10[c]	1
Reagan	1	0
Clinton	12	8[d]

SOURCE: Compiled by author from news sources.

a. Television appearances or other public events.

b. Nixon announced his full cabinet on television, December 11.

c. In addition Vice President–Elect Walter Mondale held two press conferences.

d. Includes the Economic Conference in Little Rock and attendance at the Renaissance Weekend at Hilton Head, South Carolina.

A Public Presence

The principal difference among the presidents-elect in this study in regard to their public presence during the transition is, I believe, related to their experience, self-confidence, and preferred style. Nixon and Reagan knew about transitions into major public office. Each was relatively secure about his role, with Nixon more actively involved, though not publicly; Reagan was substantially less so. Carter's and Clinton's experience was with transitions into positions of lesser importance, that is, the governor's office in Georgia and Arkansas. Therefore they used the period for orienting themselves to an executive position of a much higher order as well as to the national press and public. These differences are revealed in a general way in table 4-1.

Note that Nixon and Reagan had a limited public presence during the transition. And their statements were consistent with the dominant theme or declared purpose of their presidency. In his initial news conference, Nixon stressed organizational measures and his determination to "bring us together" following what veteran reporter James Reston called "one of the most tumultuous American Presidential elections of this century."[31] Nixon was anxious to project stability, control, and clear direction. His second news conference, a week later, concentrated on foreign policy. It was another fine example of how important it is that the president-elect not presume too much regarding his status. Following a meeting with President Lyndon B. Johnson, Nixon explained that the two men had agreed "that there be prior consultation and prior agreement" on key foreign policy decisions. He was not given a veto, Nixon explained. Instead, "what we're really trying to do is to work out as best we can a relationship which will see that the United States speaks with one voice in a vital period of 60 days."[32] It did not take President Johnson long to refute any such agreement. He explained that the agreement was merely one of his permitting the president-elect to have an observer sitting in on meetings. But "I will make whatever decisions the President of the United States is called upon to make between now and Jan. 20."[33] Nixon had come close to violating the "remember you are not the president" precept.

Nixon's other news conferences in early December were associated with appointments, the most notable being that of the designation of Henry Kissinger as national security adviser. Nixon announced his whole cabinet at once in a television broadcast on December 11. This unprecedented move was specifically orchestrated to seize attention by introducing the whole government at a time of high public anxiety. The success of the move was at least partially revealed in editorial comment: "In general, Mr. Nixon appears to have balanced his Cabinet about equally between progressive Republicans . . . and conservatives. . . . It seems a capable as well as politically balanced group and we wish for it great success; but, at a time when the country is looking for inspiration, the Nixon Cabinet is not exactly an exciting one."[34] Other statements and contacts with the press were left to staff—typically the press spokespersons. The president-elect's other public activities were primarily those of meetings with President Johnson and Vice President Hubert H. Humphrey, White House aides and various other administration officials, interest group representatives, former and present governors, economic advisers, members of Congress, foreign officials, mayors and other local officials, business leaders, and his newly designated cabinet.

In summary, Nixon's public presence was in keeping with expectations of the conventional transitions. He was among the most politically experienced candidates ever to run. Therefore it would have been phenomenal had the transition appeared disorderly and aimless. Just as unsurprising was the control of the process by Nixon himself, given his well-established manner of decisionmaking.

Superficially the evidence in table 4-1 suggests that the public presences of Reagan and Nixon were very similar. Each conducted few press conferences and, essentially, made no television or other public appearances. There were, however, important differences between the two presidents-elect that divulge variations in personality and style. Ronald Reagan was unlikely to supervise the transition and therefore to project himself as in command. His autobiography ignores the transition entirely. Chapter 35 ends with his having been summoned by his wife from taking a shower to receive the concession call from President Carter. "The polls in California wouldn't even close for another two hours. But standing in my bathroom with a wrapped towel around me, my hair dripping with water, I had just learned I was going to be the fortieth president of the United States." Chapter 36 begins this way: "Shortly before noon on January 20, 1981, Nancy and I left Blair House . . . and were driven through the gates of the White House and up to the North Portico. Jimmy and Rosalynn Carter were waiting for us, and a few minutes later, by tradition, he and I got in one car and Nancy and Mrs. Carter got in another for the drive to the inaugural ceremonies."[35] The word "transition" does not appear in the index, nor does the name of E. Pendleton James, who managed the pre- and postelection personnel search operation. It was reported that his press schedule for a four-day period in mid-December "showed only that he would visit his barber, his tailor and a meat locker and that he would receive a Christmas tree."[36]

Reagan's single press conference came on Thursday following the election. Reagan's formal statement focused on the transition organization, with special attention to a foreign policy advisory board. Most of the questions were about foreign policy, with the Iranian hostage crisis receiving heavy notice. Other topics included domestic issues, the role of the vice president, cabinet appointments, and congressional relations. In regard to the critical matter of appointments, Reagan explained that "there'll be no discussion of names until we're ready to announce the actual appointment of someone."[37]

Reagan did not personally announce his cabinet and other major appointments. This task was left most often to the press secretary. Daily statements were issued by Edwin Meese III, transition director, regarding transition organization and activities, and other preparations for governing. The president-elect's first set of appointments was introduced by Press Secretary James Brady at a press conference; subsequent appointments were announced but the designees were not present.

Reagan's most active involvement during the transition weeks occurred in mid-November, when he traveled to Washington to meet with congressional leaders and otherwise connect with Washington officialdom and insiders. On Capitol Hill Reagan exclaimed, "We're not going to accomplish anything without the cooperation of the House and Senate."[38] Reagan was eager to contrast himself favorably with President Carter. Though Carter too had visited Capitol Hill during the transition period, he was given low marks for his relationships with Congress. Reagan also hosted a dinner for Washington insiders and attended another at the home of columnist George Will, as well as meeting with President Carter and visiting the Supreme Court. The Washington trip was uniformly praised. Editorial comment in the *New York Times* was typical: "To a public thirsting for portents, [Reagan's] conduct so far suggests something encouraging: that he will be not merely a triumphant partisan but a President intent . . . on governing."[39]

During the second week of December Reagan interrupted what one reporter called his "leisurely schedule in California" to visit New York City and Washington.[40] In New York Reagan met with Terence Cardinal Cooke at his residence behind St. Patrick's Cathedral and with three black leaders who had endorsed him during the campaign (including the Reverend Ralph Abernathy). He then attended a dinner hosted by Mrs. Vincent Astor and attended by the elite of the city. His second visit to Washington coincided with the announcement of his initial cabinet selections (though he did not himself present them).

Here then was a transition process in which the public presence of the president-elect was less even than that of Nixon. Yet management and control characterized both. For Nixon that direction was centered in the president-elect. For Reagan it was obviously concentrated in the managers whom he selected immediately after the election. Reagan's distancing himself from Washington also suited the decision to focus more on the inauguration than the transition, even the appointment of the cabinet. Neustadt advised a Clinton associate: "Keep the president-elect out of Washington, except for frequent visits."[41] Reagan anticipated this advice twelve years earlier, though his visits were infrequent.

Carter and Clinton were regular presences during their transitions, though often out of Washington too. They held many press conferences, most often in Plains, Georgia, and Little Rock, Arkansas, respectively. Each also was preoccupied early in the transition with having to resolve personnel disputes over managing the formation of their governments. Lacking prior Washington experience, they were naturally inclined to send more signals as they engaged the set of issues involved in governing. Further, because of the uncertainty about their performance in office and staff capabilities, reporters were likely to ask them questions about process and organization. The similarity in their public presences makes possible a side-by-side analysis that then facilitates generalizing about their preparation and its effects.

Each held several press conferences—Carter ten, Clinton twelve. Carter regard to policy and process. Clinton, even more than Carter, created a score-card for the press and for various groups, as well as a set of expectations on sensitive policy matters that could cause trouble either at once or later. There was another feature of Clinton's public presence that contrasted with the other three presidents-elect. As table 4-1 shows, he made several attention-getting appearances in addition to press conferences. He traveled (to Los Angeles, Chicago, Washington, Hilton Head), he gave speeches, he participated actively in an economic summit, he appeared on television news shows. He left the impression more of a continuing of the campaign than a transition to governing. In fact, these activities foretold a different type of presidency, one in which the conventional transition is less apt.

The standard to be used in judging a president-elect's public presence in a transition is the extent to which it directly and positively contributes to prepa-rations for governing. A part of the decision should be the extent to which appearances by the president-elect seem to stand in place of or to compete with the outgoing administration. A continuing presence by the president-elect logically encourages comparisons and cultivates expectations. Intense discipline is required for a Washington outsider to limit appearances, given postelection interest in him on the part of the press, as well as the dramatic change in behavior required of the president-elect and his staff. After all, they have just completed a campaign in which there is a premium placed on get-ting attention. Still, the first test of their governing skills may be the extent to which they are able to focus their time and energy on what happens after January 20. The challenge is especially acute for those inexperienced in Washington ways since the early weeks of the transition are devoted to their learning what others know. It is apparent in the Carter and Clinton cases that it was necessary for them to work through, perhaps even talk about, process-es (appointments, setting priorities) that were more familiar to Nixon and Reagan and their staffs. It may also be the case that it was important for Carter and Clinton to be out front, in part to reassure themselves, in part to compen-sate for their low winning percentage of the popular vote.

The Transition and Congress

Congress, too, undergoes a transition following an election. New mem-bers are elected; returning members read their returns, comparing them with those of the president in their states or districts; new party and committee

did most of his transition business in Plains, Georgia, though his
headquarters was in Washington. Clinton, still serving as go\
Arkansas, also stayed home and, in addition, set up his transition h
ters in Little Rock. Holding press conferences in Plains and Little I
convenient for the president-elect, but it was not to the liking of
(and violates another Neustadt rule: "Put him [the president-elect
staff someplace the press will enjoy").[42] By contrast, Nixon's (
headquarters was in New York City, and appointments were not st
but presented all at once. Reagan's headquarters was in Washing
press contacts coordinated there.

The early press conferences began with statements and inquiries
appointing process. Both candidates emphasized that they would
minorities and women, but both became frustrated and defens
reporters' questions relating to diversity.[43] Reporters were also curio
how each president-elect would go about making appointments and
ing the White House. Current policy issues—in particular, the energy
Carter and the economic program for Clinton—were also subjects of

There are differences too between the public presences of these t
idents-elect. Carter moved more quickly to appointments: seven of
conferences were devoted to his selections. Clinton held five con
before his first set of appointments. Breaking with tradition, his first
with the press was a statement only, with no questions. It was inte
reassure foreign nations of the continuity of national security policy
markets of the strengthening effect of his program.

Clinton's first full press conference on November 12 touched on
topics that later resulted in problems for the Clinton administration. T
ference also displayed the president-elect's tendencies to be prolix, co
with Carter (and Nixon and Reagan). He began by stressing the imp
of diversity for appointments: "I've . . . pledged to the American peo
my Cabinet will look more like America than previous administratio
think that the great diversity of this nation can and must be a so
strength as we face the challenges that lie ahead."[44] He also announce
code of ethical conduct would be released soon. Questions ranged
over foreign and domestic policy, pacing of proposals submitted to Co
change in policy toward Haitian refugees, and lifting the ban on gay
military, among other topics. This first conference was a good exan
why a president-elect is well advised to be cautious in his early statem

leaders may be chosen. By the dictates of the Twentieth Amendment to the Constitution, the congressional installation ceremony precedes that of the president by more than two weeks. In recent decades the political parties in each chamber begin organizational adjustments shortly after the election. Orientation sessions are held to aid in socializing new members and introducing them to the forthcoming agenda.

Contrasted with the White House, Congress is a continuing body, by constitutional design for the Senate, by high reelection rates in the House of Representatives, and by staff continuity in both houses. This institutional continuity serves to acclimate the freshmen, as well as to contribute stability and predictability for others who want something from Congress. Thus there is much living knowledge about Capitol Hill and how it works. It is especially important that a president from out of town seize the opportunity to learn about Congress. As one seasoned Republican explained: "This town, the whole philosophy of this town, the whole way Washington operates is different than anything else. . . .You better know how Washington works if you're going to come up here and work it."

There is so much for the outsider to learn. The just-concluded experience of campaigning must now be set aside in favor of national leadership. "You have these two furious months of going at each other. . . . Wild activity. Suddenly, he's elected, not to keep doing that, but to work with all these people, and to be level headed, and to be reasonable, not to be on the attack." Congress is, of course, a partisan institution, but most major legislation is finally enacted with cross-partisan support.[45] Often the president cannot rely only on his own party since many issues are cross-cutting. But, as one Carter aide explained, the president is not automatically the leader even of his own party.

> [With] the congressional leadership of your party . . . you are obviously facing people who have already been there. They've been managing the process on behalf of the party. [With the Democrats] you've got 40 years of continuity and they've got their own views. There is always, I think, on the part of a newly elected president, if he's got his own [party] in control . . . on the Hill [the idea that] "together we can get a lot done."
>
> There is the notion, naively, I think, that sometimes surfaces that the president's primacy in the process will somehow be accepted by the [congressional] leadership because they are our guys. . . .

That's a fundamental misreading of the institutional politics and the constitutional relations between the congressional and executive branches. The danger is [that] the president in the transition is not yet . . . ready to really stake out and understand how to stake out a constructive but clearly independent position, vis-à-vis the legislative leadership.

So my own view is, it's time for romancing the stone, but not trying to get anything substantive done too quickly, unless you know with great precision exactly what you want and when you want it, and the leadership is ready to go and believe it's there. The danger, of course, is [that leaders tell you]: "Don't worry about it, Mr. President. We'll take care of it up there. Don't you worry about it. We've got control; we'll take care of it." At the moment the president accepts that premise, he may have lost control.

This analysis strongly suggests the need to assert leadership early but in a manner that acknowledges the constitutional and political status of Congress.

Based on his experience, another Carter aide concluded that presidential learning during the transition should include a full understanding of his status within the permanent government—one in which he has position but limited power.

I told President Carter that [his options were limited] and he didn't really like it because he thought I was denigrating his power, which I was not. . . . I said . . . I have come to the conclusion that there is only one thing that you can do, unilaterally, without getting the bureaucracy involved, or having it go through 14 different levels. . . . It is the only power you've got.

And he said, "What's that?"

And I said: "You've got the power to blow up the world. . . . Can't nobody stop you. No bureaucrat can stop you. . . . No committee has control of that. But that is not a very beneficial power. But if you want something to happen and you say, I want this done tomorrow, there ain't very much you can do to get it done tomorrow. Somebody's got to write a position paper. Somebody's got to go through this, or you've got to check with the Congress, you've got to do this. . . . And, probably, a president is not there long enough to see the results of change."

This statement offers a candid and perceptive analysis of the challenge for incoming presidents, including those with Washington experience. It informs them of the complexity of assuming leadership in a separated system. Presidents-elect need to show respect without giving up leadership and to establish authority and direction while emphasizing the importance of consultation. One former member of Congress compared Reagan and Carter in making these points:

> The people on the Hill are professionals. They respond well to somebody who demonstrates a respect, not just for the institution of the Congress, but the professional politics. . . . You don't have to be overly humble about it. It's partly attitude and style more than anything else, more than the substance of how you actually deal with the Congress. Congress . . . often disliked intensely what Reagan asked us to do, but we liked the fact that he asked us, and we admired the way he dealt with us. He always demonstrated a respect for the institution, although he might disagree with what we did. Carter never conveyed the sense of mutual respect for another politician or another point of view. If you disagreed with him, it was because you were morally wrong.

The clear point in displaying respect from the start is to create a positive working relationship, done in a way that "doesn't give away too much," "offers the potential of a little longer honeymoon," and "reassures them that here [is] a guy who want[s] to work within the Washington community."

The sensitive nature of this relationship at the point of preparing a president was acknowledged by certain respondents who urged caution and even some distance. A Reagan aide advised: "I don't think presidents are ready during [the transition] period to do serious business with the Congress." Among other things, he explained that "[presidents'] adrenalin is high, so they always overestimate their ability." In addition they are vulnerable because they are tired from the campaign, and, if the president-elect is an outsider to Washington, "he's not prepared to operate in this climate until he's been here, no matter what his background has been." In reflecting on the mistakes made with Congress during the transition, a Clinton aide stressed the lack of preparation, as well as their having concentrated more on staffing issues, including the cabinet, than on a serious review of congressional relations.

The response of a Nixon aide was revealing of problems that his president subsequently had with Congress. In speaking about pressure from the Hill regarding appointments, it was this person's view that the initial period provided an edge that should be taken advantage of, even if "they" scream.

> The thing I would keep pounding on him is: "You've got the power now. Don't listen to anybody else. Your power's going to start eroding from January 20th on. But right now, it's all yours. And do it your way." That's hard to do because [the president and his staff] are getting pulled and tugged by all these people. But there's not a thing anybody can do at that stage, and it's hard to realize that at that time. But that's the time to realize it, because that's when you can ignore all those things. And sure they're going to scream. You're going to have all kinds of problems. You're going to create all kinds of trouble. But you're still the new president. They've got to go along with you for a while.

Several aides stressed the importance of having skilled and experienced congressional liaison personnel, appointed early so as to establish communication with Congress, to reassure the members that a savvy team is moving into place, and simply to respond to incoming phone calls. Carter is generally acknowledged to have had the least effective such personnel during the transition. As one Carter aide explained: "One of the things that got the administration off on a bad foot was the difficulty that the congressional relations operation in the transition had in responding to congressional calls coming in; it had already left a sour taste by the time the administration got started. . . . President Carter waited too long to name and designate [staff]." Failures of this type reveal uncertainty and induce a lack of confidence on Capitol Hill.

Presidents-elect do not need to wonder why it is important to establish a good working relationship with Congress. For example, the budget cycle is not interrupted by elections. Therefore a new budget is being prepared for Congress by the outgoing president as the new president is organizing to assume power. Relations between the incoming and outgoing presidents can be somewhat strained when an incumbent has been defeated. "Even the most cooperative person doesn't want to share too much with the incoming [team] because (a) he's got a statutory responsibility to submit the last budget, which takes a lot of time and a lot of OMB resources; and (b) there's just always a certain sense of propriety about what you're doing." Still, the Office of Management and Budget is staffed with professionals, trained to serve each president on either side of January 20. And one Carter budget transition aide believed that, whereas President Ford and OMB Director James Lynn were "deeply hurt by losing," "Lynn's a professional and by and large . . . gave us fairly substantial access by Thanksgiving." The problem facing the president-elect is that of getting reliable numbers before the inauguration, as well as having competent aides to analyze these numbers and develop alternative proposals suited to the president-elect's priorities.

Failure to manage this important task in the constrained time period means that the new president "will lose a whole budget year, in terms of implementing a program, unless [he] can come up with revisions quickly." Thus, as this Carter aide explained:

> What that really requires is a transition staff and White House staff, and an OMB and CEA [Council of Economic Advisers] head who are really experienced hands. [David] Stockman, whatever faults one may believe he had, did more for the Reagan administration in the first three months than any single person. He made that administration effective because he was able to come up, even before you had subcabinet officers in the departments, with budget revisions which were then passed, and became Reagan's budget. . . .
>
> You just can't stress how important [it is] having somebody who understands the budget, [who] gets the president immediate revisions so his program has a chance to be implemented. We were fortunate. Although neither Bert Lance or Jim McIntyre had that experience, Charlie Schultze did.

A Nixon aide was equally admiring of the Reagan approach, much less so of the Carter effort:

> The Reagan model is absolutely textbook. They did it precisely right. . . . There is a window, as they say in the space program. And a president with any kind of a mandate at all can do it in his first year, if he moves vigorously, has a clear sense of the direction he wants to take, brings people around him who know the process. And that's precisely what Reagan did. You get in there like Carter: his folks couldn't find the men's room for the first year, and they didn't ever put their stamp on anything.

The vital personnel selection process for a new administration also brings the transition staff in direct contact with Congress. Members often want their friends or staff appointed, and several hundred appointments require Senate approval. Some aides recommend that members of Congress be brought into the transition process, perhaps on various teams. One aide expressed the view that "they ought to be courted all the time. . . . We courted them incessantly." A Nixon aide even recommended involving members of Congress in the campaign, but certainly in the transition, mostly in various task groups.

Clearly the primary recommendation among transition aides was for the new team to be sensitive to the fact that Congress performs an immediately important function in vetting and confirming presidential nominations for key positions.

> The president has got to realize that cabinet secretaries and some other major appointments have got to pass Senate scrutiny. . . . So it's very important along the way . . . that he's got to be talking to the leadership as to whether or not there is a particular problem or difficulty with a particular individual. . . . Nothing is worse than a long, drawn, tough, nasty, dirty confirmation proceeding. . . . That doesn't mean that you capitulate to them, but you've got to have a constant communication with the committees.

Of course, doing all of this right depends heavily on knowing what should be done. It is not enough to be as intelligent, say, as Carter and Clinton; being savvy too is required. A president-elect with limited Washington experience may not appreciate the ultimate importance of Congress to his success. And the most talented of his campaign aides may lack the expertise to advise him. As one Nixon aide conceded: "I didn't understand Congress. I may not, as I sit here now, understand the Congress. I certainly didn't understand when I first went [to Washington]." He acclaimed the virtues of Bryce Harlow, Nixon's congressional liaison chief with experience in the Eisenhower administration, who was "a student of Congress." "He set about to develop some coalitions. You do that really not on the issues, but you do it socially. You do it personally. You do it in terms of helping them with their constituents, know what their interests are, and cultivating those."

There is no one formula for connecting successfully with Capitol Hill since political and policy conditions vary substantially from one transition to the next. What is unlikely to vary, however, is the positive reaction on Capitol

Hill to good intentions on the part of the president-elect and his team, as reinforced by consultation and guided by a clear display of leadership.

Transition Teams

One of the manifestations of the modern transition is the creation of myriad teams for making connections with the executive departments and agencies and the Washington establishment outside the government. Many of these teams are microcosms of the challenges characterizing the shift from campaigning to governing. They provide paid jobs for campaign staff, thus bringing them together with Washington insiders. "You've kept people [from the campaign] busy and you've given them reward and a title." Solving one problem, however, may create another. Team members may believe that their familiarity with a department or agency justifies an appointment in the new administration. Personal ambition can, in turn, interfere with the teamwork required to produce a useful report.

When the department secretary or agency heads are designated, the team and its work may be competitive with, or irrelevant to, the intentions and direction favored by the nominees. For whereas one major purpose of the teams is to brief the incoming administration, some team members may have been led to believe, or convinced themselves, that they would be chosen. Therefore, transition aides had very mixed opinions about the value of these teams while acknowledging their inevitability, given the need for rewarding campaign workers and the availability of transition funds to pay them.

Transition teams differ from task forces. The former are set up to make connections with governmental units as an aid to the incoming appointees, including, in most cases, the preparation of a nominee for Senate nomination hearings. Task forces are used by presidents-elect to develop policy proposals in selected areas. Though all incoming administrations create some of both, Reagan created an extensive network of issue task forces. One Carter aide warned against issue or program task forces, especially large groups:

> I just think that they are very dangerous. . . . [They] can easily veer out of control and start setting up obligations . . . that the president must assume, positions that he must explain, choices that he must defend. . . . Generally speaking, you don't need to create task forces

of large sizes. . . . Large groups lead almost inevitably to lack of control and creating little areas of conflict within the task forces.

Another Carter aide disagreed, believing that such groups provided patronage, constituency management, and a means for testing ideas:

> A lot of this transition stuff is done because it gives you something to give people who have been working for you very hard, and it creates the impression of structure, motion, progress, control. So it's a bunch of jobs. . . . [Then] you can get a lot of people in important constituency groups who have ongoing influence over an agency or subject matter, and get them inside the tent instead of outside the tent. So they're working, and they start to get a stake in the outcomes, and the success of the administration.
>
> The problems with the substantive impact . . . are that if the agency is not staffed, if the secretary is not there, and the assistant secretaries aren't there, then the work is being done in a vacuum because it's not being done at the direction of the people who have a stake in what you do.

The key to productive use of such groups appears to be in the degree of control by a tightly organized transition structure. Neustadt advises against appointing task forces "except on substantive issues of immediate concern where advice is really needed or big shots have to be conciliated."[46] And as Brauer explained, "In 1980, as in 1960 . . . , the key decisions about personnel, policy, and organization were made by the President-elect with a relatively small number of aides and advisers."[47] In other words, the Kennedy and Reagan task forces were more closely directed and monitored and associated with the policy priorities of the president-elect. Problems with such groups develop if they are given license to generate proposals independently of, or in the absence of, the policy goals of the president-elect. And as one lobbyist noted in an interview: "I think that the task force thing was terrific if you're a lobbyist."

All incoming administrations employ transition teams. They serve as barometers of the organizational shifts away from the campaign, and they reveal the roster of tensions between the loyalists fresh from the crusade and the new governing team (which may include some loyalists). Here is how it all works, according to an aide with experience in several transitions:

You have the initial transition team put together before these appointments and they scatter out to the agencies. They are putting together briefing books. They are becoming more self-important by the day because they are the president's emissary. They get deferred to when they go to the agencies. And all of a sudden the real person is appointed. That person doesn't necessarily want these folks [the transition team]. They're perfectly happy to say good-bye to them. They have said, "Thank you for the briefing books. See ya." Then they get pressure put on them to bring some of [the transition team] to the deal and negotiation goes back and forth. Others pretty much adopt the team as their team so they become the new staff at these agencies. But it's always a tense and confusing process. . . . It often causes the first tension between the White House and the cabinet appointee because these people who were there first [the team] by definition will have good campaign contacts.

These teams also provide a more direct opportunity for the president-elect and his advisers to make connections with the Washington establishment, including the active lobbyist-lawyer-think tank population. A member of a trade transition team explained that "all the trade lawyers in town . . . believe that their reputation will be enhanced if they're on the transition team. They don't want to leave trade lawyering, so they don't want to be in the [government]. But they would be insulted if they were not picked." What was true for trade was said by others to be generally the case. "The transition team's really biggest problem is satisfying all the lawyers who want to come in, and all the people in the campaign." Some believed this practice of appointing lawyers and other interest group representatives to be an advantage:

You take the pressure groups, you get them in. There are a lot of people who don't really care about going into government. . . . So they don't have a personal axe to grind. But they know the particular area. They know that they can go in and give you good advice on positions, restructuring, reordering, and all the rest.

Others doubted the benefits of this practice, especially if the president-elect was intent on making change. One Clinton adviser found his participation partially neutralized by the established groups: "I'm really going in there with a full head of steam, and then I walk in an office and I saw it filled with everybody I thought we'd beat in the primaries." The "organized interests . . . flocked into the transition and they got put in positions." Their influence extended to the vetting process for who might be nominated. "The vetters were all from interest groups. And I think that's a big problem. The vested interests who spend their whole lifetime figuring how they're going to milk one administration, then the next, have a way of getting there first."

With too many functions being served by transition teams, and too many available funds, they become too large. Several aides made the point that most teams were unwieldy and poorly structured to serve efficiently in the transition to governing. "There are just too many people," said one, "who know too little wandering around talking." But, of course, other purposes are to be achieved: detaching the president-elect and his advisers from legions of eager campaign workers (called twenty-two-year-old "partisan kids" by one aide) by giving them terminal jobs, making connections with representatives of the "cozy little triangles" of government and interest groups, and trolling for trouble spots within the various issue networks of contemporary policymaking. It is worth reiterating, however, that realizing gains from these temporary organizations requires Washington-based know-how, thus putting outsiders at a disadvantage.

It is probably true that the bureaucracy could actually supply a great deal of what it is the nominees need to know organizationally about a department or agency. But, of course, that judgment does not account for the political tasks that have to be performed. Ironically, it is those political tasks that may create uncertainty for the bureaucracy, according to a political aide who was sympathetic to the plight of bureaucrats during the transition and early months of a new administration: "I never found a transition team that made any real effort to try to make it smooth for the bureaucracy that's there—for the people that they are going to have to manage at some point. So I have a low regard for transition teams."

Transition teams produce reports that naturally may be expected to vary substantially in usefulness, depending on the internal dynamics of the team and how well it is integrated into the orientation of the nominee. Experienced nominees like Caspar Weinberger, as secretary of defense–designate in 1980, were unlikely to rely on the work of a transition team.

I always remember what Cap Weinberger did when he took over DOD in 1980. They had a group of Reagan loyalists . . . policy types who had formed the transition team at the Pentagon. Cap's first day on the job, he fired them all, ran them all off and started fresh. . . . I think the teams can be useful if they are made up of, or very well plugged into, the people who are actually going to take over the department.

The Weinberger example illustrates the dynamics of the period. The clock is moving toward the time of governing and the start-up of a wholly new endeavor, with occasional overlap only between the campaign structure that is being dismantled or redirected and the governing structure that is being created atop a permanent bureaucracy and connected with the eternal Washington community that lives and works alongside the government. Capital-wise veterans like Weinberger know how all of this works and therefore find the transition teams of little value. For example, one such appointee explained, "I just didn't find them [the teams and their reports] useful at all. . . . I didn't use any of it. Most of it I either already knew or the pros I brought in [knew it all]. [One assistant secretary–designate] looked at the stuff [in his area] and said: 'This is superficial campaign stuff, big time.' "

Comments on the many reports and briefing books that are prepared were not very supportive, while acknowledging that their preparation was unavoidable and that they did serve some purposes. The most positive comments were that the reports were "useful" in identifying issues. Here is a sample:

A team cochair: I have no sense that anybody read the report after we submitted it. . . . No feedback whatsoever.
A former cabinet secretary: It is valuable but the truth is the bureaucracy would do it for you and give it to the designate.
A former White House aide: When there is no continuity between the people doing the work and the people who are going to be responsible in the new government, the work is collecting dust somewhere on a shelf.
An old hand at transitions in and out: Most of those books go in dumpsters almost immediately. The secretary has to connect with the career people and political appointees, set a course, and then stick to it. . . . They are somewhat helpful in the early stages but their purpose is really to get you through confirmation. Then you're working with your budget people and . . . your policy people. . . .

It's a road map, which tells you sort of where the places are that you have to go. But that's about it.

A former White House aide: I guess they can stimulate the presidents-elect or the people around them if they sat down and read those reports. They were written by serious people.

A policy consultant: Maybe they were very useful to people who actually went out and ran departments, who would look to that handbook. . . . I was more interested frankly in the kind of message that you can deliver in five sentences . . . than in those big books, because I thought that the tone of the administration was much more from those five sentences than it was the big briefing books.

A former White House aide: Those [reports] were useful. They at least gave us a preliminary idea of what issues were out there. . . . They were turned over to the cabinet secretaries. . . . We got copies of them, and it was a useful enterprise.

The aide just quoted also noted that seldom is there a "one-to-one correlation between what they [teams or task forces] recommended and what happened," which was judged by another experienced White House aide to be a very good thing:

It always seemed to me to be a mistake for transition teams to try to influence policy. First of all, they seldom end up staying at that agency. Secondly, they don't know anything so they just look stupid to everybody who is there. So then if they do stay they've gotten themselves off on a bad foot. It almost never happens that a transition team walks in, kills five regulations and people say: "God, that was smart." It just doesn't happen.

Several aides indicated that transition personnel do not take sufficient advantage of the cooperative attitude of the outgoing administration. In part this lack may be a consequence of the fact that the teams are serving patronage and campaign disassembly functions as well as preparation-for-governing functions. It may also be a result of natural wariness in regard to an administration of the other party, especially if the president-elect defeated an incumbent (as was the case in three of the four presidencies examined here). There were no party differences in these evaluations.

A Democrat: Generally speaking, the outgoing people want to help the incoming folks, even when it's an opposite party takeover. There are some notable exceptions to that. But . . . if the people coming in will exercise their responsibilities and conduct themselves in a respectful and not-crowing way; if they will come in in a respectful and courteous and professional way; and treat the outgoing people in that manner, the outgoing people will respond in kind. . . . And that's what should happen.

A Republican: It's been my experience that the outgoing team . . . wants very much to help. I think in all of the transitions I've been through . . . the people that were leaving really wanted to do the best they could to help and assist the new ones get up to speed. But it's usually not appreciated. It's often . . . the case that the new team . . . looks at the old team . . . and says, if you're so smart, how come you're leaving and we're coming in. And so a lot of really sincere, well-meaning effort that the old timers have got to offer is . . . pushed aside and ignored, because the new ones don't know what they don't know. . . . Oftentimes they don't take advantage of the opportunity that they can learn from their predecessors.

A Democrat: They appreciated our help but I think we were probably more willing to try to help than what they seem[ed] to want. . . . We were available to them more than what they took advantage of.

A Republican: We said, "Look, we're not going to play games with these people. We're not going to be partisan with them. We're going to just tell them what we know about the place, tell them about the problems, tell them what we were planning to do, walk them through it. . . . One of the toughest things was, they expected us to torque them around and to deceive them and to pull shenanigans. . . . So there was a great deal of disbelief on their part that we weren't really trying to screw them somehow.

This last respondent observed that there were departments and agencies in which outgoing personnel were less cooperative, where the attitude was: "If you want to know something, you're going to have to drag it out of me. . . . Ask me the right question and I'll tell you the right answer. If you don't formulate it in the right way, I'm not going to tell you." For the most part, however, the outgoing group was accommodating, though believing they were not necessarily trusted, and the incoming group believed that they "got very good cooperation from the outgoing people." Of course, it does not take many uncooperative or cooperative-by-the-book-only outgoing personnel to feed the suspicions of those coming in.

This terse summary of the work of transition teams was offered by a participant and long-time observer of such operations: "I think transition teams are much overdone. They should be small, they should be short-lived. They should be required to make a report in one page, and go away." A more probing analysis was offered by a respondent involved at the highest levels of transition planning. Speaking primarily in regard to work before the selection of a department secretary or agency head, he noted:

> I think there is very little value in it. I think it is busywork. It is justifiable. It makes very good sense for the president to say, I am putting transition teams into every agency so I understand what is going on. That is good political cover and it strokes policy wonks who are paying attention. But I think its value is much more in the patronage. This is a way for me to take some of those people who are piling up on my door saying, "I want a job," to say, "Go research FAA for a little while. We can employ you for 90 days with the transition." I think their work product does very little in helping to guide the decisionmaking process.

"Busywork and busy workers" are justifiable. The trick is to ensure that the product and its authors are not elevated beyond their worth. Organizationally and conceptually, multiple transitions are under way. New governing teams are replacing those currently at work, and a shift from the campaign structure is being effected. It is a demanding process that works imperfectly, yet with ample accounting for error and constant monitoring by the press. It is precisely these variable, even two-directional, tasks that justify the separation of leadership attained by the Reagan transition, with Baker in charge of forming the White House and Meese in charge of dismantling the campaign in the most positive manner possible.

Summary

This chapter has identified differences in transition performance between inside- and outside-oriented presidents-elect that happen to coincide with party labels. It has also set forth criteria for effecting the conventional transition, one primarily designed for the "let's get to work" charge so admired by Neustadt as characteristic of the Kennedy effort. By this standard, the new team conducts an orderly and purposeful process of organizing to take over on January 20. The goal is to quit campaigning and begin governing.

As it happens, creating a temporary organization to manage a permanent government is a task for which campaigning is insufficient training. In addition, outside candidacies like those of Carter and Clinton often attract staff with limited governing experience, yet with zealous ambitions for status, even to the extent of seeking then to exclude those who might truly be of help. The result is an inefficient use of the limited time for preparations to assume power and ineffective implementation of planning materials.

It is also apparent in the discussion of transition aides that no amount of "freshness" from the outside can compensate for a lack of Washington experience and a failure to comprehend the complex connections that must be made to attach a new president to an existing government. Those new to Washington are advised either to take crash courses on its ways or hire those who are in the know. And yet developments in campaigning and public access to information have made it more difficult to draw a clear line between campaigning and governing. Elaborate campaign organizations are more difficult to dismantle, the Presidential Transition Act subsidizes their continuance, and campaign-type expertise is increasingly valued in the White House. Further, outsider presidents-elect may need to continue a campaign-like presence so as to bolster status. Meanwhile, the demands of the conventional transition persist, failing, for the most part, to account for the changes that greatly complicate preparations to govern. The result is a classic portrait of institutional resistance to change in a process designed for change.

5

THE PRESS AND
THE TRANSITION

RUMINATING on the role of the press, Michael K. Deaver, longtime Reagan adviser, said:

> There is a temptation on the part of anyone who has been in public life to strike back at the press, to lash out at the unfairness of the advantage it has over each of us. And sooner or later, no matter how open you think you have been, or how friendly the relationship, the press will do a job on you. Not always a big job. Maybe a small job. But it will get you. It is the nature of the business, and what you discover is that you help your cause not at all by cursing, crying, threatening to sue, or simply falling on the floor and stamping your tiny feet.
>
> As an old wise man once said, you never pick a fight with someone who buys ink by the barrel.[1]

Presidential candidates, presidents-elect, and presidents live and work uncertainly with the press. Each has a legitimate, if competitive, function in the quest for the public interest. As Garry Wills observed: "The fight over representing the presidency is a fight for representation of the entire nation." Both presidents and the press can justify the claim to represent—one based on election, the other based on professional obligation. The relationship is bound to be strained, however. As Wills points out: "Sooner or later, all presidents blame their problems on the media, and they are right. The press and the president are linked in a natural enmity. They need each other and they resent that."[2]

The press plays an especially crucial role in the transition from campaigning to governing. In fact, many of the reporters track right through the election to the creation of a presidency. They too have campaign and job adjustment experiences as they camp out alongside the candidate–president-elect–president and his convoy. The coverage changes because the tasks are different, as are public and press expectations. The two travel-weary clusters eye each other cautiously because they are interdependent: presidents-elect and their aides want favorable stories with their new beginning; reporters want access to and information about the new administration. Both sets must know that what was (that is, the recently concluded campaign) will never be again. The news to be made is that of the creation of a new administration.

What exactly is the role of the press in the transition? Interviews with transition aides and reporters revealed similar portraits. A Carter aide: "The fact of the matter is, the interpretation, the analysis, the after-the-facts—it all comes from the media. . . . It is the mouthpiece. It's the megaphone through which it all gets heard and seen." A Reagan aide: "They are a window. They continue to be a window to the public about how the new president is perceived." A Clinton aide: "They are in some ways the keeper of the presidency. They're the ones who stay on it. In our case, they knew more about it than we did, about their own customs and mores. . . . The problem is that they have those expectations of the presidency but they don't really know the new president." For their part, reporters referred to "this enormous, idling engine of the press"; explained that they serve as "the country's window into what's going on"; and suggested that the press is "how you communicate so you don't have a choice. . . . The public's perception of you is going to be shaped by the press that you receive."

This juxtaposition of one group of fervent seekers of approval and another of professional chroniclers produces one of the more fascinating pageants in American politics. "We'll cover what's there," explained one veteran reporter, observing that the advantage then is to the president-elect who "knows why he wants to be president." There is, of course, anxiety in both camps. But the press can survive poor approval ratings more easily than can the president. And as much as the president-elect and his team may wish for positive reporting from a sympathetic press, the probability is that reporting

"what's there" depends more on performance than on journalistic preferences. "I don't conceive of my job as being a job to make the transition work
or to make the presidency work. My job, I would think, is just to sort of
report the facts."

The president-elect and his staff need to acknowledge the reality of press
coverage, of the "window," the "megaphone," the "keeper" functions, and
plan accordingly. Further, the sooner that the winners understand the role of
the press in its many forms, the better. And finally, regardless of their interdependency, the onus of responsibility for a working presidency is with those
who got elected, not those whose job is to "report the facts." Put otherwise,
the press has a continuous function to perform, whereas the place of the new
president is a more singular activity associated with who he is, how he won,
and whom he brings with him.

Inside the Window Looking Out: Transition Aides

In accepting the vital role of the press, knowledgeable and experienced
managers will incorporate coverage into transition planning and will consider how that coverage is likely to change in the postelection period. Effective
transition supervision requires developing a message or theme, making
appointments seemingly consistent with that theme, and showing tangible
evidence of control. In other words, the reality of the press's responsibility
prescribes the reporting function being integrated into transition planning by
the president-elect and his aides. No one doubts that the primary task of the
president-elect is that of creating an administration. "The most important
thing . . . for a president to do in a transition is to set up his government. He
will want to keep the press as informed as he can, but it's not as important to
keep them informed as it is that he sets up the government with the right
people."

The press can be a positive or negative force in accomplishing this primary goal of creating an administration, but which it is depends mostly on
what is in fact happening. Thus for example, a Clinton adviser observed in
regard to their transition that the press "wants to find out what the administration is going to do. You know, where is it going to go? As I said . . . we
[were] a transition without development. So we [couldn't] really answer
those questions. But they desperately wanted to get some indication." A
Reagan aide explained that "we really spent a lot of effort to try to tell the

press what we were going to do," acknowledging that the coverage could reinforce good management and clear direction.

> If their attention is directed to carrying on the themes of the campaign, and this is what the president's interested in doing, I think it can be a very positive thing. Also [a positive purpose is served] by learning about the nuts and bolts of the transition, and talking about that in low-key press stories. The fact that the transition is going well, as reported in the press, gives the public a sense of confidence in the ability of this leader to manage the government. . . . If on the other hand the press is reporting on a daily basis the bickering among the people inside the transition and the old campaign leftovers as to who's going to do what, and that there are big fights, that creates the opposite impression.

Making it all work to the new administration's advantage is no simple matter. But it is most certainly worth the time of transition managers to make an effort so as to avoid the worst mistakes, to be knowledgeable about changes in coverage (who and how), and to take advantage of the uncertainty of the period that many argue provides an edge willingly granted by the press. A Clinton aide described what should happen, but then acknowledged that they "made terrible mistakes":

> Find ways to do special things early that send the right signals to them. And that give them a sense of where the president is coming from that will at least give you a base from which to judge their daily coverage.
>
> QUESTION: Did you feel pretty good about your press relations [in the transition]?
>
> RESPONSE: No. We made terrible mistakes. We screwed it up. We went the exact opposite direction. We sent out all the wrong messages about whether they [the press corps] were going to be moved or, you know, closing the door. These were all so antithetical to the culture, that they sent signals far stronger than we intended.

How could such mistakes be made? One answer is simply the lack of Washington experience. Our system permits, sometimes even promotes, candidacies from way outside of town—for example, Watergate encouraging a search for someone uncontaminated by Washington scandals (Jimmy Carter); a poor economy and big government inviting an antisystem candidate (Ronald Reagan); and George Bush's early high approval ratings discouraging the in-town candidates, thus enticing lesser-known aspirants (Bill Clinton). Each of these winners then faced the challenge of accommodating to a press corps steeped in the continuities of Washington institutions, understanding that they would be the principal source of news from the first minute of their election. As a veteran White House reporter put it: "Everything a president-elect says in a transition is news—everything. Every word, every burp, every nod."

And so mistakes are easy to make if a transition group lacks the understanding of the complex process that has been triggered by the election. An aide to Reagan learned that "when you go from being a candidate to the nominee to the likely winner to the president-elect to the president, each of those stages exponentially focuses on you as a staff member and the amount of time that you have to spend . . . when the media grow and grow and the risks at each of those steps for you personally and for your principal grow exponentially." He noted, "We didn't know anything about Washington, D.C." For those with limited experience, one obvious solution is to include as staff people "who had made the mistakes before." This aide confessed:

> I wanted to restrict [the press], do exactly what George Stephanopoulos did. . . . Keep them out of here. Don't let them come in here. Jim Baker and other people said, "You can't do that. I know you want to do that but you can't do that. It's too big a price to pay." So it was learning the way the system worked, learning the ropes of it, learning the subtleties of how it worked, and . . . the protocols of the Congress and the media and the Judiciary and the Cabinet and all of that.

Mistakes can also be made as a result of generalizing about press coverage from the campaign experience. The press has a transition too, one involving personnel changes, an altered setting, and different attitudes—all changes that must be acknowledged and dealt with by the new team. At work in this press transition are many of the same forces occurring within politics and government. That is, many reporters are themselves moving from campaigning to governing, with all of the altered expectations implied by that shift. How important is it then that the transition staff pay heed to these changes? A Carter aide explained that it was all of one piece: "I don't know if it's more important than anything else, but it is *as* important as anything else because if you're going to govern, you are going to communicate. If you're going to communicate, you're going to have to rely on the media." So there is much to be learned by the new governing team as they observe how reporters define the jobs of president-elect and president.

Learning starts for the new team by their accepting the fact that the White House press corps is different from that covering the campaign. "The press that we'd been dealing with day in and day out of the campaign were now being supplemented by press who had been on an opponent's campaign, and some of the traditional White House press. So you're dealing with a different animal right away." A Clinton aide doubted that their transition team was fully sensitive to these changes. "I still find it fascinating that I'm on the phone with reporters who I can use a shorthand from the campaign and then other reporters who have no recollection of the campaign, all of whom are covering Bill Clinton not as the campaigner but as the President of the United States." He judged that it was necessary during the transition to learn more about how various reporters covered the president. "I don't think we focused on that nearly enough."

Senior transition aides typically know and understand this change in coverage, though some learn it only after mistakes have been made. Perhaps the most sophisticated account was that by a Reagan aide:

> First of all, they [reporters] are tired just like we are. They've been through a long campaign. They're willing to give it a rest. Secondly, they understand, usually better than the White House staff does, how governing is different than campaigning. They're different people in the campaign. They approach their jobs differently. So they're transitioning themselves during that period, even the old workhorses. And they're happy to get back into a governing mode, most of them. Most of those people have made their career in the White House rather than on a campaign trail.
>
> That should be where you start. If you start educating the old workhorses who are there, it's faster and also you learn more from them about attitudes. *They'll very quickly tell you how the press is going to relate to your president* [emphasis added].

Yet another dimension of change is that associated with what might be called the policy specialist press: those reporters who concentrate on specific substantive issues. This less political press is often quite sophisticated in regard to the history of policy development within an area and thus demands informed responses to suit its distinctive readership. A Carter aide explained the importance of this genre of reporters:

> You have a much more complicated press situation to manage because you now have the business press asking all the questions it's going to ask, or the social service press that covers the agencies and the welfare systems and the income transfer programs asking the questions they ask. They actually are a fairly sophisticated group of people. . . . They want to hear from people who are knowledgeable, who have the perspective of the new president, and are knowledgeable substantively. It's critically important that . . . [this part of] the press corps . . . doesn't come up against a bunch of political people, who are basically managing a jobs program [that is, in making appointments], managing the division of the spoils.

Everything that has been said so far illustrates how important it is for the president-elect to appoint his press aide as soon as possible following the campaign. "The press spokesman is one of the first jobs you ought to fill. And the press spokesman for the transition doesn't have to be the press secretary. It doesn't have to be the campaign press spokesman, but it's better if it is." The point is to designate someone who is familiar with the changes that are taking place and can manage the communication accordingly, both in terms of information and who will supply it.

> That's where a good press secretary can be helpful because there has to be somebody in the middle who understands both sides. And who can educate them both to each other. So you've got to have somebody who goes to the press and says, "You're in transition." They [the press] have got people moving in and out, being reassigned. They [those being reassigned] are trying to learn how to cover the presidency. So you've got to go to them and say, "Let me help you here. Here's how we're going to operate" and help them. Then you have to go to the president and the people on the inside and say, "Here's the opportunity."

Several transition aides cited the Clinton case as illustrative of poorly managed postelection communication. One Democratic aide praised George Stephanopoulos as "a very bright young man, an articulate young man, a politically astute young man, an attractive young man" who was an effective spokesman for candidate Clinton. These characteristics underscored "the youthfulness and the vigor of Clinton, and then Clinton-Gore." But the aide went on to say:

> None of the qualities that I've just described in Stephanopoulos changed after Clinton [won], but if you ask me did I think . . . that George Stephanopoulos should have been the principal press spokesman for the president, my answer then and now would be no. . . . It's nothing personal to George. It's that I think the president needed more maturity, less youthfulness. I don't think it continued to serve the president to have the principal face on television someone who looked like a college sophomore or junior.

For this person and others, the situation was not greatly improved by having Dee Dee Myers serving as press secretary. One long-time Democratic operative was quite scornful of her performance in comparison with Carter's press secretary. "Jody Powell clearly was one of the real inside people with Carter so when you were talking with him you were getting a sense of what the president thought, which you never had a sense of with Dee Dee Myers."

Among other advantages to an early appointment of a knowledgeable and an effective press aide is that of bringing discipline to postelection media contacts. The campaign staff must adjust to the emerging role of their candidate as the president of the United States. Who responds to press inquiries, and how, comes to be of substantially greater importance given the number and variation of official listeners here and abroad.

> It is a difficult time because the campaign staff move into the transition role with their contacts, their friends, their controlled leaks, their uncontrolled leaks. [They] almost turn into salesmen looking for someone to buy their product . . . the president. And the media become a vehicle for that product to be purchased.
>
> That is why I would say that one of the first appointments should be the press secretary, who then brings discipline to how

people communicate with the press, knowing that you can never shut off the pipeline from the field director in New York to the reporter from the *New York Daily News*. The question is: what information does that field director have? And I think that is something that has to be managed.

This aide also stressed the importance of the "controlled leak" or "trial balloon" "so that you know whether the idea is so stupid that it doesn't make any sense." By this aide's observation, "Jim Baker was the master of the controlled leak during the Reagan administration."

Perhaps the most important reason for entering the transition with a press operation seasoned by Washington experience is that it is a time when reporters are likely to give the president-elect and his team "the benefit of the doubt." Aides suggest that reporters are themselves eager to make contacts and create a line on the new administration; thus they have "some vested interest in being generous." Another aide noted that it is a "very tough time for the press because they want to find out what the administration is going to do; where it is going to go." Yet another observed: "Each of those members of the media now has to develop contacts . . . because now you're talking about people who are going to make or break their life for the next four years too. So it becomes kind of a dance . . . between the media, the permanently assigned White House media, and the key people in the campaign transition." One person summed it up: "If you've got a message, that's a very good time to take advantage of the press."

QUESTION: It suggests then that a conscious strategy in press relations is important. Do you think so?

RESPONSE: What it would suggest to me is that you've got to know what you're doing in the transition, and then you can get out that message. The problem with some presidents-elect, and particularly Clinton, is that they really didn't know what they were doing. They had no message to get out. They were involved simply in choosing the best person to be Secretary of Commerce, whatever that meant. . . . That wasn't a strategy. I mean that wasn't something particularly to impart to the press. So to the degree that the press was in this business, they turned the press into just speculators. Well, who's going to be Secretary of Commerce? Well, I hear—but no, he won't do it because they're looking for a black. They're looking for a woman.

One media-savvy aide stressed how important it is for a president-elect and his staff to recognize the "gift" given by the press to the new team during the transition. He underscored the importance of being suitably prepared, including an awareness of how to take advantage of this "honeymoon" in coverage:

> One of the best things about the press in transition is that that's when they are . . . at their best. You have the least kind of press hostility and the greatest opportunities to work with them during a transition that you'll ever have. I used to advise everyone who came into the White House: "The minute you get in, do every profile article they want to do. Any reporter that even says the word 'profile' get him in there and do it quick because you will never be higher in his estimation than the first day on the job. Don't pull this 'I want to wait until I know what I'm doing' because then they're going to judge you by whether you know what you're doing."

This aide judged that this period in which the new team is given the benefit of the doubt is precisely the time to "(1) form relationships with the press on a personal basis and, (2) educate them as to what you're trying to do and how you intend to do it. They're willing to listen during that point." Normally a president or his staff proposing something one aide termed "totally different" will be treated with skepticism by the press. "But during the transition, they're willing to say, 'Well, you're a new president. We'll give you a chance to see if it works.'. . . If you don't take advantage of that opportunity, you've just wasted it." As with others, this aide used Clinton as the best example of a lost opportunity. "[Clinton] threw it away by making decisions on the tax increase and on gays in the military. . . . He did not use the press during that period to build the foundation for what he wanted to do later."

Taking advantage does require being experienced enough to appear purposeful. For example, in acknowledging a honeymoon in coverage during this time, a former Reagan aide emphasized that "they [the press] will critique transition operations."

> They'll look into whether or not this crowd that surrounds him is competent or capable. Can they get appointments made on time? Can they staff up the government? Can they explain and articulate what it is they intend to do? Reagan's first transition did a great job

of that, I think. I don't think this last transition, the Clinton transition [in 1992], did it worth a damn, probably, although I didn't follow it that closely.

How then should the press be treated or managed during the transition? Transition aides have a variety of recommendations associated with their expectations of coverage, including the changes in the press corps mentioned earlier. Sometimes aides for different presidents used virtually the same language. A Carter aide: "The press is always important because of what they can do to you, either on the upside or the downside." A Reagan aide: "[The press] is important in both a positive and a negative way." Several veterans of press relations set forth rules to be followed so as to ensure that most coverage is upside and positive.

It's important to regularly feed the press from a transition organization just like it is from a campaign organization, maybe even more so. Because the horse race is over. They no longer have horse race stories they can write. They're more interested in getting a fix on what the policies might be and what the approach is going to be. They're getting more involved in the nuances of policy, the specifics. So it's important to have a regular feed going out of the transition office.

* * *

[The rules] are very easy to articulate. This is not one of those situations . . . where it makes any sense to be less than totally open with the press. I mean, one of the other things that we did in the Carter transition was [to] identify those people who were responsible for covering that transition. . . . On the policy side, it makes all the sense in the world, once you know what you're doing, to talk to these guys. . . . You've got to think through how you want to present the president-elect to the public every single day. So, yes, there has to be a press strategy. . . . Essentially what you are talking about here is a coordination between two people—the spokesperson for the transition and the presidential press secretary. It's terribly important. And you can either do a good job or a horrible job.

* * *

I don't think there are any different rules [for the transition over the campaign]. I think that as a press spokesman or as an administration

official, you have one commodity: credibility. And that credibility
comes from honesty. And there are professional, acceptable ways of
not answering a question in this town. And I think that, using the
Clinton people as an example, it took them months, to my horror,
especially on the foreign side. And I'm not sure some of them even
get it now. Words matter, especially in diplomacy and the international arena. . . . There was just this almost not understanding [that] this
isn't a campaign anymore. . . . It took them [the Clinton team] a long
time, in my opinion, to get over the hubris and the arrogance . . . to
kind of tighten up and be disciplined. This is serious business. . . .
There are so many people listening.

This third respondent illustrated the points made with a comparison of
two sets of advisers in the Reagan administration. As chief of staff, James
Baker sought "people who preferably had prior White House experience,
and if not that, executive branch experience, and it served him extremely
well." On the other hand, Edwin Meese "chose to surround himself with all
Californians; nice, well-meaning people [who] were left in the dust for about
six to nine months."

By one view, the "feed the press" advice is associated with the honeymoon period. Each needs the other, with the press anxious to "break bread
with you and all that." "So you really have to go out of your way to antagonize them, which these folks [the Clinton team] actually did do." Why should
any transition team antagonize those who are charged with providing the
daily chronicle and interpretive analysis of the passage from candidate to
president?

Some of them, at least in their heart of hearts, believed that they
didn't need [the press], believed that they really did win this campaign over the heads of the mainstream press by going to MTV and
Larry King and the alternative press, and they sold themselves on
that. And then they could let their own vile [feelings] come out.
"I've always thought you were bastards, now that I'm in power I'm
going to show you that you are."

Standards of behavior often are defined more from what is done wrong
than what is done right. Thus it was that references to the Clinton case were
more than simply to its freshness in the minds of respondents, the large

majority of whom had observed several transitions. Aides from both parties used the Clinton team to mark the downside limits of recommended press strategies. The disharmony between the press and the Clintons seemed discrepant given that most reporters were also of the "baby boom," anti–Vietnam War generation and were more likely than not to hold similar policy views. When asked about this curiosity, one of the most experienced Democratic transition specialists explained:

> It started way back. They started out being very favorable. It's sort of an incremental change, bypassing the reporters and going directly to the people; doing the talk shows. . . . Sort of thumbing your nose at the establishment got them angry. They were mad because they saw him [Clinton] more as a flawed person than their hero. They felt they weren't being dealt with straight a lot of times. And then when he came to Washington, . . . the symbolism of shutting the door just enraged them. It infuriated them. . . . And they've never gotten over it. They're still mad. And they know that Hillary doesn't like them. And they know that he basically doesn't like them either. And so it's a kind of gutty, visceral thing.

The most positive instance of press relationships and treatment for the Clinton transition in 1992 was associated with a campaign-like event: the mid-December economic summit conference in Little Rock. A Clinton aide described its success in exactly these terms, including a prophetic statement about how revealing the summit was of the subsequent administration.

> The press clearly plays a large role in setting perspectives on what to expect from this candidate and this president. . . . What we did best in that transition was the economic conference. The reason it was [successful] was [that] it captured Bill Clinton both as a campaigner and as the head of his government and as a symbol of what a young, idealistic president could do once he had the reins of power. For those three reasons it was a brilliant way of showcasing what a Clinton administration would look like.

I conclude this section on transition aides' views of the press with comments by one of the acknowledged masters of White House press management: Michael K. Deaver. First, he emphasized the importance of staying ahead of the curve—"the information curve, the leadership curve." To fall behind is to be put in the position of responding.

> And so that was the task that I gave myself: to keep . . . always . . . on the offensive. And that meant using whatever power I had to bring in everybody in the White House and pound them over the head every day as to what the priorities were. It's like I said about Clinton . . . as this week's a good example. He's had a couple of good days. He never has a good week. I wanted to be sure Reagan had a good week every week.[3]

Deaver had the following general advice for managing press relations for the various passages from candidate to president:

> My own feeling . . . is that you have to learn to be a well, not a fountain, when you're dealing with the press. You don't give off information. You listen and answer the question, and be candid at all times. And never be afraid to say "I don't know." Most people's biggest mistakes are [that] they try to give [the press] information that they don't know what they're talking about.
>
> I've found two things will happen [if you say you don't know]. One, the people will respect you for that, or, two, they won't bother you anymore because they say this guy doesn't know anything [about that]. So that's fine with me. That's just one more person you don't have to deal with. So many people get wrapped up in the business, and I confess that I did too at times, where you think you have to . . . impart some tidbit . . . "the currants of the cake."[4]

Outside the Window Looking In: Press Perspectives

How is it that reporters view the transition? What are their expectations regarding the creation of a presidency? How do reporters cover this vital period? Interviews with several veteran, mostly print, reporters produced a revealing portrait of how they understand and report on presidential transitions. I begin with this striking differentiation between a reporter's perspective on the campaign compared with the transition and with governing:

As a reporter covering the campaign you don't expect to be told the truth. You don't expect that every time you ask somebody a question that the answer is going to be the truth. In the government you expect people to tell the truth and the answers to be true. And I think that is true of the transition too. I think if I had one single thing to point at that I think has been Clinton's weakest thing, it's that he's viewed as not telling the truth and people who are around him are viewed as not telling the truth. And I think that has really hurt him. They couldn't get out of that campaign mode where every answer was spin. And to this day they're still trying to do it.

What follows is treatment of two large subjects: reporters' views of the presidency and of their own jobs in covering the transition into that office. As with the quotation just cited, the Clinton experience will be referenced often because of its currency at the time of the interviews and because these reporters saw it as a case of what should be avoided by presidents-elect and their staffs as violating standards of proper organization, sequencing, and behavior.

About the Presidency

Discussions with reporters about the transition to governing revealed quite consistent expectations about what should happen and why. Not surprisingly, these depictions were associated with their understandings of the presidency: what it represents in American government and how one should prepare to serve. Thus the conversations produced discernment regarding effective organization and behavior during the transition, relationships with and attitudes toward the press, and differences between campaigning and governing.

Reporters are professional watchers and probers. As one reporter explained, "You cannot escape 600 reporters camped on your doorstep during your transition. So you can either let them go on their own with nothing, in which no end of grief for the president can ensue. . . . Or you can say, 'Okay, we're going to use these days to talk about this or that.' " What do reporters say they want? Nothing too surprising: openness, information, dependability, access, consistency, and truthfulness are a few of the traits mentioned. Incorporated into these desired features is a search on their part for leadership qualities of the new president. One reporter referred to "a whole series of perhaps unconscious check marks on leadership and what makes a good leader":

And maybe it's not even something that you can easily articulate without sitting down and really thinking about it. But based on your experience of having seen people functioning you do sort of say, "This measures up. This doesn't. This guy can be rolled." All sorts of things. And then you begin, as the person matches up and . . . you begin to develop a picture of that person that may be positive or negative or mixed.

No one underestimated the challenge involved in the passage from candidate to president, from campaigning to forming an administration—a process made more arduous with the lengthening of the nomination and campaign period.

It must be awfully difficult for someone who has been through what these people have to go through now to get elected, this two- or three-year process, this horrible, debilitating process that they go through and then immediately to turn around and shift emphasis and maybe mind-set and all the people that you're surrounded with and suddenly try to do everything. . . . I mean, that would seem to be a pretty daunting task.

Small wonder, perhaps, that Franklin D. Roosevelt was the example given as "somebody who's good at both [campaigning and governing]." "Reagan is such an anomaly that I don't know how to put him into this. But except for Reagan, I don't think there has been anybody since Roosevelt who was good at both running and governing. It's also probably easier in a crisis. I would bet that governing in a crisis is more like campaigning than governing when times are calm."

A distinctively media perspective on the transition was offered by one reporter who focused on "words" and their evolving importance in the quest to serve in the White House. In identifying three phases of coverage, the respondent took special note of how press attention is calibrated to account for the assumption of institutional position—a person taking charge of the presidency:

As a candidate, the words he says are new the first time he says them and the second time he says them, and then they're not covered very much any more. Then when he's president-elect, and he says . . . the same words, then they're new again because he really meant it. . . . Then when he gets into office and says it, he's president. . . . Presidents who are successful use this tremendous spotlight and focus to say what they want people to hear, and not to stumble around and screw up.

Understandably, the words used by candidates, presidents-elect, and presidents are judged as suited to images reporters have of effectiveness, of "measuring up," in these complex roles. The passages are greatly facilitated, by one view, if the candidate knows why he wants to be president. "What is it he wants to do with it? They ought to know that before they get elected. There are some people who get elected without knowing, but they ought to know." This point was made primarily in the context of the ease of press coverage. Reporters want to know the answer to the very basic question raised earlier in this book: Why do you want to be president? A clear response provides an orientation for reporting and analysis. It may even offer an edge for a president like Reagan who otherwise might not be viewed favorably by the press, especially on policy grounds. What about presidents who don't have a ready answer to the big question? Here is one press perspective:

If you've got a president who hasn't defined why he wants to be president, [and] I think that is true of the last two [Bush and Clinton], you could, if you recognize that that was a problem . . . take the advice of somebody who says, "All right, now you're president but nobody knows why." Then you could use that period [the transition] to start defining it. To start drawing on what you had done in the campaign and say: "Remember that speech in Milwaukee about the middle-class tax cut? That was a seminal moment in the campaign—that's going to be one of the things that he does. . . ." But again, if you don't know what you want to do, other than sucking up to a few reporters, I think I'd suck up to the TV guys more than the print types. They have bigger audiences.

These observations imply a developmental process, one that begins with a clearly defined purpose that is then refined and applied in policy and organizational terms; one that may produce a "bigger figure, a presidential figure." Several reporters articulated how this process was expected to unfold, once again their perspectives motivated largely by their interest in coherent coverage of an institution about which they have elaborate anticipations.

Often, therefore, impressions gained during the transition carry over to service as president:

> One of the things that strikes me about the [four] transitions I've covered . . . with the benefit of hindsight you see how the transition is just like the presidency, that the mistakes that they're going to make in a presidency are the mistakes that they make in a transition. And, also, the strengths that they show in a transition tend to be the strengths of a presidency.

* * *

> There's that period [in a transition] when almost everyone really wants you to succeed. . . . It's an opportunity also if there have been things that you were afraid to say during the campaign about the deficit or the S & L crisis, or the need for tough choices or whatever. It's a time when people are willing to hear it. It's an opportunity to become that sort of bigger figure, a presidential figure.

* * *

> I think you certainly have to have a firm control of the schedule and a firm control of what . . . are the messages and impressions that you want to be generated through the transition process. The day after the election, the slate is not wiped completely clean, but it is a starting-over process. With press relations so much of the issue is: Who gets to write on that slate? Do you write on that slate? Or does someone else? Or do you control the events, or do events control you? I think that a theme is only part of it. Scheduling, discipline, decision-forcing mechanisms that mean that you're filling that vacuum every day. You come out and set the tone, the agenda. You are in control. The oldest word in the book in terms of presidential press relations is control.

* * *

> If [presidents] are going to use the time line and make a fast change, they'd better be prepared to [say], in a very detailed way, not only what they want to do, but how they get there, in the time that they select. You just can't go into office and say: "I'd like to do this and that." I think you need to have a general plan for a whole presidency, and a very specific plan for the time line you choose to emphasize in a campaign. It's generally historically true of the modern

presidents, anyway, that that early period is when you get the most done because of the traditional honeymoon.

These ruminations seemingly derive from forecasts about how a presidency should be developed during the transition: with forthrightness, control, certainty, opportunism, enlargement, planning, efficiency, discipline. By one view, if the transition meets these expectations, it will become less of a public event. Comparisons in this regard were made between Reagan and Clinton:

> This last transition [Clinton in 1992] seems to me to have been a very major news event. Maybe it would have been better for Clinton to have deemphasized it as a news event. I was trying to think back to the last comparable transition [one involving a party shift], which would have been Reagan's. It didn't seem to me to have been as public an event. . . . You had Carter in Plains and you had Clinton in Little Rock being very hands-on and trotting out these people and obviously being very involved. There was a lot of publicity given to their involvement. . . . I don't think that Reagan had that sort of involvement. And by absenting himself from the process, he may have helped to tamp down some of this attention.[5]

More generalized notions by reporters about the presidency are supplemented by specific anticipations regarding how a president-elect and his team should make adjustments from the campaign to the development of governing themes and the organization of the new administration. As it happens, experienced reporters have observed both campaigning and governing and therefore often have rather sophisticated images of the distinction between the two, naturally referring to how it was done in the past.

Discussion by reporters of the differences between campaigning and governing typically stressed pacing and scheduling, the nature of and response to opponents, and relationships with the press. Almost without exception, the Clinton experience was cited as an illustration of a failure to move effectively between the two activities. The campaign is a "rat-a-tat" exercise that operates day to day. "Government," said one reporter, "is so different."

> I think the biggest mistake is really inability to disassociate campaigning with governing. Nobody got elected president in the modern era without having busted their ass for at least a year and a half.

Campaigning is simpler than governing. To assume that because you have campaigned successfully you can govern successfully is the biggest and silliest mistake of all. . . . The biggest mistake is to assume that [governing] is going to be easy. The biggest corrective is to bring some sourpuss old hat from Washington of your party into the innermost councils the day after the election—the guy who will say, "bullshit"; the guy who will say, "You don't know how hard this is going to be."

By another view, campaigning is a problem to be overcome, or a skill to be set aside, in governing: "A lot of the energy in the campaign . . . is devoted to making sure that you respond if the other side says something." But "it's artificial." Another reporter said, "What happens day in and day out is . . . less important in the White House." An example from the Clinton administration was offered, one in which a Correspondents' Association reception for the new press secretary, Mike McCurry, was interrupted by phone calls from the White House and Camp David regarding comments by Speaker Newt Gingrich on a Clinton priority: "So they decided to do this hit on Gingrich on Monday. And they got some pretty good press out of it. But I can't imagine it matters. That's sort of a campaign-type thing."

Most reporters agreed that the Clinton team had a distinct campaign orientation. Their critiques often revealed their own preferences regarding how the White House should be managed:

[The Clinton] administration employs campaign tactics all the time every day in every way, in their dealings with reporters, in their dealings with Congress, in their dealings with their Democratic colleagues, because they think they . . . know the operating technique of point/counterpoint, and answering a charge, and getting in the same news cycle as your opponent, and taking your opponent's argument and taking it apart, and providing the research and evidence to diminish his argument.

This reporter was then led to articulate a conception of a successful presidency as one featuring "a connection between the governed and the governor in which they have a fundamental understanding and belief in what they think the core of that president is about." Clinton did not achieve this connection in the transition or after, and therefore he had a "communications problem." The reporter continued, "If people don't think they can understand what your presidency is about, fundamentally about, then it becomes about anything any day. Then it's ephemeral. It's nothing. It has no standing. It has no foundation, no base." A reporter who makes this judgment about a presidency will obviously be a hard sell, further encouraging that president and his aides to seek other means of public contact. So it is that poor press relations can get still worse.

One of the complications in achieving the ideal presidency is the quantum change in communications in the last decade that has quickened the pace during the campaign and added "political hit men" to the candidate's innermost advisers. "In the old days," one reporter explained, "a news cycle was twenty-four hours, and now it's about an hour and a half." A consequence of the so-called CNN effect is that the new team enters office prepared always to make a quick response, thus enhancing the campaign-like approach of a White House staff.

> The pace has gotten noticeably more frantic. It always was pressurized. But I think that [the communications] dimension has been a very important part of almost totally obliterating any attempt [in advance] to think about transitions. I think also that the mind-set is so different. . . . The kinds of abilities, the kinds of talents, the kinds of sensibilities that are invaluable in the hurly-burly of a campaign are often not at all what you want in planning a government. So that there's such a premium on the political hit men. There's such a premium on the image makers. That's obviously true in any administration. But campaigns are virtually all image. . . . So the Carvilles of the world become the kings of the campaign because they master that environment. Then also, it diminishes the role of the thinkers.

It was, perhaps, these developments that influenced one reporter to conclude that the "campaign component" has come to be important for the "bully pulpit portion [of the presidency], and that's a lot of what the White House is." His observation was that campaigning "continues to be part of the modern-day White House, but it is not the engine behind the government. It is a loudspeaker for the message that the whole government is trying to convey."

The demands are even greater, therefore, if an administration is to be successful by the criteria stated above, that is, in fostering a connection between the "governed and the governor" that is rooted in core beliefs that form the engine of government. Adaptations of those governing principles to short-term developments may have to be made instantaneously. The "bully pulpit" comes to be more than the occasional reiteration of political and policy themes. It is, as well, a constant spray of reaction to ongoing events that are reported instantly. The Clinton team mastered the quick response without fully integrating their rejoinders into a larger policy base since new skills were clearly required to meet new challenges. It is in this context of change that the Clinton experience may have been a transition in a transition—the creation of an administration for a new and emerging politics. It is not surprising in a representative democracy to have politicians respond to trends and operate within the events that designate them; most would say that is precisely how it should work. The developments in question are those generating a quantum increase in communication forms and speed. Future evaluations of the Clinton presidency will likely consider these changes in accounting for what was done in preparing for office.

How do reporters assess the personnel issues associated with organizing a new administration? For those I spoke with, the short answer is: realistically. "By 11:00 o'clock on election night, people are not sitting around thinking: 'What really should be our policy on agricultural price supports?' They're thinking: 'Where am I going to get a job?' " The distance is short between postelection thoughts about employment and "backbiting and the rivalries" since "everybody can't be accommodated in all the top jobs." The rivalries are among those who shared the "spaceship" that is the campaign apparatus and between them and the party's policy and governing establishment, from whom cabinet and major subcabinet selections will be made. The initial scoring of the president-elect's leadership qualities may well be the extent to which this competition is effectively managed or at least moderated.

Experienced White House observers had clearly in mind what a president-elect needed to assist him during this demanding passage from candidacy to presidency. He has to identify the most versatile among his staff, quickly appoint and organize his White House staff, create a loyal circle of aides to help him identify the meaning of his election, understand that personnel will be interpreted as policy, and appreciate that the press is forever aiming to grasp the meaning of the new administration. Obviously, getting the White House staff and loyal inner circle set, with a press spokesperson designated, suits the needs of the press. But it is apparent, at least to reporters, that accomplishing these goals is mutually beneficial and, quite possibly, in service to the public interest.

Many of these points were illustrated in my conversations with reporters, with reference to the Clinton experience because it was the freshest in their memory and, even more, because they believed it was not done to suit their expectations. Some emphasized how important it was to learn the right lessons from campaigning. The danger is that those who are good at campaigning may assume "that the lessons [they've] learned in the campaign do carry over . . . [and yet] the environments are so different." The temptation, then, is to react to problems in governing by concluding, "Oh, we'll go on the road and make a few speeches, take a few polls—that kind of bullshit."

Clearly much of what an administration becomes is centered in the new people who are brought into governing. For reporters, "people stories are always easy to focus on." They are also a rather parsimonious means of reporting if people do represent policy. As one reporter explained, "You have this whole cast of characters to play with and to tell people about. This is sort of giving the shape of the administration in a tangible way. I think that's the thing we focused on." The attention given to people was amplified in 1992 by Clinton's own stress on personnel, specifically on diversity of appointments; and as well by television coverage. "[Television] tends to put the focus on personnel and personalities, and I think a lot of us [print reporters] absorb that because it is easier. It's more compelling to talk about individuals."

Reporters had a rather refined view of the nature and relative importance of appointments, much of it self-serving in the sense of producing a coherent presidency to report on. What follows then is a composite of assessments. "It's very hard for the president to make new friends, to get to know people whom he hasn't known before to a degree that he feels like he can rely on them. Not impossible, but hard." As a result, he will work with those he knows and knows well. The campaign concludes with "a very small circle of people you really trust." These "friends" as loyalists should then be positioned during the transition as confirmation of the shift from campaigning to governing. They know what was said in the campaign, they come to be oriented to the new task in the transition, and they are then in a position to make the turn to governing once in the White House. As described, these loyalists serve as the satellites around the main star, thus meeting the expectations of creating a presidency and with the advantage of orienting the press to the new team. One reporter argued:

I argue strongly you would need to have someone in the White House who remembers, knows, internalizes, and believes in every one of your campaign promises, so when you're breaking them, you know you're breaking them and why. . . . I think you need to have people whose personal loyalty to you is absolutely, totally, unbelievably unquestionable; that you couldn't dream in a million years that they would ever, ever [be disloyal]. You need that kind of support in bolstering the White House.

Due to the substantial growth of White House operations, management skills are also required, but the campaign is also a large operation and thus such talent should be available, with adaptations to meet the governing challenge. "You need a chief of staff who knows how to delegate and isn't afraid to do it, who is a strong enough person and is confident enough that he surrounds himself with other really good people. . . . You [also] have to think about how they look to the country."

These discussions consistently led to a critical analysis of the Clinton experience, noting the effects in press coverage as a consequence. Attention was directed to Clinton's decision to select the cabinet first and to emphasize diversity. Here is the clearest presentation of this view:

So much focus was put on the diversity and politically correct combinations of the makeup of the cabinet, whereas really the White House staff is where all the power resides. A lot of the senior people on the deputy assistant level of the White House didn't even know they had a job until just a day or two before the inauguration. People who had been loyal all through the transition, who have enormous say in what goes on, did not know.

Their anxiety was reflected in the press coverage, because these were the people who became the friends of the reporters, basically, in the foxhole existence of the campaign. And still they're our only friends, basically in what was essentially a news blackout during the transition in Little Rock. . . . And these people, with whom really the essential power of governing will reside, were not told that they had any authority until well past the end of the transition.

A related analysis stressed an issue basis for emphasizing the early appointment of the White House staff. For this reporter, that is where the "toughest, biggest issues . . . end up [that will] involve the twenty people that you put as senior White House staffers." The Clinton transition, however, failed "to have a cluster group that was focused on the White House, so that I think they failed to understand that, while Bob Reich may be able to do a lot of interesting things at Labor, or Donna Shalala may be doing important things at HHS, they're not the things that will either leave your historic mark as a president, or get you into really deep trouble."

The public face of the administration is another factor in the staff–issues–press relations configuration of a new administration. Basically agreeing with several transition aides, one reporter spoke for several others in regard to the press operations of the Clinton transition and early White House: "All these people who look sort of like kids. . . . They had no heft. They had no gravitas." Others judged that the problems of the White House staff went beyond appearances. "The [Clinton] White House staff has been second-rate; he didn't focus on strengthening a lot of those offices with the best possible people. . . . So he devalued the White House staff."

A number of other press management criticisms of the Clinton transition arose, perhaps related in part to disappointments. For many, there was optimism, even excitement, about the new administration—a new generation, new ideas, a fresh start:

> There we all were in Little Rock. Look, we're part of something exciting too. All of us who covered him, a lot of us were going to the White House. That's a big deal. We kind of got a reward by being in the right place at the right time. And we're really, really interested in if this guy is going to succeed. I think at that point there was a tremendous amount of good will. . . . In Little Rock . . . every night he would try to go out to dinner. . . . There was a lot of camaraderie still, just like you had during the campaign. You'd grab your person and take them out to dinner. . . . After a while, the press starts to write these guys off because they can't seem to get anything right. You've been given the wrong information a hundred times.

However chummy the arrangements in Little Rock, many reporters were unhappy—some because they had to travel to Little Rock, "a godforsaken place, if truth be told"; others because there was so little news to report. Among those expressing disapproval of Little Rock were Washington reporters who had not traveled with the candidate. And because the appointments were strung out during December, "he kept the press corps in Little Rock until, in fact, late on Christmas Eve so that he could meet this artificial deadline that he had foolishly set for himself. In the process I'm sure that he earned himself a lot of ill will with many of the very people that he has to depend on to get his story out."

Of course, reporters expected that the time in Little Rock would be a busy time and one in which they could prove their worth. Not surprisingly, their egos and ambitions are on the line too:

> They're going to be expected to write about something every day. They're going to be desperate to file every day for their own institutional and personal benefit. . . . Maybe they want to be White House correspondents, and part of what they're there for is to prove that they should be the White House correspondent.
>
> I can tell you that every day at the *New York Times* they will sit down at 11:00 o'clock and plan for a story from the transition before they know what's being said. The same with the networks. So you have this enormous vacuum that is set up there, compounded as I said by the egos and the ambitions of the reporters. Something is going to fill that vacuum. And if you don't fill it . . . it's going to be filled by bad news. It's going to be filled by rumor. It's going to be filled by stories of indecision and failure to make decisions. It's going to be filled by stories of infighting and backbiting and rivalry.

Being in Little Rock with little to report was "one of the most frustrating experiences of my reporting career. Phone calls were unanswered. Simple 'get to know you' sessions couldn't be scheduled." Another reporter elaborated: "What the press wants is information . . . and . . . we didn't get very much."

> We expected to learn what Clinton was going to do. In Little Rock we hardly ever found out. There was . . . essentially a blackout. Any information that we gathered came extremely roundabout and not directly from the operation that was put down there. So we expected some of the openness that we had gotten during the successful days of the Clinton campaign and got none of it.

* * *

There were the stakeouts at the governor's mansion—you know, vans. Nothing would be happening. You'd try to spot cars going in to see who was coming. I don't know if that was any less orderly than other transitions, but there was a kind of madcap, kind of bizarre aspect to our life in Little Rock. . . . They could have developed really good relations with us. And . . . that's when a lot of the themes began to be set, like the breaking of the promises, and the fact that they just didn't seem ready for prime time.

The consensus was that the failure to fill the vacuum was by no means intentional. Rather it was attributed to inexperience, a lack of understanding, and a failure to adjust to the new role. Many staff were still in the campaign mode. The most serious criticism was directed to the press operation itself. A part of the problem was attributed to the emerging relations with the White House and Washington press corps—all very much part of the transition. "The time to prepare your good relations with the press is when you arrive in Washington," one reporter declared. But, of course, if the transition headquarters is in Little Rock, then adjustments have to be made to accommodate to Washington coming there, or to preparing material for those members of the press in Washington who are unlikely to travel to Arkansas. None of these arrangements was well handled, according to most reporters I spoke with.

Neither Dee Dee Myers nor George Stephanopoulos received good grades from the press: "Dee Dee Myers was a great traveling press secretary and . . . she should have been kept as the number two in the press office." In one of the harshest reviews of the operation, a reporter did not limit comments to the transition period, concluding that the problems carried over to the new administration for two years, to the great detriment of the president:

One of the things that's made the Clinton presidency work less well is that they have this completely inadequate White House press operation. It's just pathetic. It's just awful. Dee Dee Myers was a good campaign press secretary, but she was not prepared to be the White House press secretary. And George Stephanopoulos, he was disastrous. They've both been awful in different ways in terms of being the president's chief spokesman. The president complains about not getting his message out. In two years, he has not had an effective person explaining what it is he's trying to do, or available to reporters to give their reasoning behind things. . . . It's been unbelievably damaging.

Another of the experienced hands at White House coverage was "a bigger fan of George [Stephanopoulos] than a lot of reporters," but was no less critical of the press operations. In this review, however, the president-elect was implicated for "talking too much and saying things without recognizing their news value." Thus part of the problem for Clinton was too much news, not too little, yet a lack of control and direction:

> We're intuitively averse to the idea of controlled news. But when you see it done well [as with Reagan], there's a sort of beauty to it in that it's remarkably effective if the president has only A to say, and only A is on the television news that night and the newspapers the next day. . . . [Clinton] had a whole series of things that screwed up what were supposed to be some of the messages. The economy was supposed to be a message. Ethics was supposed to be a message, with the series of "We're going to have the most ethical administration. . . ." As someone who has covered several [transitions and inaugurations], I took to resenting deeply their constant references to things they were doing for the first time ever, which were demonstrably not only not for the first time ever, but almost a total pattern of things presidents do. . . . I always find the Clinton people to have insulted your intelligence as reporters, as if you were like, born yesterday and never heard of Nexus. It just infuriates me still.

The economic summit held in Little Rock in mid-December was a good example of the mismatch between the new team's approach to the transition and the press expectations of what should go on during this time. Many reporters I spoke with believed that the time might better have been used for formulating the economic plan rather than conducting a seminar. It "was a quintessential Clinton type of event" with "long sessions and schmooze about things to decide things." The president-elect should have had his economic plan ready "from day one," thereby signaling both the priority for his administration and the proposals for change. That would have suited the press. That would have produced the news they were looking for. "The notion that resources already stretched to the limit would be diverted for a pointless talkathon; it was a very bad mistake . . . to have the president in particular, and the vice president, sit there hour after hour."

Still, the astute reporter was getting an impression of the working style of the new administration—one less sensitive to traditional hierarchy and governing practices, one unprepared to act in expected ways.

> It took a lot of time away from doing the things they should have been doing. . . . It did showcase the president as being incredibly articulate and smart. But so what? If you look at that economic summit, it had all the seeds of everything that was wrong with his administration. People fawning over him and talking about how smart he was, and what did the economic summit do? Nothing. If it had a message to communicate, it was that the deficit was a problem and they were going to have to do something about it. . . . There were like 1,800 [similar meetings] after that.

The most positive view of the summit identified it as an extension of the campaign and as a display of Clinton's "ability to listen, engage" which in turn "got people thinking about economic policy." However admirable a quality, one reporter stated, "it's not sufficient to make people think that you feel their pain when you're governing," where "expectations are different."

These discussions with seasoned reporters revealed a clearly etched rendering of how a president-elect and his team should perform during the transition. It is a portrait drawn from experiences of the past and is, therefore, self-serving in many respects. It eases one's task if change is not required. The Reagan and Clinton cases were freshest in the minds of the reporters with whom I spoke. They offered contrasting styles: Reagan more conventional in meeting the expectations of the press, Clinton much less "by the book." As several reporters noted, however, important changes have occurred in the technology of communication, many of which have yet to be fully absorbed even by those most experienced in the craft. Thus it was that the Clinton transition from the press perspective was different, seemingly failing to meet the expectations of the past. Perhaps they were witnessing the first transition of the future—more possibly due to changes in campaigning *and* governing, changes not well understood either by the press or by the Clinton team but that influenced behavior nonetheless. Certainly the penchant of the president-elect himself to communicate directly and frequently with the public was confounding to the press, as was his apparent disinterest in streamlining his press operations to suit prior patterns of communication. By his second term, Clinton had established a workable method sensitive to his talents and more responsive to the needs of the press.

About the Press

Reporters, too, experience a transition following an election. After all, they are reporting on politics and government, both of which are changing. And different news organizations handle the transition differently. Some assign reporters who covered the winning candidate to the White House, others bring in new reporters, and many carry over with those who had previously covered the White House. Because careers are involved, some jockeying and rivalry occur, which may influence coverage. Naturally, then, the advantage goes to that president-elect with savvy aides who understand what is happening in the press's transition.

A shift in people covering the candidate-now-president-elect is accompanied by a not-so-subtle change in the coverage itself. This change has several dimensions. I begin with the physical and managerial. One respondent noted, "The reporters covering the campaign want to take some time off. Most reporters are human beings and they're exhausted." David M. Shribman of the *Boston Globe* provided details at a conference on transitions:

> These people have been away, basically, for a year. They've been in a sensory deprivation unit for a year. They haven't spoken to their husbands, wives, families. They only know where they were this morning by checking the local phone book in a hotel . . . . So all of our crack reporters are going to want to be in Florida and the Cayman Islands for the next 75 days. . . . They're sick of who they're covering. They're also sick. They have sinus infections that began about the second week in May, haven't been treated since then. . . . So we're going to sit and talk in grand terms about how we're going to cover this pageant of democracy?[6]

Shribman also pointed out that relatively little planning goes into covering the transition period, compared with the national conventions (yet both occur every four years).[7] In part, perhaps, the reason is that the convention is a part of the campaign, the actual nomination having been settled in the primaries. The transition, on the other hand, represents a shift in subject. In the words of another reporter, "I suppose you could say that the transition is [when] you stop covering the horse race and you start getting into more substantive stuff."[8]

One important change in the style of coverage is associated with the metamorphosis in roles from candidate to president-elect. The expectations that reporters have of themselves shift with the election of a president. They may even come to identify their future with that of the candidate, "unconsciously ... acquiring a vested interest in the success of the candidate you're covering ... the journalistic phenomenon of going native. If the guy loses, you're back covering agriculture." With his election, however, "the vested interest flips almost on its head to being critical, to show that you can be tough enough to cover the White House, and that you're not going to be in the tank for him ... because the last thing that any bureau chief wants is someone who's going to be soft." This shift may surprise the candidate and his aides, who have come to believe that they were on good terms with the reporters covering them, only to see them "turn into tigers the day after the election." According to this reporter, there are two "press biases" that should be acknowledged by strategically sensitive presidential candidates and future White House staff:

> One is that they [reporters] are in favor of a good story, and the other is, they're against whoever's in power. Now, if you think about it, both of these impulses worked for Clinton during the campaign, and against him once he became president, because during the campaign, the good story was the challenger, the outsider, the new generation, all of those clichés, the bus trips. And, of course, there were people who were tired of Bush, and the whole notion of four more years to the press corps was a threat, not a promise, because it was really twelve years. The instant [Clinton] won, a lot of that flipped because now he was in power, and therefore you are much more critical. You have spates of stories within days after the election about disarray and backbiting.[9]

Accounts by other respondents suggested a related component to the shift from more favorable to more critical treatment. Believing that the "campaign press" had given the winner "a free ride," the "institutional White House Washington press" is determined "to hold him to a strict standard, starting now." One such White House reporter confirmed this interpretation, particularly in regard to Clinton. Those covering his campaign "were very . . . sympathetic to him and agreed with him on policy. . . . But when Clinton came into the White House, you also had this group of reporters who were basically White House reporters, like myself, that had covered him some, but also covered Bush and didn't feel that allegiance." The result was a "split in the press corps early on" and "more of a jolt for the Clinton people since they had had a press corps that . . . was sort of more sympathetic than the White House press corps."

Another interpretation of this phenomenon for transition and early White House staff to consider is that an "exhausted" campaign press may be on vacation in the immediate postelection period, with the more "cynical" or "jaded" Washington-based corps taking over. As it happens, this latter group may be less knowledgeable about the president-elect's statements on the campaign trail. For Clinton, one reporter judged that "it had some impact on the gays in the military thing" because "reporters looking at that issue for the first time gave it more attention and pushed harder for it as a story than people who had been in the campaign, who didn't think it was news."

The greater number and variety of press covering the president-elect, compared with his role as a candidate, have still other effects. First is the "greater intensity of focus"—a phenomenon that seemingly must be experienced to be realized since many winners and their staffs are unprepared for it. Then there is "the sense of time."

> In a campaign, you've always got to be pushing for a story that you can produce that night. . . . There is very little capacity . . . to dig into a story in any depth, to allocate a lot of resources for a long period of time in the hopes that you might produce something. The perfect example of this . . . was Whitewater. The *New York Times* spent three days on the story, didn't produce very much, they're on to something else. They couldn't afford in the middle of a campaign to really dig into it. The instant you're elected, you've got four years. . . . The whole mentality in the press corps changes [as does] bureau decisionmaking . . . [regarding] what is worth investing. How much is it worth to invest resources?[10]

In the case of Whitewater, "Hillary Clinton said over and over again: 'Whitewater is not going to be an issue. We dealt with it during the campaign. We know how to do that.'"

What is the role of the press in the transition, as viewed by experienced reporters? And are they "at their best" during this period, thus providing a honeymoon for the emerging administration? Or is the treatment during this time mostly a consequence of adjustments in coverage and uncertainty about the direction and shape of the new team? Is it true that the press is willing to go easy on the president-elect during the transition period, as certain White House staff believe? If so, how does that square with the judgment above that the press transition is from the more sympathetic campaign reporters to the more critical Washington-based reporters? Is the "honeymoon" less a matter of intent than of the circumstances of a change in leadership? Discussion by reporters of their role in relationship to the incoming administration helps to answer these questions.

Perhaps the explanation regarding the honeymoon is found in the press's role as reporters interpret that role during this time. The shift in coverage from candidacy to preparation for the presidency is driven by conceptions and expectations of fitting behavior for each activity. But the change is subtle and accompanied by a substantial overlay of tolerance of the preparations themselves. Therefore, the new team has several degrees of latitude if they understand how reporters are doing their jobs and nurture them. They may want to avoid inviting or forcing the press into a more critical posture too early by alienating them.

Recall the remarks of a former Reagan aide in speaking about the press's role during the transition: "One of the best things about the press in transition is that that's when they are their best." This aide recommended, therefore, that the president-elect and his staff take advantage by providing open access. Here is how several reporters described interactions during this time:

> We view the transition and the first few months, not as time to assess, but as time to straight cover. What they do has much more meaning than . . . why they did it . . . . So it's sort of the clearest, most pristine moment of straightforward news coverage, because everything they announce, say, talk about is covered straight, or relatively straight.
>
> * * *
>
> It seems to me that you've got 100 days where people are going to give you the benefit of the doubt. Then if your 100 days go well, maybe you have until the end of that year. But chances are that's going to be your period of maximum opportunity. And that window closes.

The strong focus on the major appointments to the White House staff and the cabinet contributes to good relations during the transition. One reporter explained that with so many new faces, and old faces in new jobs, the press has an opportunity to inform the public about the cast of characters that will be governing the nation. Another stressed that "the press is easy. Our demands aren't much. A few tips on cabinet members or White House staff positions and a chance to speak to whoever is writing the inaugural address; we buy off fairly easy in that period." Asked whether most reporters "want the president to succeed," this reporter asked, "Succeed in what? . . . Do I want Ronald Reagan to succeed in cutting the budget? No, not particularly. Do I want him to be a failure as president of the United States? No." This point was expanded upon later in the interview:

> You asked me before: does the press want the president to succeed? I think the public wants this president to succeed. In almost any campaign if you have a poll in December in which you ask . . . how people voted for president you will find that the president got a higher percentage of that vote than he did in the election. People want to be for the president. So they want him to succeed. We're not impervious to that. If they [the new team] give us stuff to write about that helps them make that point, we'll write about it.

To summarize: reporters do have different and more elevated expectations for the transition than they had for the campaign and do, therefore, make critical judgments as to whether the winner is doing it right. Their standards for the good transition are drawn from their experience with and understanding of the presidency. Within this framework, however, their reporting is more straightforward and less critically analytical than it will be later; yet it is typically more demanding, comprehensive, and intensive than during the campaign. The task, then, for a new team eager for favorable coverage, is to comprehend both the shift in expectations and the measure and form of latitude in coverage due to reporters' interpretations of their responsibilities in the transition.

As with other topics, it was exactly the seeming failure of the Clinton team to comprehend or account for these shifts that led several respondents to criticize the Clinton transition performance. Said one reporter, "They really could have developed good relations with us." Why did it not proceed more smoothly? Reporters offered a number of explanations. Whereas reporters naturally focus on people—who is getting what job—the diversity determinant was considered to be "a big mistake." It provided the press with a continuous test and invited "bean counting" among various interests. Further, diversity appeared a campaign-oriented, not a governing, criterion. One reporter believed he should have said, "'Hey, I'm getting the best people for these jobs, and you'll be surprised when you see the result.'"

In fact, continuing the campaign more than preparing to govern was a common motif in the discussions of the Clinton transition. What this meant from the press's perspective was that the new team had not acknowledged the shift in expectations among reporters. Clinton and his closest aides were literally unprepared to manage the transition or to turn it over to those with experience who could so manage (and several such persons were available who had worked on preelection transition planning). Therefore much of the campaign press relations team was carried over to protect the candidate (now president-elect), to guard what was released, to provide quick responses to criticism, to develop campaign-like themes, to promise more than could be delivered. The recollections by reporters were uniformly unflattering and apparently not moderated by time. One example:

> I think a smart transition, a smart White House is one that gives some thought about what the story of the day may be. You can't always dictate it because things happen. But you can at least make an attempt to get your point of view across. . . . But instead [with Clinton] there was day after day, week after week, month after month, of nothing but sitting and waiting and excuses from the official spokespeople about why they couldn't tell us anything.
>
> QUESTION: How do you explain that?
>
> RESPONSE: Well, Clinton personally dislikes the Washington press corps because . . . he considered himself badly beaten up in the New Hampshire primary . . . and he didn't think he could trust that the press would convey his message as he wanted it conveyed. . . . He thought that somehow he could do without them, go around them, convey it personally by force of his personality, town hall meetings . . . go to individual markets. He can't do that. . . . Those are all useful things, and could help. But it's too complicated a world to simply say that you could ignore one part of the infrastructure of Washington that is there specifically to convey your message.

For several reporters, the retention of George Stephanopoulos as a press spokesperson, along with Dee Dee Myers, suggested a failure to make the necessary adjustments following the campaign. Reporters expected to be fed stories about the plans of the new administration, plans that clarified the direction in policy and personnel. Best of all for the press was to have these stories be direct and truthful as well as somewhat integrated (as with policy and appointments, a goal complicated by the emphasis on diversity). It would be hard to overstate their doubts about Clinton's press aides being able to accomplish these goals. As noted earlier, Stephanopoulos was judged an advantage in the campaign and even in Little Rock because it was not Washington:

> You take that same person and you put him under a sign that says, "The White House," and all the impressions are different. What seemed feisty and youthful in Little Rock seems a little whiny and immature in the White House. Same guy, different sign he's standing under, metaphorically as well as literally. And that's part of what the transition has to do. I think that they made the mistake of having the transition so much like the campaign, and . . . would use those mechanisms, those strategies, those systems that worked in the campaign, but failing to understand the need to make that transition.

Dee Dee Myers was consistently judged to have had a similar profile: capable in the rapid-fire pace of campaign communications, poorly trained for the White House, and lacking the experience in government and for dealing with veteran news people. "Dee Dee has a way of kind of wading into it and getting in deeper and deeper and deeper, because . . . she doesn't have that background."

> They used Dee Dee Myers in the campaign as a lightning rod and a deflection, and to get a quick response to the traveling press, not understanding that . . . the role of the White House press secretary . . . sets forth administration policy. It can be a proactive role. . . . George Stephanopoulos was obviously a terrific campaign communications chief, because he was quick and he understood politics and policy, and maybe very good at that role in the White House. But he was not good as a public spokesperson. They were stuck. They didn't have anyone. And so they put him out there.

Observing that "they were stuck" is itself a conclusion about whether the Clinton team was prepared to make the transition to governing in the conventional manner. Had they been so prepared, they might have appointed Mike McCurry at the start.[11] As it was, in appointing Myers, the White House was "stuck" in another way, according to one reporter. Given their "diversity" criterion and the relatively few women in major White House staff positions, it was not simple to replace Myers once she was appointed.[12]

Comparisons were made between Clinton's press operation and that of other recent presidents. Marlin Fitzwater with Bush and Jody Powell with Carter were praised as being savvy about the role of the press and the workings of the government, as well as being in the loop and possessing an accommodating style with reporters: "I think the whole press corps knew Marlin, had some kind of working relationship with him. He understood . . . even to the point of some of the personalities at the briefing that you have to handle in particular ways."[13] Equally, "Carter had a great advantage. . . . You could really tell from Jody what was going on. I mean, he was very good."[14]

In responding to a question about "a model transition," reporters typically cited that of Reagan in 1980, though one noted, "But it worked best because it fit Reagan . . . [and] compensated for the president's weaknesses." Questioned whether the Clinton transition also may not have fit Clinton well produced a response revealing of this reporter's expectations (which were a fair representation of others as well).

> It fit him well in that it made him comfortable. But it didn't fit him well in that it didn't compensate for his weaknesses. And it didn't fit him well in that it didn't prepare him for once he took office. And it didn't fit him well in that he didn't make that transition he needed to make. So it may have been a transition that he liked, but it didn't do the things that needed to be done.

Concluding Comments

In his reflections on service in the White House, much of it as the president's press secretary, Marlin Fitzwater summarizes relationships with the press this way:

> We work together, within steps of each other, within seconds of the

Oval Office, and within earshot of the world. Yet we conduct private inner wars to submerge the personal and policy conflicts that drive us. It is a world of personal strategies in which everyone has a plan for dealing with everyone else. No wonder it burns people up. But it is also very exciting, adrenaline producing, and intellectually addictive. . . .

Press secretaries do not make policy, nor does the press. But together we make a difference at the margin. Together we are an appendage to the presidency that ties the daily deliberations of government to the American people.[15]

Appendage they may be, but the press is permanently affixed to the presidency. Thus Fitzwater's story, along with those of Larry Speakes (Reagan) and Jody Powell (Carter) before him, is an account of his temporary service in the process of tying the government to the people.[16] The press, on the other hand, like Congress, the bureaucracy, and the courts, is a more permanent fixture. A change in the presidency, then, results in different people filling every room and office in the White House—every place, that is, except the press quarters. There is turnover, to be sure, as those covering the successful candidate's campaign are often assigned to the White House press corps while others are assigned to other beats.[17] But there is substantial continuity in at least three senses: first, in the number of reporters who carry over from one administration to the next (by one count about half of the approximately sixty who constitute the White House press corps);[18] second, in the news organizations represented; and third, in that those reporters leaving the White House typically do not leave journalism, and thus their experience may influence other coverage as well as affect their replacement in the White House (after all, most remain colleagues in the same news organization).

This chapter's recounting of the press's role in the transition is striking in the extent to which the reflections of transition aides and experienced reporters correspond. There is substantial agreement in regard to the critical tasks performed by the press, the importance of selecting a skilled press secretary early in the transition, the shifts that occur in personnel and coverage within the press, the opportunity for the president-elect to gain favorable coverage, and the need for a strategy on the part of the new team to take advantage of so-called straight coverage.

At the same time, however, the discussions revealed intricate developments that invite serious consideration of important changes in transitions.

Most of the evaluations of recent transitions were drawn from conventional perspectives of the changes required to move from campaigning to governing. By these standards, Nixon and Reagan were judged to have had effective transitions, Carter less so, while Clinton was uniformly criticized. At the same time, however, journalists in particular emphasized important developments in communication and the generational shift represented by the Clinton candidacy. The winner in 1992 was the first president born into the television age. Why would he make the mistakes in organizing to govern that were attributed to him? Possibly because he never intended to govern in the traditional way. In accepting the limits and opportunities of a new era of communication, perhaps he instinctively sought to develop a nonconventional style of governing—one in which campaigning carries through as a political resource in national policymaking and implementation; campaigning as a style of, not a substitute for, governing.

Professionals in the mass communication business—the reporters—were the most critical of the Clinton transition. The reason may be simply that many of the developments facilitate direct communication between the White House and the public, which in turn encourages continuous campaigning and a reduced role for the press, or in Fitzwater's analysis, tying "the daily deliberations of government to the American people." As one reporter explained about Clinton's effort to "go around" the Washington press, "He can't do that. . . . It's too complicated a world." No one will argue about the complications, but they affect the press too and provide alternative channels for the president to reach the American people. Bill Clinton has certainly availed himself of those channels.

6

"THE BIGGEST MISTAKE" AND OTHER LESSONS

PRESIDENTS are expected to meet unreal expectations in a real-world setting. Mistakes will be made. There is no one formula for meeting an inconstant challenge. The demands on ordinary mortals during the election and after are bizarre. Hyped-up campaign vagabonds are expected suddenly to create an interim, elaborate organization to accomplish a goal for which most are ill prepared both by reason of their background and recent political experience. One former aide explained, "A transition is like assembling and then tearing down a multimillion dollar corporation in a span of ninety days. It doesn't exist November 5, and then it is built up, and then it is destroyed January 20. So there's a lot of chaos. You're going to make mistakes. It's a question, I think, of minimizing mistakes."

A common discovery is that "the whole philosophy of this town, the whole way Washington operates, is different from anything else." If the president-elect and his aides are not Washington-wise, then they are advised to get help. They may have campaigned against the government they are now presumed to lead. Even reformers, however, need to know where and how to make change. And so what got applause on the campaign trail may not serve well as a basis for relating to those in the permanent work force of the national government, those whose support may be needed if the new president is to lead effectively. Paradoxically, this new and challenging mission comes at a point of triumph—of having won taxing nomination and general election battles that leave the victors exhausted to the point of numbness. Then, "like flicking a light switch," the winner is asked to form an administration that will direct and manage the permanent government. A Reagan and Bush aide spoke for many:

> It's horrible. . . . They [transitions] are absolutely horrible. I've done them from the outside. I've done them from the inside where we won, and I've sat in the inside where we lost. And I can tell you, none of them is pleasant. They are all awful. But it's worse transitioning in, never having been in government. It's pretty overwhelming.

All may be "horrible" due simply to the enormity of the challenge, yet be harrowing in different ways. For there is no escaping the prime variable in transitions: the person as president-elect. They are all different, and yet they must somehow accommodate to anticipations related to images that are carried over from one administration to the next. That process of adjustment is at the core of politics in a separated system. The new president represents change; the living images represent stability. Fitting the new into the familiar requires adroitness, typically including clarity of message and integration of personnel. Presidents-elect must come to be seen as fit for the job in order to do the job. One aide reflected: "A president, a great president, does represent something greater than himself. That's a very important part of the presidency. You have to assert presidential authority in your own party and with Congress. . . . I don't think it's that hard to do, but you've got to do it. And you can't do it halfheartedly." A Reagan aide believed that a future president should begin to think of himself in that role "months in advance," leaving all of the managerial issues to staff aides.

> People tell me that athletes have a game-day face that they have to put on. They start thinking days before the big game, and they start hating their opponent, and they start thinking about how they're going to react in certain situations. It seems to me there's something to be said in the same way in becoming president. . . . You ought to start thinking about your role as president a couple of months beforehand, and what kinds of challenges you're going to face, and how you're going to react, and the five things I never want to do, and the five things that I always want to do if I can.

It is all of a piece. Thinking ahead demands knowledge and understanding of the permanent government and the status of the presidency in that government, that is, knowing how Washington works. Thinking ahead accepts that the president will be seen as more than the person, as encompassing aides and appointees. Presidents will be viewed as greater than themselves; their challenge is to master that enlargement so that it will be seen as a presidency deserving of regard. This process of transformation was illustrated graphically by a reporter in reflecting on the Clinton transition:

> In the sense of making himself larger than himself, not only did he not accomplish that at all, and that, of course, became a huge problem for him later on because he diminished himself relative to the presidency, as opposed to the other way around, but I really believe that back then [in the transition], they weren't thinking in those terms at all. They were thinking during the campaign [that] he had diminished the distance between himself and the public. He created all this intimacy with the talk shows, and he was a regular guy, and he stopped at McDonald's, and they continued that [in the transition]. Remember the other thing he did during the transition was he walked down Georgia Avenue. Now that was a good thing, but I don't think they got . . . the larger-than-life part. They got the man-of-the-people part. But I don't think they had any concept about creating a presidency.

The enormity of the challenge, the individuality of the effort, the unlikelihood of learning from the past, expectations exceeding capacity to achieve—these and other factors preclude an error-free transition. Still, is there a biggest mistake? And how important is the transition for subsequent governing?

A Biggest Mistake?

Transition aides and reporters identified several "biggest mistakes" that could and have been made during the transition period. Most frequently mentioned were the failure to establish leadership, mismanagement of the time and the opportunity, misjudging or mishandling appointments, and failing to relate properly to Congress. In fact, these mistakes are variations on a theme of not being prepared to complete the shift from campaigning to governing and therefore of a failure to have projected competence and clear direction. For one reporter, this required a conceptualization of "the transition as a bridge from the campaign to governing, in a communications sense." Another concluded that the biggest mistake "is really the inability to disassociate campaigning [from] governing." Responses from transition aides were consistent with these judgments—all stressing leadership in setting a course and displaying control.

> The biggest mistake that can be made is to portray a sense of confusion, chaos; something said one day and contradicted the next day, so that it shows that the president is not in charge and does not have good leadership skills. That then . . . creates an impression that carries over into his governing.
>
> * * *
>
> The biggest mistake you can make is to appear not to have a strategy and be inconsistent. . . . That's what people want more than anything else is consistency. . . . I'd be sure that my goals were short enough that I figured out where I was going between now and the State of the Union. . . . If I did that right, the rest of it would take care of itself.
>
> * * *
>
> To go out there and walk away from what you promised the people you were going to do. That is in my mind the absolute worst. The rest of this stuff comes and goes and a lot of it is just the rhythms of living here, the fun and games. . . . Everybody makes mistakes in appointments. Everybody gets embarrassed. Every party has got their turkeys. Some of that comes and goes.

Very much associated with the more general points regarding leadership were the comments about transition management. Presumably a president-elect averting confusion and chaos by displaying leadership comprehends what is necessary to manage effectively between the election and inauguration. Clearly a smoothly operating transition is one important test of the new president, "your first identity," according to one cabinet member. It is a time for signal sending to a most attentive professional audience: the press, bureaucrats, members of Congress, the outgoing administration, lobbyists, the international community. Voters may be taking a rest from politics, but official Washington is fully engaged. Therefore a biggest mistake, in the words of one observer, is "not understanding the importance of the transition. . . . People have to understand that this is an absolutely essential part of making the leap from being a candidate to being president."

An important component of management is the time factor. "If you don't recognize that three months is a short period of time in which to get your hands around the federal establishment, that's a big mistake," said another former aide. After all, the government in a separated system is continuous by design. Certain functions must and will be performed whether or not the new administration is prepared to participate as expected. Those who do the government's work under pressure of deadlines "will come back and . . . say that 'the White House doesn't have their act together. . . . Well, we don't have any choice, let's just put the regulation out.'"

It was also judged to be a mistake not to realize the advantages offered a new team: "You start fresh. He's now the president-elect and put together his administration, and we'll cut him the slack of a little bit of time." But, of course, that time has to be used effectively as all of Washington watches. The same person added, "If you get off on the wrong foot, if you pick the wrong issues to work, priorities get misguided, he'll waste his first six months." A reporter confirmed this assessment, noting that "if you don't take advantage of [the opportunity], then it's lost forever, and it's not retrievable." Admittedly, however, it may require a certain level of experience to realize the opportunity, again handicapping candidates from far out of Washington. Bill Clinton was the most recent example, as one respondent recalled: "He had never run something big. He had never dealt with foreign policy issues that have sapped a lot of his energies. I think he wasn't prepared."

Mistakes regarding appointments were also mentioned by several aides. The comments about appointments are, at root, concerns about whether the president-elect and his aides fully understand the tasks of organizing and programming an administration. "It's easy to misjudge people," said one aide. "And if you have a bad transition, where you do that for whatever reason, it's hard to recover. You only need one or two or three bad actors and you've got a real problem. And it's hard to get rid of cabinet officers. It's hard to get rid of top staff." In direct reference to the Clinton experience, one aide concluded:

> The biggest mistake was being so slow to get off the dime. I mean, it took forever to get the cabinet and the White House staff. . . . So

going too slow . . . in building their government, not asserting presidential authority in Washington and in your own party, those are two pretty big mistakes that you can make in a transition. . . . I can give you a scenario where [had] Clinton come out of the box [in 1993] like gangbusters . . . 1994 would never have happened.

Another aide agreed, noting that slowness "is a common mistake. . . . They always believe that if I say Joe Schmo on Thursday, I will be able to announce it on a Friday and he will take position on the following Friday or send his name to the Senate for confirmation the following Friday. It doesn't work that way." It was this person's view that the process had to start much earlier than anybody imagined.

Some respondents were moved to add relationships with Congress to the list of biggest mistakes.

I think if there is a biggest mistake, it is in the relationship to the Hill. That's the greatest risk to long-term governing relations. All the other stuff is a matter of time. . . . You can adjust White House staff. You can make some changes in personnel. But if you get off on the wrong foot institutionally with the Congress, they never forget and it's almost beyond the personalities and the structures, the committee relationships with the agencies.

* * *

If you make a bad relationship with a member of Congress, it is really hard to turn that around once you start governing. All the forces in Washington are, almost by . . . design, geared toward driving people apart and pitting people against each other. . . . So you just can't dig a hole for yourself before you even start.

A reporter warned against another form of error in relating to the Congress, that of being "usurped" by congressional leaders. The reporter made specific reference to Clinton, who "put his . . . fate [in the hands] of Democratic congressional leaders. . . . I tend to think that is an example of making a big mistake you can't remedy."

Biggest mistakes are typically the result of unfamiliarity with Washington and the complex relations of the national government. It seems curious that a candidate and his staff could win the nomination and election without being fully knowledgeable about the role of the presidency in governing. But we know that can happen. The next question is whether mistakes, born out of ineptitude or innocence, make any difference, or whether a mostly error-free transition ensures successful governing.

Importance of the Transition for Governing

The transition is typically judged to be an opportunity for a positive start in governing. It is a chance for the president-elect and his team to establish credibility, to move beyond the campaign by displaying organizational agility and a capacity to adapt. Like any successful preview, a well-managed transition can generate highly positive anticipations about the feature attraction. The transition, in the words of various respondents, is "important for the start-up . . . it's your first identity," "sort of a shakedown cruise," "to set the tone," "an incredible launching pad."

These judgments about the importance of the transitions were uniformly drawn from what I identified earlier as the conventional perspective. By this view, a transition's value is measured by the extent to which a president-elect prepares himself to govern in the standard mode. Notable among the criteria is whether the new team effects a shift from campaigning to governing, clearly specifying a distinction between the two activities. Here are the markers as set forth by a Reagan aide:

> If the transition has gone well, [it] has continued to carry over the good effect of the election; and . . . has built the confidence of the people and the press that this is a president who knows what he's doing. And so it supports the impression the people have of the president's ability to govern. Also the substantive work that's done, like the strategic plan, means that you're not saying: "Well, what are we going to do now?" Or have too many objectives, or scatter your shot, or you don't have the relationship with Congress. The transition is the time to be ready; that preparation is absolutely critical to doing a good job of governing. It's important for the impression the people have of the ability to govern.
>
> On the other hand, if the transition goes badly, in the sense that papers are filled every day between people vying for positions, or different factions within the president's inner circle arguing about

policy issues, or . . . the president making statements that are silly, this can undermine then a good start to the presidency.

Other Republican aides offered similar tests. All believed that Nixon and Reagan used the transition effectively to launch governing presidencies and that Carter and Clinton were less successful in achieving that goal.

It's important because you've got to transform a campaign into a government. You've got to move from a campaign mode into a governing mode. It's important for the three reasons I said: people, ideas, and organization. You've got to develop those. . . . The Clinton administration didn't do this during their transition period. . . . Can you overcome it? Yes, you can but you start at a disadvantage. Why do that?

* * *

It kind of establishes the credibility test for the president's ability to manage the executive branch. . . . I think establishing the president's role as the head of the executive branch and the leader of the free world is pretty much set within the first ninety days of a transition.

* * *

The transition is the last opportunity to sort of reenergize your intellectual batteries. You've got one more pause until you're the man for the next four years, or even longer. [It is] the first opportunity . . . to try to take what you've been saying ad nauseam for a year and a half now, and actually translate that into policy and real legislation.

These orderly thoughts about the transition unquestionably represent the dominant outlook. Clinton aides, too, weighed their own transition and its importance by relying on the standards of the conventional perspective, yet provided strong hints of another method for assuming office.

[The transition] can't hurt you that much but I just think it can be a missed opportunity. I think in some sense ours was a missed opportunity. We did some very good public things in the transition—the economic conference, coming to Washington, some of our announcements and all that. But nothing you can do publicly in those . . . days . . . can even approach the importance of laying that base in that time. That's what my own bias would be. I would rather trade off all public benefits during that transition for being prepared to take office.

Note that this person appeared to hold to the conventional perspective of preparation to govern over more public and campaign-oriented activities. Yet did a more preparation-for-governing perspective suit Bill Clinton? The same person said, "I think maybe no when he was elected . . . but I think now [1995] he would see the wisdom in it." Another Clinton aide emphasized their interest in "gearing up, getting the American people ready." This person explained that "every transition will by necessity be dramatically different and will reflect the strengths and the weaknesses of the candidate. The fact that ours was not as disciplined as I would want said something about all of us."

However effective by the standard criteria, do "good" transitions ensure successful governing? Can an administration recover from a "bad" transition? Aides provided interesting views on these questions. The prevailing thinking is that a good transition is no guarantee of success in office, whereas a bad transition may result in seriously crippling effects.

> If you do kind of a cost-benefit analysis that says, will your governing be a lot better if you have a great transition, the answer might be no. But if you ask, can a bad transition kill your ability to govern, the answer is often yes. So I think the opportunities to do great damage are greater than they are to do great benefit. But I do believe there are marginal benefits to be achieved by a good transition.
>
> * * *
>
> So I think doing a bad job in the transition will normally lead to doing a bad job in governing. Doing an effective job in transition doesn't mean you're going to be effective in governing, but at least it is an important criterion of whether you're going to be successful.

One respondent doubted that even a bad transition would have long-term consequences. "But, boy, it has short-term consequences, I mean really short . . . you know, one-month consequences." An example given was that of removing the ban on gays serving in the military for Bill Clinton.

> That was to me the reflection of a bad transition. And it's in that first month I think that more people are conscious of who the president

is, first impressions. Then they go on to their own business, and don't have to think much about the president. "Oh, yes, we know about him. He's the one who wanted gays in the military." So I guess you can say [the transition's] important at least to the degree that it can screw up things, if it's not done well, or as well as possible. Can it be helpful? I don't know. . . . It can certainly hurt you. Can it help you? I don't know.

Journalists' views were very much in accordance with those of transition aides in regard to the importance of the transition for subsequent governing. Special stress, however, was placed on the importance of first impressions as an advantage in the early months, given that press coverage at this time is likely to be more favorable than later. It is the time when "you sow your seeds," as one person put it. "If you don't get that right, it's going to be very, very difficult to correct it." Most subscribed to the conventional perspective, as illustrated by the following response:

If you can't run a transition, how in the world are you going to run a government? So that problems you have then are problems you'll repeat later. . . . It illustrates how you're going to run the government. It is this period of time where you have an opportunity to prepare for your presidency, because once your presidency starts, there is no time for thinking; there's only time for doing. You need . . . to devise a strategy, take advantage of the very limited amount of time you're going to have with maximum clout.

Observe that the expectations underlying this view are that the president-elect will prepare himself to govern in the standard way, that "maximum clout" is related to classic preparation by which the new president abandons the campaign mode in favor of an insider-Washington governing mode.

First impressions are very important to reporters in providing an orientation for subsequent coverage. As noted earlier, the transition and the early months of the new administration typically feature straight reporting. A good transition, therefore, is one in which the president-elect and his team portray a clear and consistent image for governing. A bad transition projects confusion and is thus unsettling for reporters looking for cues, at a time they believe is beneficial for the new president. As explained by one reporter, the

Clinton team, in particular, "didn't provide a solid base on which to use the honeymoon . . . in order to make a point and get something done, which I think is an imperative." Can an administration recover from a bad start? "Yes, I assume you can recover from anything. But I think it makes it immensely more difficult, because if you have a cracked foundation, you have to dig it up and repour the cement. You have to have another transition." Another reporter related the importance of first impressions to the public's attention span, but with the important side benefit of capitalizing on favorable coverage:

> As the American attention span gets shorter and shorter, it becomes more important in that it affects your ability to do something right off the bat, and that affects your ability to do more things. So it's important that you position yourself to be seen to succeed in your first few weeks in office. . . . By and large, I think the president is going to be profoundly pleased with the coverage. There will be a little carping, but not much. . . . We will gushingly cover whatever news conferences and speeches he makes. So they'll get a lot of upbeat coverage.

Much of the analysis by aides and reporters amounts to judgments about whether the transition produces a presidency in conventional terms by the inauguration. By one view, "the personal transition of the president-elect is probably the most important" factor in achieving a suitable passage from campaigning to governing. And, as it happens, a president-elect who proceeds by the precepts of the conventional transition reduces uncertainties for bureaucrats, members of Congress, and the press by conforming to existing norms.

But what if political conditions are undergoing significant change, as associated with dramatic developments in communication and demographic changes among voters? A revised perspective of the transition may well be necessary as befitting a shift in the relationship between campaigning and governing, indeed, in what constitutes governing itself. The Clinton experience is the prime case for examining these matters. I turn first to the realities of the conventional transition as explored in this book, then consider a revised perspective that emerged in 1992 and continued after.

Realities of the Conventional Transition

Two subtexts have permeated this treatment: the tests of an effective transition are drawn from a conventional perspective that distinguishes between campaigning and governing, and a revised form of transitioning is emerging that is less sensitive to that distinction. It is not unusual in the midst of change for there to be a carryover of criteria, particularly in the absence of new measures associated with restyling a process. Therefore the basis for evaluating whether a president-elect and his team have a successful transition is the conventional perspective. I expect analysts will continue to rely on it in the near future, even as conditions change and in the wake of successful employment of a campaigning style of governing by the Clinton administration after the 1994 election.

What are the realities of the conventional perspective that serve as tests of the contemporary transition? The following points are drawn from the analysis contained in these chapters. Based as they are on the wisdom and observations of those participating in campaigns and transitions, the lessons are presumably useful to future presidential candidates and their aides.[1]

Presidents-elect arrive in Washington with a background and operating style that help to explain their behavior and approach during the transition. This reality aids in identifying the strengths and weaknesses of presidents-elect in meeting the tests of the standard transition. Those like Nixon, whose whole career was Washington-based, can be expected to meet those standards. Those like Reagan, who was staff-dependent and experienced in managing a large government, can be expected to hire those familiar with what is expected. Those like Carter and Clinton, unexpected winners lacking Washington experience, face a significant challenge in meeting the tests of the conventional perspective. Among the problems faced by the outsiders is the loss of time, a precious asset, in having to acquaint themselves with the standard expectations. One implication of this reality is that the capacity of candidates to meet the tests of the conventional transition may be known well in advance, and thus hard-headed analysis by them should identify the problems to be corrected.

Political conditions may produce presidential candidates with limited stature and presidents-elect unprepared to effect a conventional transition. It is a fair reading of history to suggest that Watergate yielded the Carter candidacy by encouraging a candidate from outside Washington, and the successful Persian Gulf War yielded the Clinton candidacy by discouraging more credible Democratic candidates. Neither Carter nor Clinton could rely on national standing as an asset in the transition. Further, lacking stature, they were likely to be subjected to greater scrutiny in official Washington by those uncertain of their abilities and intentions.

Presidents-elect who win convincingly with a clear message and collateral support for their party in Congress have an advantage in effecting the conventional transition. Of the four presidents receiving special attention in this book, Reagan clearly had the greatest advantage by reason of his election. Essentially this reality identifies the ideal conditions for the conventional transition—conditions that encourage talk of a mandate. Whether it can be shown empirically that voters intended to empower a president in that way or not (and it normally cannot be so proved), a strong showing for the president and his party in Congress reassures official Washington and the press, not to mention the president-elect and his staff, that the transition has a theme and a message. In Reagan's case, it also permitted him to withdraw from detailed involvement, allowing his staff to manage the organizational and policy planning aspects of the transition and him to concentrate on broader themes.

Preelection transition planning must be done as though it were unnecessary, even dangerous. One of the eerier aspects of the campaign as preparation for governing is that candidates refrain from revealing that they are planning ahead. This "Dewey superstition" (a reference to Thomas E. Dewey's overconfidence in 1948) is universal and ingrained. No amount of rational argument is persuasive to candidates who, like others, have unsound fears. Therefore preelection planning, which all candidates arrange in some form, must proceed as if it were not occurring. If, as a consequence, the candidate avoids personal involvement in and control of the exercise, the result can be harmful later in the transition itself. Put otherwise, there are benefits for the president-elect in paying attention to preelection planning—in how it is organized and what it is producing.

Preelection planning isolated from the campaign organization invites distracting conflicts after the election. The Dewey superstition may encourage the candidate and his staff to separate the planning and campaign staffs to the extent even of having little coordination between the two. A price will be paid later for this structure as the campaigners come to believe that the planners are positioning themselves for the spoils of victory. However awkward the arrangement, integrating the two organizations through the campaign leadership is preferable. Of course, the less campaign managers are familiar with governing, the more difficult it becomes to effect a workable integration.

Transitions lacking a theme will be given one. The conventional transition is facilitated by a theme or clear set of purposes related to the election. A theme provides an orientation or context within which to evaluate appointments and policy proposals. The question is one of who controls how the new administration is characterized: those managing it or those reporting on and critiquing it.

An assigned theme will have a long shelf life. If others have gone to the trouble of creating a theme from their observations, the theme will then continue to serve as a lens for viewing the new administration. First impressions do make a difference. Thus it was that the failure of the Clinton administration to establish a coherent theme led many reporters and others to fix on diversity as a motif, as well as on such early policy issues as removing the ban on gays in the military. Judgments were rendered that the new team was not ready for "prime time," a view that dominated much of the first term.

Placing campaign workers is a substantial management task in the conventional transition. The growing size and complexity of national campaign organizations leave the president-elect and his closest aides with an enormous placement chore following the election. Many, if not most, campaign staff want positions in the new administration. Funds are now provided, which assist in short-term assignments. But these assignments, too, can lead to expectations of jobs in the new administration. The new team will be judged by how well this placement process is administered. The process may be facilitated by splitting transition management tasks—separating, for example, the task of creating a White House staff from that of dissolving the campaign staff (such as in the Reagan transition).

In solving one problem (placement), transition teams and task forces create other problems. The standard judgment is that transition teams and task forces are inevitable and that they serve the vital postelection function, along with inauguration planning, of placing and paying campaign staff. Many such teams also perform marginally useful transition functions, including the preparation of briefing documents for incoming officials. On the other hand, these interim appointments can promote the expectations of an already anxious and ambitious group of office- and access-seekers. Meanwhile top-level appointments are being made of persons who may then create a structure independent of the temporary transition units for connecting with department or agency bureaucrats and the emerging White House. Many of those in the temporary units (the teams and task forces) understandably wish to be a part of the new structure, again creating the unusual management problem of ensuring that busywork by participants be seen to be of value without its actually interfering with the efforts of the top-level appointees to take over.

The outgoing administration can be helpful, but the new administration has to overcome several impediments in order to take advantage of this potential assistance. Most of those in a position to aid the new administration were not, themselves, involved actively in the campaign. They are genuinely willing to provide useful information to the incoming team, which is understandably skeptical of such offers, especially if they just defeated the incumbent. Further, not everyone in the outgoing group is likely to be cooperative, thus feeding the mistrust of the new team. Clearly it requires experience and savvy to know when and how to realize this potential advantage of accepting assistance from those on their way out.

The press corps tracks the conventional transition from campaigning to governing. The change from candidate to president-elect is accompanied by a change in press coverage. Many of those covering the winning candidate will move to the White House press corps, where they join veteran national reporters. Coverage is adjusted to suit the expectations reporters have of a president-elect as opposed to expectations they had of a candidate. For the most part, these expectations draw from the conventional perspective of the transition.

The press corps primarily engages in straight reporting during the transition. Often referred to as a "honeymoon," straight reporting is an advantage to the president-elect and his new team if they meet the expectations of the conventional transition, that is, one with a coherent theme and proper sequence. To be effective during this time, therefore, a press relations strategy must account for the changes that occur in the press corps and how reporters view the purposes of the transition and how the purposes relate to governing.

These realities are rooted in the standard adaptation from the frenetic, short-term, self-centered campaign to the more composed, longer-term, other-directed governing process. While all transitions are acknowledged to vary with the president-elect and his immediate staff, many experienced observers in the Washington community have rather explicit expectations about how the winner ought now to prepare to serve in the White House. As I have shown, Nixon and Reagan were judged to have done reasonably well by these tests, Carter measurably less so, and Clinton was deficient, even a disaster by some accounts. As a final exercise, I turn to the Clinton case to probe whether there may not be lessons in his deficiency for future transitions.

The important question is this: Was the Clinton transition the first of a new form? If so, how might that form be perfected so as to provide an altered perspective, one with different expectations regarding the passage from campaigning to governing?

The Clinton Case: Preparing to Govern by Campaigning

The transition is a process of introducing and integrating change into institutions, of absorbing what's new into what's there. Stephen Skowronek deals with this basic issue in *The Politics Presidents Make*. The individuality that different persons as presidents exhibit can be disruptive to the communities that the permanent government cultivates.[2] As Skowronek has shown, an important variable in this adaptation is the extent to which the new president is synchronized with public moods, agenda shifts, and governmental evolution. These factors help to shape the expectations that the Washington establishment has of new presidents. If a president-elect tries to move too far beyond these expectations, he opens himself up to substantial criticism. His daring may be unintended, a result more of inexperience, perhaps misunderstanding, than of design. Whatever the explanation, such a performance is bound to induce uncertainty among presidency watchers and draw substantial criticism of the unfamiliar from those comfortable with the prevailing norms.

I believe that Bill Clinton's transition is a case in point. This person from Arkansas was not prepared to become president in the expected way. He was not daring to be different; he did not know how to be the same. I believe the explanation of his behavior is rooted in who he is—his strengths and weaknesses—and how he won. He represents changes in the post–World War II period that have come to affect the presidency, as well as the other institutions of government. This is by way of suggesting that the standard perspective of the transition as outlined in this book is no longer applicable in the same way. Bill Clinton's ineptness in meeting the demands of the standard transition and his emerging proficiency in creating a campaign-oriented governing style will likely alter future expectations of this important passage from candidacy to presidency. However imperfectly, the Clinton style of serving reflects change and will have an impact on future presidencies.

The personal skills of Bill Clinton, the first president born in the post–World War II era, are well publicized. He is extremely bright, an avid student of public policy issues, extraordinarily personable and empathetic, an accomplished orator, and compliant negotiator. He is a public person. Less well advertised, yet complementary to those listed, are his abilities as a contemporary analyst and director of public opinion. In his revealing book about "winning the presidency in the nineties," Clinton White House political consultant Dick Morris specified his client's skills in reading polls and reviewing advertisements. While reporting on the 1995–96 period, Morris made it clear that the traits were long-standing. All presidents want to know about their status in the polls. According to Morris, Clinton supplemented interest with expertise:

> After two hours of reviewing each question, I realized that Bill Clinton's need for the micromanagement of polling had not lessened as his responsibilities had increased. . . .
>
> Then came the president's real objection: 'If you control each aspect of the media and the polling, how can I control the process? How can I get different options and choices? How do I keep control? . . .
>
> I answered, 'You'll keep control, total control, the same way you have for seventeen years with me. . . . You're better at reading polls than any pollster I know. I'll work with you the way I always have. I'll clear everything with you constantly. I'll talk with you when we develop the questionnaires for the polls, when we get the results back, when we script the ads, when we test them, and before we run them. You'll be right there every minute.' "[3]

Possibly more surprising was the president's interest and involvement in the campaign advertisements that were so much a part of Clinton's political recovery following the 1994 election.

> The president became the day-to-day operational director of our TV-ad campaign. He worked over every script, watched each ad, ordered changes in every visual presentation, and decided which ads would run when and where. . . . The ads became not the slick creations of admen but the work of the president himself. . . . Every line of every

ad came under his informed, critical, and often meddlesome gaze. Every ad was *his* ad. . . .

"Remember how we did it in Arkansas?" he asked me at a strategy meeting while the others looked on curiously. "We'd give the facts to rebut the negative ad first, always the facts up front, and then we'd counterpunch with our own negatives."

Clinton always loved the actual process of writing and designing ads. As involved as he was in the '95 and '96 ad campaigns, he missed actually sitting at the table, the way he had in Arkansas, and participating in the process. Once, as he wistfully contemplated the start of the actual campaign, he said, "I'll miss writing all those rebuttal ads. You'll have all the fun."[4]

Here, then, is a politician with rare talents. He not only *thinks* he can manage campaign activities, he is determined to do so and is familiar with many of the basics. His devotion to campaigning and other public exercises is unprecedented, thereby raising doubts that he could be expected to conduct a conventional transition upon being elected in 1992. Bill Clinton in person represented a change that had yet to be fully absorbed in the working government or acknowledged by presidency watchers: that of the greater publicness of agenda setting and policymaking. Thus Clinton and his most intimate aides (not including Morris in 1992) lacked the incentive and the experience to effect a conventional transition from campaigning to governing. They may also have questioned the relevance of any such passage. Yet they were not prepared to substitute a crisply defined and reality-tested alternative process, one so well designed for the effective implementation of campaign-oriented governing as to impress or persuade official Washington.

And so the transition was judged to be a failure. It disappointed those expecting the standard creation of an administration. It disoriented those seeking to report on and interpret what was happening. Big mistakes were made, as gauged by the conventional transition. It is apparent now, however, that the most important shortcoming was that the Clinton team was not experienced or knowledgeable enough to effect a different type of transition (nor, perhaps, was the Washington establishment prepared to accept any such change). The newcomers represented change but lacked a sophisticated strategy for implementing it in a manner that would be convincing even to friends of the new administration. Lacking a convincing rationale for a new order, most interpreters declared the transition incomplete. And so it was, as tested both by the standard criteria and by its not having offered an alternative model suited to the new president's preferred governing style. The case was further complicated by the fact that the Clinton team tried to do both: meet the standard criteria while preparing to govern differently. Yet they lacked the experience and desire to accomplish the first and the finesse and knowledge to accomplish the second.

This analysis has concentrated on the period between the election and the inauguration as a time for making adjustments from campaigning to governing. Clearly the transition for the Clinton team would extend beyond that period, given their instincts for integrating campaigning into governing. Detailing this extended transition is a subject meriting separate treatment. Suffice it here to state that there was strong resistance (from a variety of quarters) to the Clinton style during the first two years even as there were adaptations to a more public, campaign-oriented policy process (most dramatically illustrated by the battle over health care reform, where opponents battled hard for public support, relying on television ads).

It was with the loss of Democratic majorities in Congress that the Clinton administration refined its campaigning style of governing. Freed of its interdependent relationship with congressional Democrats and, indeed, of the responsibility for setting the agenda, the president and selected aides concentrated on designing and refining an altered approach to governing.[5]

What are the basics in this revised perspective on transitions? First, the purpose itself is altered. The shift is from campaigning for office to campaigning for policy. The conversion from the campaign is less in style and method than in objective. Accordingly, political consultants and pollsters do not recede in favor of those with experience in traditional governing. Rather they have a prominent place in the daily functioning of the White House. One test, then, during the transition is the extent to which the president-elect is able to integrate these specialists into the organization without disrupting the functioning of the regular White House staff. Advice given from the conventional perspective for the president-elect to play a limited public role is replaced by that from the revised perspective for the president-elect to bolster his public status on policy issues. His professional reputation is enhanced less by his experience and work in government (though these attributes are hardly irrelevant) than by his demonstrated ability to communicate with the public. Precursors for all of the developments were evident in the Reagan White House, as managed by Michael K. Deaver; all were accelerated substantially in the Clinton White House.

Richard E. Neustadt, among others, has identified estimates of public prestige for the president by other power holders to be among the potential sources of strength.[6] And Samuel Kernell has recorded that "going public" has become a staple of presidential influence, even a substitute for bargaining.[7] Public status in the Clinton revised perspective for the contemporary transition is a substantial modification of these renditions. It is policy specific, issue responsive, interactive, and continuous. The public status strategy is applied at the formative and expressive phases of public opinion. Polls are taken continuously in regard to major issues as well as daily concerns of various groups. Influenced by poll results, policy discourse is oriented to these matters, using the bully pulpit of the presidency and, as needed, television advertisements, paid for with privately raised funds, to gain support for the president's position and record. Response to opponents is instantaneous, thus requiring careful preparation to anticipate counter positions.

Hugh Heclo observes that campaign-oriented presidents are a vestige of a larger phenomenon. "Not just presidents but everyone with an active interest in what happens in Washington now engages in continuous efforts to orchestrate, amplify, and inject the presumptive voices of the American people . . . into the formulation and management of national policy. This is the permanent campaign."[8] Thus there are forces contributing to the changing role of the president in the separated system. Split-party government has been a common feature in recent decades—80 percent of the time from 1968 to 1998—thereby limiting a president's political status. Debt and deficits have dominated the domestic agenda since the 1980s, thereby defining policy options. A revolution has been wrought in communications, information dissemination, and the technology of polling, thereby facilitating public debate of policy issues.

Yet the FDR model of the policy-active, politically advantaged president lives on to shape the expectations of many. With expectations high, status weakened, powers shared, options limited, and job approval tested constantly, presidents are naturally tempted to yield to a more public-oriented strategy for enhancing their standing. Presidents vary in their preference for and their ability to engage in a more public-oriented style of governing. Bill Clinton has that talent and likes using it. With the loss of Congress in 1994, conditions were suited to his outside style. He was given the time to travel, prepare responses, and raise money; he was released from responsibility of working with Congress; and he could justify a change in staff operations to expedite a more campaign-oriented governing mode.

As practiced by Clinton, the public status–campaign-oriented style included the development of an advantage not previously identified by students of the presidency. I call it "voice." Not satisfied in public debate simply to say no by vetoing congressional Republican initiatives, President Clinton developed a positive message in regard to lesser matters. Voice features constant monitoring of the interests and concerns of ordinary Americans, sympathetic exposure of these matters in a "family values" setting, exhortation for a community solution (typically but not always involving government), liberal use of executive orders and other presidential prerogatives that avoid congressional participation, and little deference to jurisdictional boundaries between public and private or levels of government. That an issue might be judged outside the president's usual domain is no barrier to his declarations. Examples include school uniforms, curfews, reading specialists, cops living next door, Internet development, flex time, v-chips, 911 use, and hospital stays, to name a few (he made forty separate proposals in his speech accepting the nomination in 1996). Properly done, there is reason almost every day to reinforce the president's presence in national, state, and local public affairs.

The point of these developments for present purposes is simply that President Clinton has refined a campaign-oriented style of governing that may well influence the next transition. He has found an outlet for his activist ambitions and a reason to maintain a public presence. The consequence is an enhancement of his influence in the separated system in exactly the manner identified by Neustadt: perception of his legitimacy and backing by other power holders.

Future presidents may now be expected to organize and prepare staffs and make appointments so as to campaign effectively for policy and political standing. Political consultants, the "hired guns," don't seek new clients in this revised transition. They have new challenges in serving their candidate, who has now become president. Pollsters do not retire. Their data provide evidence for where and how the continuing campaign is going, as well as which group is focusing on what.[9] White House staff is as oriented to the outside for building pressure within as it is to the inside for generating a record to display without.

The test of an effective transition in the new conditions is how well all of this is managed in the weeks after the election, perhaps with displays of its workability so as to hit the ground campaigning. The conventional work of the White House has to be done too, but in this new context. Clinton may have failed on both scores in 1992, but his experience since, especially in 1995–96, surely vindicates his initial reluctance to forget the campaign mode. It is the Clinton practice since 1994 that the next president will have to strive to incorporate into conventional arrangements for his own transition. Clinton's presidency, therefore, is genuinely "transitional" throughout.

From Campaigning to Governing

Transitions are themselves in transition because the presidency is changing both in how persons get elected and how they serve. Informed observers of our government and politics have firmly in mind what constitutes a successful transition. Basic to their views is a clear distinction between campaigning and governing, accompanied by guidelines for ending one activity and starting the other. But each of these activities has evolved in response to political, institutional, and policy developments and, further, they have become less distinct. As for campaigns, technicians supplement, sometimes supplant, politicians as strategists. The president's postelection team includes many specialists from the election industry, the so-called hired guns. Those subscribing to the conventional perspective have a healthy skepticism about the positive effect for governing of presidents-elect continuing to consort with such people. The hired guns know about campaigning. By the conventional perspective, they are dysfunctional for governing and should go away after the election is over. Presidents-elect should turn to experienced Washington hands and establish ties to other elected officials in Congress and at other levels of government (persons presidential candidates used to campaign with, thus creating an interdependency useful later in governing). That the political consultants do not depart in favor of those with Washington experience is explained in large part by changes in governing, in doing the job of being president.

The changes in governing are just as obvious as those in campaigning, but less recognized as affecting the transition. The developments themselves are dramatic: frequent split-party control between the White House and Congress; emergence of "mega" reform issues like welfare, trade, and health care; concentration of policymaking in various budgetary vehicles (resolutions, reconciliation packages, debt limit extensions); greater public and group participation in policymaking; talk radio and other forums for policy debate; and Internet developments, with the instant availability of documents and commentary and access for the public to government institutions. Many observers lament these developments. For some, elections should settle a policy debate that takes place during the campaign. The winners should then effect a smooth transition, during which they send signals through statements, appointments, and organization as to how they will govern. Alas, voters have not been so accommodating. Mixed messages are sent even when one party wins at both ends of Pennsylvania Avenue (as in 1976 and 1992). And presidents have learned how to manage, even win reelection, under conditions of split-party control (in fact, only under those conditions in the post–World War II period).[10]

Since history seldom reverses itself, it is predictable that if campaigning is changing and governing is changing, then the transition from the new campaign to the altered governing process will also undergo a transformation. Future presidents will prepare to govern more publicly from the start, seeking to integrate public opinion specialists into the White House staff not merely for their polling results but also for input in policymaking decisions. Anxious to establish and enhance their public status in a more communal style of governing, presidents will play to the outside. What some call the "permanent campaign" will become an important feature of governing, one that will invite imitation by other power holders.[11] And whereas split-party results may have contributed to these developments, we may expect single-party transitions to exhibit similar patterns.

The use of political consultants is not new, nor is their being brought into the White House. Their status beyond campaigning and into governing has grown and matured during the Clinton administration, however. "Going public" is not new either, but it has been modified from a strategy of presidential leadership to a more general manner of public policymaking. Understandably, these developments will have an impact on future transitions to the extent of requiring revisions in the conventional perspective about how a president should prepare to serve. A revision is not a substitution, however. Many of the same expectations will hold in regard to the sequence of appointments, the specification of a theme, linking up with Congress and the bureaucracy, and developing a strategy for press relations. Application of these rules and lessons, however, will occur in the altered context of governing having become a more public and participatory enterprise, even as voting turnout remains low.

It is also worth emphasizing that the Clinton transition in 1992 satisfied neither the conventional perspective nor its revision. It was properly dubbed the worst. At the same time, however, Clinton and his aides were the first to reflect so *completely* the lessening of the distinction between campaigning and governing (with the Reagan White House a precursor). Therefore we await the clear specification of the revised rules that will come with experience, not the musings of outsiders or the haranguing of those clinging to the canons of the standard transition. Meanwhile one may expect future presidential candidates to take notes on the governing adjustments made by the Clinton White House during its first full term as revealing of the changes likely to affect future transitions.

Finally, this question: is a campaign style of governing a positive development for a democracy? If so, then surely the transition should aid in preparing the president-elect and his team to do it effectively. If not, then there is a larger problem to be solved, given developments in recent decades. Dick Morris, Clinton's resident political consultant and polling guru for the 1996 election, acknowledged the importance of the question and responded this way:

> The emphasis on polling . . . naturally gives rise to the question of whether it has become a substitute for leadership. Voters have never much liked the idea that candidates merely spout what pollsters have told them the public wants to hear. It smacks of opportunism. But Clinton used polling for a different purpose: as a tool for governing, as a technique to facilitate progress in a democracy. Polling for him was not a onetime test of opinion. It was a way of conducting an extensive dialogue with the public.[12]

In his statement, Morris offers the most constructive interpretation, one most favorable to him and his client. That is to be expected. What is of special interest, however, is his acknowledgment of the central function of polling for governing, which, of course, he views as positive. Morris also noted that: "When the polls indicated that his [Clinton's] position on an issue was unpopular, he would usually ask for a study of how he could convince people of his point of view."[13] This statement suggests a presidency that on many major issues governs on the basis of a continuous testing of public attitudes.

In fact, my question has roots in one of the oldest dilemmas of representative government: whether to serve as the delegate or the trustee. The trustee preserves the distinction between campaigning and governing; delegates are much less the purists, seeking throughout their service to mirror the interests and concerns of their constituents. The so-called permanent campaign can be viewed as the constant search for what the public wants, perhaps informed by political leaders eager to continue to serve. We normally apply these representational forms to legislators, not presidents, who lack a constituency in the usual sense. A strong case can be made, however, that Jimmy Carter was the trustee, Bill Clinton the delegate. As a sign of the times, it is relevant that the trustee lost badly in his reelection effort, while the delegate won handsomely.

Presidents-elect in the twenty-first century will prepare for office acknowledging many of the standard realities identified by those experienced observers quoted in this book. But they will also integrate the lessons drawn from the transition judged worst in modern memory; even more, perhaps from its efforts to recover. Future presidents will not be expected to prepare to serve as pure delegates; they will, however, have to ready themselves for a wider and more active public role to be effective in policymaking.

I conclude with my opening statement: persons become presidents. I am impressed with the manner in which these persons become magnified through the passages from candidate to nominee to president-elect to president. Their voices are amplified through ceaseless coverage and with the talk of those now speaking for them; their musings are reported as future policy; they are "handled"; they travel as the group they are becoming; they are seldom alone and increasingly with us electronically. A person-oriented contrivance materializes before our very eyes—for example, the Reagan presidency; the Clinton presidency—one charged to manage a public-oriented government; one that changes through the period of service and that will disappear once out of office. The sensitive and challenging task of fashioning this improvisation is expected to take place quickly and efficiently even as it is made more difficult to accomplish.

I do not anticipate any significant interruptions to these developments in the ways of doing our politics. If anything, there is a stronger than ever public mood to have outsiders serve in government, with term limits. Therefore transitions will continue to be frequent and likely to trace inexactly the rigorous demands of a citizen-led separated government. New persons as presidents can benefit from the experience of others only if they grasp that their own ordeal is singular.

NOTES

Chapter 1

1. Several scholars make this point regarding presidency-centered analysis, stressing the realities of the separated system. See, for example, Richard E. Neustadt, *Presidential Power: The Politics of Leadership* (Wiley, 1960); Charles O. Jones, *The Presidency in a Separated System* (Brookings, 1994); Mark A. Peterson, *Legislating Together: The White House and Capitol Hill from Eisenhower to Reagan* (Harvard University Press, 1990); and Michael Foley and John E. Owens, *Congress and the Presidency: Institutional Politics in a Separated System* (Manchester, UK: Manchester University Press, 1996).

2. Many fine studies and reports describe, analyze, and prescribe for the transition from one president to the next, and most of them stress organizational issues. See, for example, Laurin L. Henry, *Presidential Transitions* (Brookings, 1960); Carl M. Brauer, *Presidential Transitions: Eisenhower through Reagan* (Oxford University Press, 1986); Stephen Hess, *Organizing the Presidency,* rev. ed. (Brookings, 1988); James P. Pfiffner, *The Strategic Presidency: Hitting the Ground Running,* 2d ed. rev. (University Press of Kansas, 1996); and several reports by the Brookings Institution and the National Academy of Public Administration. Emphasizing organizational matters is not necessarily devoid of policy preferences. For example, a memorandum to the president-elect entitled "Harnessing Process to Purpose" (1992) from the Commission on Government Renewal (sponsored and published by the Carnegie Endowment for International Peace and the Institute for International Economics) offered many organizational recommendations reflecting the policy preferences of the commission.

3. Samuel Kernell, *Going Public: New Strategies of Presidential Leadership*, 3d ed. (Washington: CQ Press, 1997), p. 57.

4. Actually, the average service for all presidents to Clinton is five years. Just two presidents since 1951, Dwight D. Eisenhower and Reagan, served two full terms; two others were elected to two terms: Nixon and Clinton (currently serving). There are three two-term, same-party presidencies in the postwar period (Franklin D. Roosevelt and Harry S. Truman, John F. Kennedy and Johnson, Nixon and Ford), and one three-term, same-party presidency (Reagan and Bush). Of all presidents, just eleven of forty (to Clinton) completed two full terms (with Franklin D. Roosevelt serving three plus and Grover Cleveland serving two nonconsecutive terms). Of these eleven, five completed two terms in the first forty-eight years—Washington, Jefferson, Madison, Monroe, and Jackson—when there were but seven presidents total. That leaves just six presidents serving out two (or three in FDR's case) terms from 1837 to 1992. Three other presidents were reelected but failed to serve out their second term (Lincoln, McKinley, and Nixon).

5. The incumbency return rate fell below 90 percent just once between 1974 and 1996 (at 88 percent in 1992); likewise the reelection rate as a percentage of House membership fell below 80 percent just once in that same period (also in 1992). Norman J. Ornstein, Thomas E. Mann, and Michael J. Malbin, *Vital Statistics on Congress, 1997–1998* (Washington: Congressional Quarterly, 1998), p. 61, table 2-7.

6. This view distinguishes my emphasis from that of other transition studies that focus on the postelection period and into the first year of the administration. Pfiffner defines transition this way: "In reality the shift of power between administrations extends from the election until the new president has established his control over the government" (p. 3). My interest here is more in the preparation mentally, politically, and organizationally to assume office on January 20, the day that, according to President Eisenhower, presidential authority is transferred (cited in Pfiffner, *Strategic Presidency*, p. 1).

7. Nicholas Johnson, "Questions They Never Get Asked: How Would the Candidates Govern?" *Washington Post*, July 12, 1987, p. C7.

8. Richard E. Neustadt, "Memorandum to James Baker," December 1, 1980, p. 1. Copy sent to author and quoted with permission of Neustadt and Baker.

9. Sometimes these lame-duck sessions happened with substantial turnover in Congress and a new president having been elected. Particularly dramatic cases in this century occurred in 1912–13, 1920–21, and 1932–33.

10. That is, after Congress established a uniform date for elections. Before that time, states varied in the time set for the election, with some even holding contests in odd-numbered years since members would not meet anyway until December of the odd-numbered year. See *Guide to Congress*, 3d ed. (Washington: Congressional Quarterly, 1982), p. 636.

11. Carl Brent Swisher, *American Constitutional Development*, 2d ed. (Houghton Mifflin, 1954), p. 722.

12. One might well ask why the change in dates could not have been effected through ordinary legislation, given that the inauguration date of March 4 was originally set by an act of Congress and Article I, Section 4 provides that Congress may set a different day for meeting (and had exercised this discretion in the past). The explanation is found in the term lengths provided for in the Constitution: two years

for representatives, six years for senators, four years for the president and vice president. To change the dates would, perforce, shorten the terms of the sitting members. Therefore, a constitutional amendment was needed to legitimize the reduction in term length of all officials elected in 1932. Edward S. Corwin, *The Constitution of the United States of America: Analysis and Interpretation* (Government Printing Office, 1964), p. 1371.

13. Normally, however, the old Congress does not meet during the period between the election and the inauguration.

14. Lame-duck sessions are summarized in Congressional Quarterly, *Guide To Congress*, 3d ed., p. 971. The lame-duck session in 1994 dealt with just one measure: the General Agreement on Tariffs and Trade (GATT).

15. The letter is contained in *Presidential Transition Act of 1962*, H. Rept. 87-2432, 87 Cong. 2 sess. (GPO, September 19, 1962), pp. 7–10.

16. *Presidential Transition Act of 1963*, Hearing before the House Committee on Government Operations, 88 Cong. 1 sess. (GPO, 1963), p. 11. See also the testimony of Herbert E. Alexander, who served as the executive director of the president's commission, pp. 21–25. The only slightly contentious issue that arose during the hearings was a concern about paying the "carfare" and other expenses of job seekers.

17. A total of $72,000 was provided to Hubert H. Humphrey under the Presidential Transition Act. Comptroller General of the United States, *Report to the House Committee on Government Operations: Audit of Ford-Carter Presidential Transition Expenditures*, December 23, 1977, p. i.

18. Ibid.

19. *Presidential Transition Act Amendments*, H. Rept. 94-1442, 94 Cong. 2 sess. (GPO, 1976), pp. 2–3.

20. 102 Stat. 985.

21. The Reagan transition in 1980 established a private corporation, the Presidential Transition Foundation, to solicit funds. These funds were audited by a private accounting firm. Outside support was needed since the number of personnel involved totaled over 1,500. Just 311 of these staff were paid salaries from Transition Act funds. Presumably others were paid from monies raised by the foundation. As explained in letter from Elmer B. Staats to Jack Brooks, Chairman, House Committee on Government Operations, March 2, 1981.

22. *Presidential Transitions Effectiveness Act*, S. Rept. 100-317, 100 Cong. 2 sess. (GPO, 1988), p. 6.

23. Ibid., pp. 6–10.

24. Paul C. Light was active in this transition reform package as a staff person for the Senate Committee on Governmental Affairs. He describes the work on the legislation, with special attention to the preelection planning funds in *Forging Legislation* (Norton, 1992), pp. 133–35. As he observes: "Despite allotting $200 million in public financing for the presidential candidates, the federal government gave absolutely nothing for [pre-election] transition planning" (p. 134).

25. *Presidential Transitions Effectiveness Act*, pp. 18–21.

26. Ibid., p. 19.

27. Ibid., p. 20. However important the problem cited by Eizenstat, the corporate CEO analogy is a weak one, given a change in partisan control of a highly political office.

28. The growth was due primarily to additional entitlements and to a major increase in regulations. Much of this increase resulted in a heavier workload for state and local governments, where employment more than doubled; federal government employment actually decreased during this time. See U.S. Department of Commerce, Bureau of the Census, *Statistical Abstract of the United States, 1998* (GPO, 1997).

29. There also may be important effects of split-party government that extend to single-party government. That is, a congressional majority party may, under split-party conditions, get used to opposing the president, thus presenting a new president of the same party with a significant challenge in working with Congress.

30. Stephen E. Ambrose, *Nixon: Ruin and Recovery, 1973–1990,* vol. 3 (Simon and Schuster, 1991), p. 14.

31. In Clinton's case, the relatively low turnover of cabinet secretaries during the first term resulted in a large number resigning after the election. Of special importance were the shifts in foreign and national security policy, where all major positions changed hands.

32. See Michael Nelson, ed., *Guide to the Presidency,* 2d ed., vol. 2 (Washington: Congressional Quarterly, 1996), pp. 1690–92.

33. Neustadt, "Memorandum to James Baker," pp. 8–9.

34. I have employed the male reference because to date there has not been a female president. I expect one will be elected early in the next century. I foresee that the problems encountered and the lessons learned are mostly gender neutral.

35. Richard E. Neustadt, *Presidential Power and the Modern Presidents: The Politics of Leadership from Roosevelt to Reagan* (Free Press, 1990), p. 248.

Chapter 2

1. Stimson Bullitt, *To Be a Politician,* rev. ed. (Yale University Press, 1977), pp. 21, 33.

2. Theodore H. White referred to "the principle of Legitimacy in American Presidential politics." His reference was primarily to the succession of "great chieftains of war and diplomacy, men who have previously sat in the Cabinets in Washington, men who have already inherited the White House as Vice-Presidents." Though the concept of stature implies legitimacy, the succession referred to by White no longer appears applicable. *The Making of the President, 1960* (New York: Atheneum, 1961), p. 64.

3. The contrast with an incoming Congress is striking. Members are sworn in with little ceremony, with family and friends in attendance.

4. There are other considerations as well, such as the capacity to raise the necessary funds. The fund-raising factor, however, is less directly related to how a transi-

tion might be managed than the other matters (though it suggests an organizational facility that is relevant).

5. Paul T. David, "The Presidential Nominations," in Paul T. David, ed., *The Presidential Election and Transition, 1960–1961* (Brookings, 1961), p. 4.

6. Richard M. Nixon, *Six Crises* (Doubleday, 1962), p. 296.

7. Ibid., p. 299.

8. Ibid., pp. 300–01.

9. Bush appointed five former Reagan cabinet secretaries—three of whom were appointed to their positions by Reagan the year before Bush's election; two others served in different cabinet positions for Reagan. See Charles O. Jones, *The Presidency in a Separated System* (Brookings, 1994), pp. 110–11.

10. Carl M. Brauer, *Presidential Transitions: Eisenhower through Reagan* (Oxford University Press, 1986), p. 127.

11. Stephen E. Ambrose, *Nixon: The Triumph of a Politician, 1962–1972*, vol. 2 (Simon and Schuster, 1989), p. 13.

12. Richard M. Nixon, *RN: The Memoirs of Richard Nixon* (New York: Grosset and Dunlap, 1978), p. 248.

13. Ibid., p. 250. One call from his upstairs neighbor was for another purpose. Rockefeller asked Nixon up to seek his support in exchange for Rockefeller's support should the convention deadlock (p. 251).

14. See Ambrose, *Nixon,* pp. 38–47. See also Theodore H. White, *The Making of the President, 1968* (New York: Atheneum, 1969), p. 48.

15. White, *Making of the President, 1968*, p. 45.

16. Ibid., p. 50.

17. In his memoirs, Nixon describes how he expected a late move by President Johnson in 1966 to influence the election. Johnson met with President Nguyen Van Thieu of South Vietnam in Manila, issuing a communiqué. Nixon crafted a critical response that was printed in full in the *New York Times*. Johnson replied in a subsequent news conference, further acknowledging Nixon's prominence on the major issue of the time. See Nixon, *RN*, pp. 273–76.

18. Ibid., p. 279.

19. As quoted in William Safire, *Before the Fall: An Inside View of the Pre-Watergate White House* (Doubleday, 1975), p. 43.

20. Nixon, *RN,* pp. 278, 279.

21. White, *Making of the President, 1968,* pp. 59, 61. In fact, Nixon wrote just two articles for *Reader's Digest* in 1967: one eulogizing John Foster Dulles (July 1967), the other on racial issues, prompted by urban riots (October 1967).

22. Ambrose, *Nixon,* p. 106.

23. Nixon, *RN,* p. 280.

24. Robert B. Semple Jr., "Nixon Gives Views on Aid to Negroes and the Poor," *New York Times,* December 20, 1967, p. A22.

25. Nixon also ran twice for the House of Representatives and once for the Senate. Though not quite matching Clinton's total number of campaigns, he did have substantially more national election experience than Clinton.

26. Nixon, *RN,* pp. 272, 287. Of course, he had also visited many of these states

as part of the "Congress '66" effort. Nixon was still holding out the chance that he might not make the run, but his visits at least ensured that many governors would remain uncommitted until he made his decision.

27. White, *Making of the President, 1960,* p. 64.

28. Ambrose, *Nixon,* p. 104.

29. Nixon, *RN,* pp. 285.

30. Ibid., p. 297.

31. As recorded in Congressional Quarterly, *Guide to U. S. Elections* (Washington: Congressional Quarterly, 1975), p. 345.

32. Martin Schram, *Running for President, 1976: The Carter Campaign* (New York: Stein and Day, 1977), p. 6.

33. Jules Witcover, *Marathon: The Pursuit of the Presidency, 1972–1976* (Viking, 1977), p. 143. Rosalynn Carter reports this typical conversation during her campaigning: "I'm Mrs. Jimmy Carter. My husband's running for President." "President of what?" "President of the United States." "You've got to be kidding." *First Lady from Plains* (New York: Fawcett Gold Medal, 1984), p. 106.

34. Jimmy Carter himself observed in his book, *Why Not the Best?,* that he "lost my feeling of awe about presidents" when, as governor, he met Richard Nixon, Spiro Agnew, and several presidential hopefuls. (Bantam Books, 1976), p. 158.

35. Burton I. Kaufman, *The Presidency of James Earl Carter, Jr.* (University Press of Kansas, 1993), p. 15.

36. Ibid.

37. Carter, *Why Not the Best?* p. 159.

38. Witcover, *Marathon,* pp. 106–07.

39. Carter, *Why Not the Best?* p. 159. See the account of these meetings in Betty Glad, *Jimmy Carter: In Search of the Great White House* (Norton, 1980), pp. 207–13. "Generally, he was advised to run against Washington" (p. 211).

40. Quoted in Witcover, *Marathon,* p. 111.

41. Even still, he was second to Morris Udall, who announced on November 23. Two other potential candidates withdrew earlier: Kennedy on September 23 and Minnesota Senator Walter Mondale (later to run with Carter) on November 21. See Charles O. Jones, *The Trusteeship Presidency: Jimmy Carter and the United States Congress* (Louisiana State University Press, 1988), p. 27.

42. The text of the announcement is printed in *The Presidential Campaign, 1976,* vol. 1, pt. 1 (Government Printing Office, 1978), pp. 3–11.

43. *Atlanta Constitution,* December 13, 1974, p. 19a.

44. Glad, *Jimmy Carter,* p. 488.

45. Schram, *Running for President,* p. 377.

46. As printed in *The Presidential Campaign,* pp. 1–2.

47. David S. Broder, "Georgia Governor Declares '76 Bid," *Washington Post,* December 13, 1974, pp. A1, A9. Broder also reported that Carter acknowledged that he would accept the vice-presidential spot on the Democratic ticket, though he had no interest in the vice presidency——a rather unusual statement for a newly announced presidential candidate.

48. Wayne King, "Georgia's Gov. Carter Enters Democratic Race for President,"

New York Times, December 13, 1974, p. A18.

49. Witcover, *Marathon,* p. 529.

50. His win was very much like that of Kennedy in 1960, which was also centered in these same regions. The congressional results were similar.

51. See White, *Making of the President, 1968,* pp. 239–46. Reagan headed the California delegation and received 182 delegates on the first ballot (won by Nixon with 692 delegates).

52. Lou Cannon, *Reagan* (Putnam's, 1982), p. 191. Cannon also reports that, in any event, Nancy Reagan was not interested in living "the life of a senator's wife in Washington."

53. Quoted in Michael K. Deaver with Mickey Herskowitz, *Behind the Scenes* (Morrow, 1987), p. 73.

54. Lou Cannon, *President Reagan: The Role of a Lifetime* (Simon and Schuster, 1991), p. 35.

55. Ronald Reagan, *An American Life* (Simon and Schuster, 1990), pp. 147, 150.

56. Cannon, *Reagan,* pp. 194, 198. Reagan even briefly considered a third-party bid (p. 197).

57. Ibid., p. 198.

58. Deaver, *Behind the Scenes,* pp. 63–64. Deaver states that this incident occurred in January 1976—clearly an error since Reagan had, by then, already made his announcement.

59. Martin Anderson, *Revolution* (Harcourt Brace Jovanovich, 1988), p. 43.

60. Ibid., p. 45.

61. Reagan, *American Life,* p. 203.

62. Ibid., p. 204.

63. Reagan was critical of Carter in this regard: "The problem with Carter is that he tries to do everything at once and he tries to do too much of it himself." Quoted in Anderson, *Revolution,* pp. 56–57.

64. Reagan, *American Life,* p. 161.

65. Lou Cannon, "Reagan Announces, Urges Strength at Home, Abroad," *Washington Post,* November 14, 1979, pp. A1, A2. The speech was judged to have a "more moderate tone" so as to attract "middle-of-the-road voters." Robert Lindsey, "Reagan, Entering Presidency Race, Calls for North American 'Accord,' " *New York Times,* November 14, 1979, pp. A1, A24.

66. Theodore H. White, *America in Search of Itself: The Making of the President 1956–1980* (Harper and Row, 1982), p. 249. See also Cannon's description of Nancy Reagan's role in the 1980 campaign organization in *Reagan,* pp. 65–87.

67. White, *America in Search of Itself,* p. 249. Also see accounts in Anderson, *Revolution,* pp. 328–31; Cannon, *Reagan,* pp. 227–40; Deaver, *Behind the Scenes,* pp. 85–102; and Edwin Meese III, *With Reagan: The Inside Story* (Washington: Regnery Gateway, 1992), pp. 3–13.

68. Reagan, *American Life,* pp. 213–14. Cannon explains that Nancy Reagan was crucial in preparing the decision. "She knew what it took to get him to make a painful decision" (*Reagan,* p. 255).

69. Cannon, *President Reagan,* p. 70.

70. Later Ford would help Reagan in another way. He was asked to run with Reagan as his vice-presidential candidate. He declined but did think about it. The effect was to make George Bush a second choice for Reagan, thus avoiding a potentially serious convention floor battle. Charles O. Jones, "Nominating 'Carter's Favorite Opponent': The Republicans in 1980," in Austin Ranney, ed., *The American Elections of 1980* (Washington: American Enterprise Institute, 1981), pp. 77–78, 94–96.

71. James Reston, "Carter's Secret Weapon," *New York Times*, March 21, 1980, p. A27.

72. Jones, "Nominating 'Carter's Favorite Opponent,' " p. 63.

73. Ibid., p. 90.

74. David Maraniss, *First in His Class: A Biography of Bill Clinton* (Simon and Schuster, 1995), p. 451.

75. Peter Goldman and others, *Quest for the Presidency, 1992* (Texas A & M University Press, 1994), p. 33.

76. Maraniss, *First in His Class*, pp. 436–37.

77. Ibid., pp. 442–43.

78. For an account, see ibid., pp. 444–47.

79. Goldman and others, *Quest for the Presidency*, p. 37.

80. Maraniss, *First in His Class*, p. 452.

81. Goldman and others, *Quest for the Presidency*, p. 38. Maraniss reports that the decision by Clinton to run was quite tortured. Rumors were rampant, including one that his wife, Hillary, might run instead. Maraniss also notes that Hillary was, herself, surprised by his last-minute declaration to run (*First in His Class*, pp. 452–53).

82. Maraniss, *First in His Class*, p. 456.

83. Ibid., p. 460. Goldman and others report that Frank Greer "had helped seed the crowd with claqueurs for Clinton" (*Quest for the Presidency*, p. 40).

84. Goldman and others, *Quest for the Presidency*, p. 39. Senator Charles Robb, Democrat of Virginia, was another, but he was experiencing personal problems and a bitter party squabble with Governor Douglas Wilder.

85. From an ABC News/*Washington Post* survey as reported in "Public Opinion and Demographic Report," *American Enterprise*, vol. 2 (September–October 1991), p. 91. By contrast, the mean ABC/*Washington Post* results for four readings on Bush's handling of the job were approval 76 percent, disapproval 21 percent.

86. An ABC News/*Washington Post* survey as reported in "Public Opinion and Demographic Report," *American Enterprise*, vol. 2 (November–December 1991), p. 97.

87. As reported in "Public Opinion and Demographic Report," *American Enterprise,* vol. 2 (May–June 1991), p. 84. The Wirthlin Group survey April findings showed 44 percent, right direction; 47 percent, wrong.

88. As reported in Ronald D. Elving, "McCurdy Bows Out of Race; Cuomo Teases Again," *Congressional Quarterly Weekly Report*, October 19, 1991, p. 3049.

89. Mary Matalin and James Carville (with Peter Knobler), *All's Fair: Love, War, and Running for President* (Random House, 1994), p. 244.

90. It should also be noted, however, that Clinton tried for a preemptive strike on "race baiting," so as not to fall prey to a Willie Horton–type ad. "I want to tell you one thing: I understand this tactic and I will not let them get away with it in 1992." Quoted in Dan Balz, "Gov. Clinton Enters Presidential Race," *Washington Post*, October 4, 1991, p. A1.

91. Ibid., p. A16.

92. Robin Toner, "Arkansas' Clinton Enters the '92 Race for President," *New York Times*, October 4, 1991, p. A10.

93. Quoted in Maraniss, *First in His Class*, p. 461.

94. Goldman and others, *Quest for the Presidency*, p. 43.

95. Matalin and Carville, *All's Fair*, p. 87.

96. Goldman and others, *Quest for the Presidency*, p. 78.

97. Ibid.

98. Ibid., p. 227.

99. Two years into the Clinton presidency, Elizabeth Drew wrote: "If Clinton is to save his presidency . . . he must restore the moral authority and the stature of the office he holds." "Desperately Seeking Stature," *Washington Post*, December 11, 1994, p. C1.

Chapter 3

1. Carter had served as cochair of the Committee to Elect Democrats in 1974 (an offshoot of the Democratic National Committee), which he used primarily as a means for recruiting contacts for his run for the nomination in 1976. Clinton chaired the National Governors' Association and the Democratic Leadership Council— important posts but unlikely to make his name a household word.

2. This aide suggested that their campaign was "idiosyncratic" on this point.

3. As the respondent observed, "Sometimes it's not clear what the campaign's all about, not clear what the election's all about. Those of us in the political business or people who study it and comment on politics and the press . . . are always trying to establish some sort of intellectual framework to explain what happened. But I think lots of times they [pundits and those involved in the campaign] don't really understand."

4. As one aide noted, "People used to say, well, you know, poor old Reagan is kind of simple. He only has two or three things he's interested in. Absolutely right. . . . But with Clinton, you know, I don't think they ever know where they are or where he is."

5. Edwin Meese III, *With Reagan: The Inside Story* (Washington: Regnery Gateway, 1992), p. 57. James P. Pfiffner notes: "Clinton got spooked in the summer of 1992 when George Bush accused him of 'measuring the drapes in the White House.'" Pfiffner quotes Thomas "Mack" McLarty as saying that Clinton did not want "a major transition organization." *The Strategic Presidency: Hitting the Ground Running*, 2d ed., rev. (University Press of Kansas, 1996), p. 150.

6. The Speaker does not have to be a member of the House of Representatives, though all have been.

7. John Ehrlichman, *Witness to Power: The Nixon Years* (Simon and Schuster, 1982), p. 43. Note also Carl M. Brauer, *Presidential Transitions: Eisenhower through Reagan* (Oxford University Press, 1986), where it is noted that Haldeman read extensively about previous White House staff operations and Nixon's staff consulted with Eisenhower staff "and with a study group on transition based at Harvard's Institute of Politics, headed by Franklin Lindsay, chairman of Itek Corporation" (p. 130).

8. Brauer, *Presidential Transitions*, p. 221.

9. Meese, *With Reagan*, p. 57.

10. Ibid., p. 58. Brauer reports that Bill Casey, the campaign manager, initially opposed the creation of the James group because of its potential distraction from the campaign and possible press attention. *Presidential Transitions*, p. 225.

11. Adam Clymer, "Staff Quietly Plans for a Reagan Presidency," *New York Times*, September 14, 1980, p. A. 32.

12. Brauer, *Presidential Transitions*, p. 225.

13. Meese, *With Reagan*, p. 59.

14. Brooks Jackson, "Reagan's 23 Teams Feed Him 'Hot' Ideas for How to Run U.S.," *Wall Street Journal*, October 24, 1980, p. 1.

15. Charles L. Heatherly, ed., *Mandate for Leadership: Policy Management in a Conservative Administration* (Washington: Heritage Foundation, 1981), p. vii.

16. Brauer, *Presidential Transitions*, p. 175.

17. Quoted in Haynes Johnson, *In the Absence of Power: Governing America* (Viking, 1980), p. 295.

18. James Fallows, "The Passionless Presidency: The Trouble with Jimmy Carter's Administration," *The Atlantic*, May 1979, pp. 40, 42.

19. Brauer records that Carter sought a ruling from the Federal Election Commission (FEC) to exclude transition planning costs from "qualified campaign expenses" so as to be able to raise private funds for the purpose. The FEC split along party lines, thus denying the request (*Presidential Transitions*, p. 180).

20. The names and positions of the team are identified in Bruce Adams and Kathryn Kavanagh-Baran, *Promise and Performance: Carter Builds a New Administration* (Lexington, Mass.: Lexington Books, 1979), pp. 14–15.

21. Remarks at "Conference on Presidential Transitions," Brookings Institution, October 26, 1996, p. 42.

22. Watson even met with Frederic V. Malek, Nixon's assistant for personnel, who supported Ford in 1976. As reported in Adams and Kavanagh-Baran, *Promise and Performance*, p. 14.

23. Apparently Watson himself was interested in being the domestic policy adviser. Upon learning of this, Eizenstat "didn't know whether to laugh or cry" since he (Eizenstat) "had been doing policy for Jimmy Carter when he was running for governor" (ibid.)

24. Earlier press coverage of the FEC ruling against permitting the Carter campaign to raise private funds had already caused nervousness among campaign staff since the Watson group was deluged with résumés from job seekers.

25. Laurence Stern, "Transition Unit at Work for Carter," *Washington Post*, August 9, 1976, pp. A1, A2.

26. Quoted in Carl P. Leubsdorf, "Unprecedented Effort Under Way to Plan for a Carter Administration," *Baltimore Sun*, August 13, 1976, p. A1.

27. Hobart Rowen, "Carter Transition Team Readies Data," *Washington Post*, October 26, 1976, p. A2.

28. Of course, the so-called talent inventory program (TIP) of the Watson group was already well known among the campaign staff, and several thousand résumés had been collected over the course of the campaign. For details on TIP, along with a special Women's Talent Bank, see Adams and Kavanagh-Baran, *Promise and Performance*, pp. 11–31. See also Dom Bonafede, "The Carter White House—The Shape Is There, But No Specifics," *National Journal*, December 25, 1976, pp. 1799–1801; and Joel Havemann, "The TIP Talent Hunt—Carter's Original Amateur Hour?" *National Journal*, February 19, 1977, pp. 268–73. Bonafede wrote an excellent series of articles on the Carter transition.

29. Adams and Kavanagh-Baran, *Promise and Performance*, p. 19.

30. Robert Ajemian, "The Transition: '*Proceed and Be Bold*,'" *Time*, November 15, 1976, p. 25.

31. Pfiffner reports that Clinton earlier had a "low-visibility effort" managed by a low-level campaign operative, John Hart. Hart's job was limited to "doing background research and liaison with the General Services Administration about office space and other provisions of the Presidential Transition Act." *Strategic Presidency*, p. 150.

32. Ruth Marcus and Edward Walsh, "A Call for a 'New Patriotism,'" *Washington Post*, November 4, 1992, pp. A1, A25. This report noted that Thomas "Mack" McLarty, "a boyhood friend of Clinton" who later served as chief of staff, "was added to the board—at Clinton's direction." A campaign aide was quoted as saying, "I think he wanted someone there who would be his voice at the table. All the other folks . . . are sort of political acquaintances or people who are close to Mickey, not to the governor."

33. Al Kamen and Ruth Marcus, "Clinton Isn't Rushing on Transition," *Washington Post*, November 6, 1992, p. A20.

34. "Conference on Presidential Transitions," p. 41.

Chapter 4

1. Remarks at the Woodrow Wilson International Center for Scholars, Smithsonian Institution, June 13, 1996, at a conference on "*Presidential Power* Revisited." It should be noted that Neustadt wrote one of the principal transition memos for the Kennedy group.

2. Roger B. Porter, "Of Hazards and Opportunities: Transition and the Modern Presidency," paper prepared for Conference on "*Presidential Power* Revisited," p. 28.

3. Stephen E. Ambrose, *Nixon: The Triumph of a Politician, 1962–1972*, vol. 2 (Simon and Schuster, 1989), pp. 223–25.

4. The split in the Senate going into the election was 57 Democrats, 43 Republicans; after the election it was 56 Democrats, 42 Republicans. Two seats were decided later: Republicans won the Georgia seat, Democrats the North Dakota one. Subsequently a Republican won the Texas seat held by Democrat Lloyd Bentsen Jr. when he joined the Clinton cabinet. Jeffrey L. Katz and Ceci Connolly, "Women, Minorities Rock Records, But Ideology Will Barely Budge," *Congressional Quarterly Weekly Report*, November 7, 1992, pp. 3557–64.

5. Quoted in Ambrose, *Nixon*, p. 227. Ambrose explained that the "obvious answer was 'talk shop.' " He also noted that following breakfast on November 7, "his aides came over, and they began the process of creating a Nixon Administration" (p. 227).

6. This aide observed that Carter appointed the cabinet first and told them: "It's your show. . . . The White House staff never quite caught up in trying to manage the process."

7. Elizabeth Drew, *On the Edge: The Clinton Presidency* (Simon and Schuster, 1994), pp. 22–23. Mrs. Clinton also played an active role in the designation of other key appointments. According to Drew, "After Clinton interviewed candidates, his wife interviewed them" (p. 28).

8. Hamilton Jordan, "What Not to Do," *Washington Post*, November 9, 1992, p. A21.

9. Richard E. Neustadt, "Memorandum on Organizing the Transition," September 15, 1960, p. 5. Copy supplied to the author. Clifford concluded in his memo that "certain White House functions must begin immediately." "Memorandum on Transition," November 9, 1960, p. 2.

10. Richard Darman, who was appointed by Baker as executive director of the White House transition, understood that he was "a cultural and ideological outsider," thus a "Washington insider" to many of the "Reaganauts." "Their version of the purity test," he said, "was one I could not pass." *Who's in Control? Polar Politics and the Sensible Center* (Simon and Schuster, 1996), pp. 36–37.

11. Remarks at "Conference on the Presidential Transition," Brookings Institution, October 26, 1996, pp. 44–45.

12. As reported in James Bennet, "Clinton's New Year's Eve: Looking Back," *New York Times*, January 3, 1997, p. A20.

13. Neustadt, " 'Lessons' for the Eleven Weeks," Summer 1992. Copy sent to the author.

14. In his first news conference after the election, President-elect Clinton stated that he would change the policy of the Bush administration of returning Haitian refugees. He specifically stated, "I can tell you I'm going to change the policy." "Clinton Renews Past Pledges at Post-Election Session," *Congressional Quarterly Weekly Report*, November 14, 1992, p. 3645. Such statements were viewed by many Haitians as very encouraging, and they began building boats for a mass migration. Before his inauguration, Clinton found it necessary "to avert a flood of Haitian boat people" headed for the United States by agreeing to station United Nations observers in Haiti and to persuade "deposed President Jean-Bertrand Aristide to appeal to his countrymen to stay at home." John M. Goshko and Douglas Farah, "Clinton Aides Try to Halt Haitian Flight," *Washington Post*, January 12, 1993, p. A13.

15. A related piece of advice for assistants to the president was provided by Donald H. Rumsfeld, who served as chief of staff to Ford. One of "Rumsfeld's Rules" is: "Don't play President—you're not. The Constitution provides for only one President. Don't forget it, and don't be seen by others as not understanding that fact." "Rumsfeld's Rules," privately distributed (1970, rev. May 8, 1980), p. 2.

16. Quoted in Hedrick Smith, "Transition Shaping up As a Very Fast Pit Stop," *New York Times*, November 16, 1980, sec. 4, p. 1.

17. It is interesting to note, however, that Nixon's "deliberate approach" was reportedly the subject of comment in Washington. One person noted, " 'Waiting for Nixon' has become something of a parlor game around this capital." In part this mood was the result of a Nixon selection process that was tightly controlled, with little public vetting of the candidates for each position. Max Frankel, "Washington Is Feeling Somewhat Uneasy about the Unhurried Pace of Nixon's Entry to White House," *New York Times*, November 21, 1968, p. 27.

18. The delay was a result of a search for a woman or minority representative, with several potential candidates declining to accept. Terrel H. Bell was the person initially recommended by the transition team. Harrison Donnelly, "Reagan Names Career Utah Educator to Head Department of Education," *Congressional Quarterly Weekly Report*, January 10, 1981, p. 111.

19. Stated in a press conference on November 12, 1992. Reprinted in "Clinton Renews Past Pledges at Post-Election Session," p. 3643.

20. At one point late in the appointment process, representatives of women's groups were critical of Clinton for not selecting women to more of the important cabinet positions. The president-elect responded angrily, making reference to his critics as "bean counters." "[They're] playing quota games and math games," he said. Ruth Marcus, "Clinton Berates Critics in Women's Groups," *Washington Post*, December 22, 1992, pp. A1, A12. E. J. Dionne Jr. pointed out that "presidential Cabinets have always been the product of a similar kind of bean-counting. What's changed is the nature of the beans we count." "He'd Better Count Beans," *Washington Post*, January 12, 1993, p. A17.

21. Quoted in Haynes Johnson, *In the Absence of Power: Governing America* (Viking, 1980), pp. 41–42. See also Carl M. Brauer, *Presidential Transitions: Eisenhower through Reagan* (Oxford University Press, 1986), p. 190.

22. I stress again that the differences associated with the political parties are special to these cases. The other contemporary cases of Democratic transitions under conditions of party switching—Franklin D. Roosevelt in 1932 and John F. Kennedy in 1960—were more like those of Republicans—Dwight D. Eisenhower in 1952, Richard M. Nixon in 1968, and Ronald Reagan in 1980—than like Carter or Clinton.

23. Neustadt, "Lessons," p. 2. Copy supplied to the author.

24. Neustadt offered similar advice: "Be immensely courteous to the outgoing White House but don't agree to share responsibility for anything." Ibid., p. 2.

25. It should be noted that this respondent was not that sanguine about how often it happens in this way.

26. This Clinton adviser observed that it was important for the president-elect to "reassert presidential dominance in the Democratic party because we have been for years in a circumstance where we had all these fiefdoms operating on their own." As a matter of fact, Clinton did not achieve this goal; quite the opposite, the Democratic chieftains from Capitol Hill asserted their dominance even during the transition period.

27. Richard E. Neustadt, "Historical Problems in Staffing the White House," Memorandum to James Baker, December 1, 1980, p. 2. Copy supplied to the author.

28. The final "count" among cabinet departments included four women (including the first female secretary of state), three African Americans (including one of the women), one Hispanic (though a second was nominated for United Nations Representative), and six white males. The president expressed his aims this way in a news conference: "I believe that one of my jobs at this moment in history is to demonstrate by the team I put together that no group of people should be excluded from service to our country and that all people are capable of serving. So I have striven to achieve both excellence and diversity." Transcript of News Conference, "I Have Striven to Achieve Excellence and Diversity," *Washington Post*, December 21, 1996, p. A16.

29. Jeffrey H. Birnbaum, *Madhouse: The Private Turmoil of Working for the President* (Times Books, 1996), p. 157.

30. Neustadt advised this: "Return most of the Federal funds to the Treasury. . . , thus avoiding temptations to spend it on campaigners, raising their hopes for permanent employment, creating a *prima facie* case for that, thereby unleashing intense jockeying for advantageous access to agency payrolls. That jockeying will badger civil servants, distract incoming White House aides, and subject new department heads to constant observation." "Lessons," p. 1.

31. James Reston, "From Promise to Policy," *New York Times*, November 7, 1968, p. 20.

32. R. W. Apple Jr., "Nixon Says Johnson Gives Him Key Role on Foreign Policies," *New York Times*, November 15, 1968, pp. 1, 32.

33. Roy Reed, "President Denies Nixon Will Share Policy Decisions," *New York Times*, November 16, 1968, pp. 1, 16.

34. "The Nixon Cabinet," *New York Times*, December 12, 1968, p. 46.

35. Ronald Reagan, *An American Life: The Autobiography* (Simon and Schuster, 1990), pp. 222, 225.

36. Elizabeth Wehr, "Presidential Transition Offers Insights into Character, Style of Reagan Administration," *Congressional Quarterly Weekly Report*, December 27, 1980, p. 3658.

37. "Reagan Press Conference," *Congressional Quarterly Weekly Report*, November 8, 1980, p. 3351.

38. Quoted in Irwin B. Arieff, "Reagan Courts Legislators in Visit to Hill," *Congressional Quarterly Weekly Report*, November 22, 1980, p. 3393.

39. "Courtship in Washington," *New York Times*, November 20, 1980, p. A34. Reagan even met with Senator Edward M. Kennedy, Democrat of Massachusetts, at Kennedy's request. "It was a courtesy call," in that Kennedy had never met Reagan. Quoted in Arieff, "Reagan Courts Legislators," p. 3394.

40. Steven R. Weisman, "Reagan Refuses to Give Answers on Cabinet Jobs," *New York Times*, December 8, 1980, p. D10. Reagan mostly stayed at his secluded home, keeping in telephone contact with officials at the transition headquarters in Washington.

41. Neustadt, "Lessons," p. 1.

42. Ibid., pp. 1–2.

43. At his press conferences on December 18 and 20 (before his appointment of Patricia Harris as Secretary of Housing and Urban Development), Carter was asked several questions about the number of women and blacks being appointed. See "Text of Dec. 18 News Conference," and "Text of Dec. 20 News Conference," *Congressional Quarterly Weekly Report*, December 25, 1976, pp. 3393–96, 3396–99. As noted earlier, Clinton responded harshly to criticism by women's groups that he had not met their expectations. See Marcus, "Clinton Berates Critics."

44. "Clinton Renews Past Pledges at Post-Election Session," p. 3643.

45. David R. Mayhew shows that over 90 percent of major legislation is passed by two-thirds majorities in one or both houses, with support of majorities from both parties in most cases. *Divided We Govern: Party Control, Lawmaking, and Investigations, 1946–1990* (Yale University Press, 1991), pp. 121–22.

46. Neustadt, "Lessons," p. 1.

47. Brauer, *Presidential Transitions*, p. 226.

Chapter 5

1. Michael K. Deaver with Mickey Herskowitz, *Behind The Scenes* (Morrow, 1987), p. 139.

2. Quoted in Charles O. Jones, "The Presidency and the Press," *Harvard International Journal of Press/Politics*, vol. 1 (Spring 1996), p. 116.

3. Michael K. Deaver interview, February 10, 1995, p. 8. Quoted with permission of Deaver.

4. Ibid., pp. 27–28.

5. This reporter's recollection confirmed the intent of the Reagan staff to play down the transition as a major news event, wishing to focus instead on the inauguration.

6. Remarks at "Conference on Presidential Transitions," Brookings Institution, October 26, 1996, pp. 116–17.

7. Ibid., pp. 112–13.

8. This reporter modified these comments by noting that "the press never stops covering the horse race . . . who's up, who's down." The race itself is different, however.

9. There are two interesting variations of these biases. In 1980 the assassination attempt on Reagan muted the criticism early in his administration by creating a story favorable to the president. In 1996 Bob Dole was less of an interesting story and, in any event, he was also in power during the early part of the election year, thus subject to criticism. Clinton, on the other hand, very nearly assumed the role of the challenger, given the dramatic loss of the Congress to the Republicans in 1994.

10. Watergate would be another such example.

11. Of course, McCurry was not among the Clinton intimates from campaign days. In fact, he had worked for Mario Cuomo and Senator Bob Kerrey previously. Douglas Jehl, "President Is Ready to Move on White House Shake-up," *New York Times*, September 23, 1994, p. A23.

12. For details, see Jeffrey H. Birnbaum, *Madhouse: The Private Turmoil of Working for the President* (Times Books, 1996), pp. 153–93.

13. For evidence on this point, see Marlin Fitzwater, *Call the Briefing! Bush and Reagan, Sam and Helen: A Decade with Presidents and the Press* (Times Books, 1995).

14. This view of Powell was not uniformly held. For example, see comments by James Deakin, former White House correspondent for the *St. Louis Post-Dispatch*, in Kenneth W. Thompson, ed., *The White House Press on the Presidency: News Management and Co-option* (Lanham, Md.: University Press of America, 1983), pp. 15–16.

15. Fitzwater, *Call the Briefing*, pp. vii–viii.

16. Larry Speakes with Robert Pack, *Speaking Out: The Reagan Presidency from Inside the White House* (Scribner's, 1988); and Jody Powell, *The Other Side of the Story* (Morrow, 1984).

17. For details, see Michael Baruch Grossman and Martha Joynt Kumar, *Portraying the President: The White House and the News Media* (Johns Hopkins University Press, 1981), especially pp. 36–80; and Stephen Hess, *The Washington Reporters* (Brookings, 1981), especially pp. 24–46, 47–66.

18. According to a 1991 survey conducted by Stephen Hess. See Hess, *News and Newsmaking* (Brookings, 1996), pp. 20–32.

Chapter 6

1. These realities are not in the form of "how to" advice. There are several such works produced by those who have been involved in transitions, like Harrison Wellford and Donald Rumsfeld, as well as several studies by the Brookings Institution, the National Academy of Public Administration, and others. Likewise, James P. Pfiffner's work, *The Strategic Presidency: Hitting the Ground Running*, 2d ed. rev. (University Press of Kansas, 1996) provides a strong message for presidents-elect, as does Stephen Hess's book, *Organizing the Presidency*, rev. ed. (Brookings, 1988).

2. Stephen Skowronek, *The Politics Presidents Make: Leadership from John Adams to George Bush* (Belknap Press of Harvard University Press, 1993).

3. Dick Morris, *Behind the Oval Office: Winning the Presidency in the Nineties* (Random House, 1997), pp. 10, 143.

4. Ibid., pp. 144, 148.

5. Morris describes the conflicts that developed within the White House staff during this time, with Leon Panetta, Harold Ickes, and George Stephanopoulos as more traditional versus Morris and the pollsters as designing change (with Erskine Bowles facilitating their work and influence). See, in particular, ibid., chaps. 5–10.

6. Richard E. Neustadt, *Presidential Power: The Politics of Leadership* (Wiley, 1960), chap. 4.

7. Samuel Kernell, *Going Public: New Strategies of Presidential Leadership*, 3d ed. (Washington: Congressional Quarterly Press, 1997).

8. Hugh Heclo, "Presidential Power and Public Prestige: '. . . a snarly sort of politics . . .' " paper prepared for conference on *"Presidential Power* Revisited," Woodrow Wilson International Center for Scholars, Smithsonian Institution, June 13, 1996, p. 9.

9. This is not to suggest that such persons will receive White House staff appointments (though some may), rather that they will become important in decisionmaking beyond strictly election-oriented strategy. Thus, for example, several of the political consultants for Clinton were paid from outside funds and did not have official White House positions.

10. See, for example, David R. Mayhew, *Divided We Govern: Party Control, Lawmaking, and Investigations, 1946–1990* (Yale University Press, 1991).

11. Seemingly we are already observing this development on Capitol Hill as congressional leaders perform a more public role than in the past. There are even frequent job approval ratings for the Speaker of the House, a rarity in the past. Several governors, too, have been active in campaigning for policy.

12. Morris, *Behind the Oval Office*, p. 338.

13. Ibid.

INDEX

217